Finding Ralphy

Ralph De Tunstall Sneyd 1862-1947

Sneyd
Nec Opprimre Nec Opprimi

Marion Aldis and Pam Inder

ACKNOWLEDGEMENTS

We would like to express our gratitude to Ralph's grandsons and their wives - Colin and Joyce Shenton and John and Sue Sneyd - who have been kinder to us than we could ever have dared hope and without whose help this book could never have been written. We would also like to thank the following individuals and institutions who have helped us in various ways:

Patsy Allen, Alan Badnall, Jean Bode, Bridget and Bob Boyd, Cathy Braddock (Nicholson Institute), Peter and Susan Brandreth, Mrs Boulton, Christine Chester, Chez (Leicester Pagan Alliance), Paul Connor (Alton Castle), Professor Cooper (Leicester University), Arnold Corden, Angela and Alun Davies, Angela Druce (Etwall), Barbara Fishburn, Chris Fletcher, Gayle Gibson (Vancouver), Annie and John Gilman, Mr and Mrs Henshall, Mrs Hodgkinson and family, Deb Klemperer (Potteries Museum), Father Michael Lang (Brompton Oratory), Lynn Maranda (Vancouver Museum), Dr Merry (Leicester University), Father Michael Miners (St Mary's, Leek), Tony Moult (Alton Parish Council), Sue Notley, Jodi and John Peck, Doug Pickford (Leek Post and Times), Ray Poole, Graham Riley, Frank Roden, Maxine Rowlinson, Rev Chris Scargill (vicar of Onecote), Paul Smith (archivist, Thomas Cook), Averil, Judy and Humphrey Scott-Moncrieff, Mr and Mrs Sutton, Chris Tatton, Gary Thorn (British Museum archive), Bob Trubshaw, and the staffs of Keele University Library Special Collections, the Nicholson Institute in Leek, and Fearns and Marriott of Leek.

PEOPLE MENTIONED IN THE TEXT

This account is not fictionalised in any way. All the people
we mention exist, all the events actually happened, but in a
few cases people have asked not to be named and so we have
used pseudonyms to protect their identity.

COVER PHOTOGRAPH
RALPH DE TUNSTALL SNEYD AS KNIGHT 1902

CHURNET VALLEY BOOKS
1 King Street, Leek, Staffordshire. 01538 399033
www.leekbooks.co.uk
© Marion Aldis and Pam Inder, and Churnet Valley Books 2005
ISBN 1 904546 39 0
(978 1 904546 39 9)

CONTENTS

REFERENCES

This is not an academic book - but nonetheless it is a serious piece of historical research and we have tried to source our references. However, the majority of the documents we have used belong to members of Ralph's family or are in other private collections and are not listed or catalogued. Many of the press cuttings Ralph kept, and from which we have sometimes quoted, have had the dates cut off and often we do not even know in which newspaper they appeared. Quite a lot of other information has come from conversations with people who knew, or knew of, Ralph De Tunstall Sneyd, or acquired items from his collection. Some of them asked not to be named. Of the material that is in the public domain, Susanna Ingleby's diaries are in the Special Collections of Keele University Library. All other documents are referenced in the text.

WHAT IS THAT WORTH TODAY?

In Ralph's time the UK currency was pounds, shillings and pence - written £-s-d. For those unfamiliar with pre-decimal currency: 12d = 1s and 20s = £1. A sum comprising shillings and pence was often written as follows 10/6 (10 shillings and 6 old pennies). Where sums of money are mentioned in the text we usually follow them with their modern equivalents (in terms of purchasing power) eg. £2 in 1882 [£123]. To arrive at these conversions we have used Lawrence H. Officer, *Comparing the Purchasing Power of Money in Great Britain from 1264 to 2002*, Economic History Services, 2004. The sums refer to purchasing power in 2002 and are converted from the precise year for which they appear. This means that some figures may seem inconsistent. For small sums we have given the full conversion but for larger amounts we have rounded it up or down to the nearest pound.

WELSH

Ralph did not speak Welsh and neither do we. We have quoted the inscriptions on his banners exactly as they appear in the sources (newspaper reports and Percy Brentnall's novel) that we have used. We are, however, aware that the language may be incorrect and if so we apologise to any native Welsh speakers who may read this book.

Ralph De Tunstall Sneyd as he chose to appear in his book of poems

The Staffordshire World of Ralph De Tunstall Sneyd

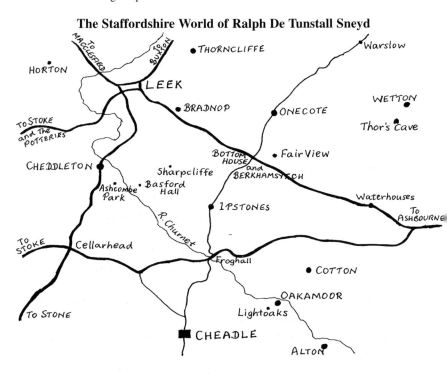

Cheddleton Station

Chapter 1
Meeting Ralph

Leek, Staffordshire, October 1998

I place the small letter, ink faded to sepia, on to the shining white surface of the photocopier. Nina takes the copy and I carefully remove the letter and turn it over. The sequence is repeated. I hand the original to Pam who places it on a pile and then delves into the seemingly bottomless trunk. Joyce takes another letter from the brown paper-covered book and hands it to me.

Nina yawns.

'Do you want to stop now and go to bed?' I ask.

'No,' Nina glares at me. 'He was my great-great-grandfather and I want to do his letters!'

I knew better than to argue with a determined ten year old - especially one who is descended from Ralph De Tunstall Sneyd.

We continue, rhythmically. Flash and whirr punctuate our movements. An efficient production line.

Colin comes in from the lounge where he has been watching the news, leans on the door jamb and watches us - looking redundant in this female hive of labour. Pam turns to him.

'Do you remember your grandfather Colin?' I hear her ask as I put another letter in the eager machine.

'Not very well. I was only ten when he died. He didn't come to see us very often.'

He pauses. We do not speak. We place, press and retrieve. The pile on the table grows higher. Joyce carefully unpicks another book. We work in silence. Colin watches.

He adds, thoughtfully, after a long pause, 'I do remember my cousin John saying that one day our grandfather visited them in Leek and asked my aunt where my uncle was. 'At work of course', she replied. He stared at her for a while and said, 'Work. At work. How very curious!' It seemed such an odd thing to say - but then he never worked himself, as far as I'm aware. But no, I didn't know him well at all.'

'That's the end of the books. I'll re-stitch them tomorrow,' says Joyce.

'Now, some more tea. You'll stay and have another bite before you go won't you? And time for bed for you Nina.'

Nina ignores her grandmother and tidies the pile of letters - her small hands touching the very words her great-great-grandfather had written. Pam continues to dig into the trunk. Colin returns to the television.

Back in our homes we ploughed through the mounds of photocopies, carefully re-reading the documents we had seen at Colin and Joyce's, marvelling at our good fortune.

When we were working on our previous book, *Finding Susanna,* we had given a reading at Ipstones Village hall from Susanna Ingleby's diaries. She was Ralph's aunt but had brought him up from infancy. Colin and Joyce had seen the talk advertised in the paper and come along on the spur of the moment. Fortunately for us they had liked what they heard and invited us to see the huge archive of family papers which Ralph De Tunstall had kept. Amongst them was a series of books made up of the letters he and his aunt exchanged over the eleven years he spent at boarding school. He had asked his aunt to keep them - even as a small child Ralph had a sense of history - and what became apparent to us as we read the diaries and letters was that Ralph had been a very unusual boy. He did not become any more ordinary as he grew up....

It soon became clear that writing Ralph's story would pose many problems. For a start, the information we had was patchy. We could reconstruct the first 29 years of his life in considerable detail but thereafter - with 56 years left to go - the documentation became thinner and we were heavily reliant on secondary sources and second-hand memories.

Although most of our research was done together, we divided the writing between us. Emails flashed between us several times a day:

'Deeply respected Colleague - I seem to remember we had a document about... Have you still got a copy of it? And what do you know about....?'

'Yes I have a photocopy - will scan and send as an attachment. Do you want the full works about... or the abbreviated account?'

'Full works, please.'

'OK'

'Great - you get two extra packets of Smarties for that!'

Smarties were our currency. I even managed to find some Thai ones when I was in Chiang Mai for two months and brought them back for Pam! Being halfway across the world presented no problem - emails made it like being in adjoining rooms.

Many happy hours were spent together in our homes, in pubs, restaurants and hotels, and in the Green Man B&B in Leek. Amazingly, people soon became accustomed to the two slightly plump, slightly eccentric ladies who had lunch, tea, drinks, and anything else that was on offer, and who spread their papers over the tables for hours at a time. Research is so very enjoyable! We read and re-read each other's work, altering, re-writing, adding, subtracting - in the end every chapter was a joint effort

We hope you will enjoy getting to know Ralph. He was a gentle, complex and much misunderstood man.

Ralph De Tunstall Sneyd was born at the height of the Victorian period and brought up as a 19th century gentleman. The Sneyds were an old Staffordshire family - the earliest reference to a Sneyd in the county came in a mediaeval document relating to lands held in the parish of Tunstall, hence Ralph's rather ostentatious name. His father and aunt had grown up on a large estate in a grand house, with a dozen live-in servants. As the eldest son, Ralph's father, John William Sneyd, expected to inherit it all. But he had quarrelled bitterly with his father, the Reverend John Sneyd of Ashcombe Park - and in 1872, when Reverend Sneyd seemed on his death bed and little Ralph De Tunstall was ten, John William had to face the reality of his disinheritance. Today expensive lawyers can often overturn wills, but in February 1873, when his father finally died, John William Sneyd had no such redress.

The Basford estate, which John William inherited from his grandfather, consisted of a fine house, Basford Hall, a handful of farms and several hundred acres of land. To most of us it would seem more than enough but it was scant compensation for John William. He became bitter in ways that probably only a Victorian landowner could. Not only was the estate he had loved and learned to care for snatched from him, but it went to his younger brother, Dryden. Rural society in the 19th century was still almost feudal. It was Dryden, not John William, who was invited to sit on local committees, whose opinion was canvassed and whose patronage was sought.

To make matters worse, John William's own tenants at Basford recognised his reduced circumstances and were often less than respectful. Family friends courted Dryden but snubbed John William, not inviting him to their homes and not returning calls. Victorian society was unforgiving; a son at loggerheads with his clergyman father was automatically in the wrong - no matter if John William actually seems to have been in the right. Worse, the quarrel had not been resolved before his father's death.

Social status, breeding and position were important in the 19th century, although Victorian society was, in fact, very fluid. Industrialisation and urbanisation brought wealth to many able men of relatively humble birth. Within a generation, their kind would be accepted in polite society, but only when they, and more importantly their wives, learnt the prevailing social niceties. Victorian literature is awash with cruel - or comical - examples of people desperately trying to get their feet on to the social ladder and failing. Strict and ever-evolving rules of etiquette existed to keep parvenus on their toes and in their place.

An equally strict code governed relationships between the social classes. Speech, dress, education - matters like where you sat in church or what time you ate your meals - indelibly marked your place in society. A gentleman's child might love his nursemaid more than his often-absent mother, or visit the gardener's cottage and play with his children - but at no point would he have been allowed to see himself as their equal. And when he grew up the social gulf between them would widen. It is almost incomprehensible to us today that, far from seeing inclusiveness as an ideal, most Victorians would have seen it as shocking and dangerous.

To Ralph's father and aunt, a stable society depended on everyone knowing their place. The French Revolution had taken place a bare generation before they were born, a chilling lesson of what could happen to people like themselves if the masses ever got out of control. They allowed themselves to be convinced that the social order that so benefited them was divinely ordained. The lines from *All Things Bright and Beautiful* reflected this attitude perfectly: *The rich man at his castle, The poor man at his gate. God made them high or lowly. And ordered their estate.*

Not that the Sneyds ignored their poorer neighbours. In their view it was the job of the gentry, even comparatively impoverished gentry as they had become, to set an example. They helped the deserving poor with gifts of food and clothing and pious advice. But they could be pitiless to those whose misfortune was deemed to be their own fault - through drink, idleness or petty crime. They expected gentlemen to play a part in their community. John William was a J.P. and, as a young man, an officer in the Yeomanry. His father, an overwhelmingly ambitious man, had been even more active, a conscientious magistrate, a member of turnpike committees, a Poor Law commissioner, and a mover and shaker in all things important in North Staffordshire. One of Aunt Susan's perennial complaints was that Ralph seemed incapable of 'doing good' in the County, as her generation expected.

The Sneyds' credentials were impeccable. They were gentry who had lived in the area for generations and who traced their ancestry back to the Mercian kings, but John William's position as a disinherited son was hugely embarrassing. And Aunt Susan's history was little better. Married in 1860 to the Reverend Charles Ingleby, an abusive, homosexual husband who treated her abominably, she had fled home after a mere eight weeks. Her family and friends supported her, but nonetheless she was still a disgraced wife in the unforgiving eyes of Victorian society. Their chequered histories made their precise social status somewhat ambiguous and inevitably this must have rubbed off on little Ralph. Perhaps it fostered his sense of singularity, of not being like other people.

As we worked, we began to realise that much of what Ralph thought and experienced would be difficult for modern readers to comprehend. The world he grew up in is, to us, a foreign country. Conversion from one branch of Christianity to another, for example, would today scarcely merit a comment; in Ralph's day it almost caused his family to disown him. We are a less religious society but we have a widespread wariness of the occult. Ouija boards are seen as dangerous and their sale is banned in parts of the USA; in Ralph's day 'table tapping' and séances were innocent party games. Today, opium is a class A drug and even possessing it is a crime; in Ralph's day it was an over-the-counter remedy, as available as aspirin is now and used as routinely and unthinkingly. Modern agony aunts urge us to follow our hearts and marry for love; in Ralph's youth parents dictated who their children could or could not marry and being 'in love' was not a good enough reason to wed. Family background was hugely important, even better when backed up by land and money, and money alone would do if the wife was prepared to learn to adapt to her husband's social milieu. Love and friendship counted for much less.

Attitudes changed dramatically in the 85 years of Ralph De Tunstall Sneyd's lifetime. The First World War was the great catalyst and society was never the same again after 1918. Gone was the old deference to authority; mass experience of incompetent upper class officers and of the wider world saw to that. But the changes had begun much sooner. By the late 1870s British farming was in the doldrums as imports of grain and tinned meats undercut prices, and farm rents fell. More and more of the younger countrymen, tenant farmers and labourers alike, moved to the towns to find work or emigrated to the colonies. Those farmers who remained were forced to keep costs to a minimum and cut jobs and wages. Many of the old landed gentry sold their estates or let them and moved away. Villages shrank. As a result of free universal education after 1880, younger people were more knowledgeable and questioning than their forbears had been. The social fabric that Ralph's father and aunt had set so much store by was beginning to wear thin well before 1914.

The process of change accelerated after the war. A million young men were dead. Schemes to find employment for returning soldiers resulted in men training for jobs that they could not previously have dreamt of doing. The social ladder was becoming easier to climb. Although the 1920s and 30s saw much poverty and unemployment, working men were less constrained than before by fear of their betters and behaved in ways that would have been unthinkable when Ralph was a boy. The General Strike of 1926, for example, although eventually a set-back for trade unionism, elicited much less in the way of reprisals than Ralph or his father could ever have imagined. As a young officer in the Yeomanry in 1842, John William Sneyd had ridden into Stoke-on-Trent, sword in hand, to break up a starving mob whose only crime was to demonstrate against bread prices.

Ralph had to come to terms with a world which was overturning the old certainties, one that was increasingly compassionate and egalitarian. Born in the age of the horse and the steam train, he saw cycling become popular in the 1880s and 90s and witnessed the effect it had on village life. For the first time in history countrymen could travel further from home in an evening than they could walk and the effect this had on patterns of marriage has been well-documented. He witnessed the invention of first the motor car and then the aeroplane. He would travel in both. In Ralph's youth there was an excellent local and national postal service with three or four deliveries a day. It was possible to send a local letter in the morning and to receive an answer the same day. For more urgent communication there was the telegram. These services remained in force throughout his life, but by the early 1900s the telephone was beginning to supersede them. Private phones were still a rarity but messages could be passed via the local post office to summon the doctor or the midwife, or distraught relatives to a deathbed, with hitherto unknown speed. Ralph and his neighbours saw the coming of wireless and television. Newsreel images of the wider world were shown in cinemas in Leek. Little by little, horizons were widening and people were becoming better informed.

Ralph lived through four reigns and he witnessed the abdication crisis of 1936 - a tremendous shock to traditionalists like the Sneyds. *Hark the Herald Angels si-ing, Mrs Simpson's got our King!* children sang that Christmas. Ralph was not greatly interested in politics but he saw 19 prime ministers come and go - and he had the opportunity to vote in 20 national elections. He was a Conservative, as his family had always been. He feared the Liberals for reasons both general and personal. They wanted to *do away with the law of primogeniture*, he is reported as saying at a Conservative party meeting: *There would then be nobody with sufficient money to keep up the grand old houses you see in many parts of England. Everything must have a head, but the Liberals would like to overthrow heads. It is not right that there should only be working men or gentlemen. We must have both classes. How would it be if we were all hands or feet? It would be ridiculous. We must have hands and feet with the trunk and the head that contains the brains. So it is with society.*

Ralph could not rid himself of the belief that it was the gentry, *the brains*, who should be in charge of society. Yet he lived to see the Labour party come to power in Britain for the first time under Ramsay MacDonald in 1924, he saw them return in 1929 and 1931, and again under Atlee in 1945, incontro-vertible evidence that the old order was changing and the country was 'going to the dogs'.

What is going on! *...The present government seem to be in league with Moskow to ruin England. With the dumping of <u>slave</u> grown wheat & timber & now oil... Already my little income is crumbling from the effects of this Russian competition...* lamented Ralph's cousin, Bertha, in one of her of her diatribes to him, confusing the personal and the public good in the time-honoured way of the ruling class.

Ralph was well travelled, but latterly his world centred on the small corner of Staffordshire around Leek. Things changed more gently there, old fashioned beliefs and attitudes lingered longer. Even so, the abiding memory people have of 'Mr Sneyd' is that he was an old fashioned gentleman, courteous, considerate, kind - but out of his time.

THE SNEYD FAMILY TREE

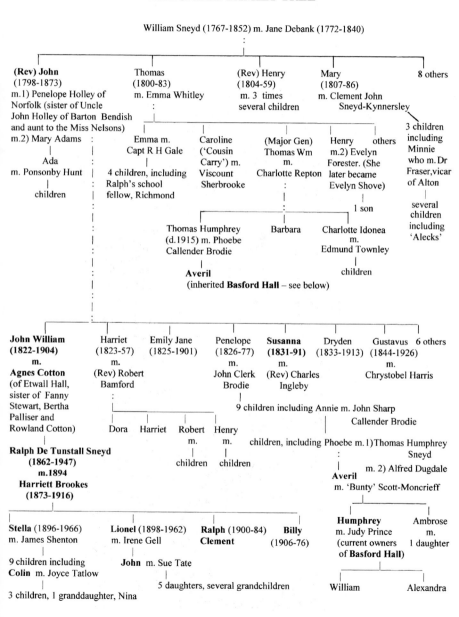

William Sneyd (1767-1852) m. Jane Debank (1772-1840)

(Rev) John (1798-1873) m.1) Penelope Holley of Norfolk (sister of Uncle John Holley of Barton Bendish and aunt to the Miss Nelsons) m.2) Mary Adams — Ada m. Ponsonby Hunt — children

Thomas (1800-83) m. Emma Whitley

(Rev) Henry (1804-59) m. 3 times several children

Mary (1807-86) m. Clement John Sneyd-Kynnersley

8 others

3 children including Minnie who m. Dr Fraser, vicar of Alton — several children including 'Alecks'

Emma m. Capt R H Gale — 4 children, including Ralph's school fellow, Richmond

Caroline ('Cousin Carry') m. Viscount Sherbrooke

(Major Gen) Thomas Wm m. Charlotte Repton

Henry   others m.2) Evelyn Forester. (She later became Evelyn Shove) — 1 son

Thomas Humphrey (d.1915) m. Phoebe Callender Brodie

Barbara

Charlotte Idonea m. Edmund Townley — children

Averil (inherited **Basford Hall** – see below)

John William (1822-1904) m. **Agnes Cotton** (of Etwall Hall, sister of Fanny Stewart, Bertha Palliser and Rowland Cotton)

Harriet (1823-57) m. (Rev) Robert Bamford

Emily Jane (1825-1901)

Penelope (1826-77) m. John Clerk Brodie

Susanna (**1831-91**) m. (Rev) Charles Ingleby

Dryden (1833-1913)

Gustavus (1844-1926) m. Chrystobel Harris

6 others

9 children including Annie m. John Sharp Callender Brodie

Dora   Harriet   Robert   Henry
                    m.   m.
                  children children

children, including Phoebe m.1) Thomas Humphrey Sneyd m. 2) Alfred Dugdale

Ralph De Tunstall Sneyd (**1862-1947**) m.1894 **Harriett Brookes** (**1873-1916**)

Averil m. 'Bunty' Scott-Moncrieff

Stella (1896-1966) m. James Shenton — 9 children including **Colin** m. Joyce Tatlow — 3 children, 1 granddaughter, Nina

Lionel (1898-1962) m. Irene Gell — **John** m. Sue Tate — 5 daughters, several grandchildren

Ralph (1900-84) **Clement**

Billy (1906-76)

Humphrey m. Judy Prince (current owners of **Basford Hall**) — William

Ambrose m. 1 daughter — Alexandra

Ashcombe
The Sneyd family seat

Ralphy aged 6 with his Aunt, Susanna Ingleby, and father, John William Sneyd.

Susanna's, and below, young Ralphy's, drawings of Armitage Cottage. It is notable that his aunt left out the pottery works surrounding the cottage.

Hawkesyard Hall, near Armitage, the home of Josiah Spode III.
Ralph went to parties there as a child.

Tixall Lodge, near Stafford, home of Mr and Mrs Mayne. Ralph and his father and
aunt spent several Christmases there.

John William Sneyd

Susanna Ingleby nee Sneyd

Gustavus Sneyd

Dryden Henry Sneyd

Lea Fields
Abbots Bromley

Major-General Thomas Sneyd

Rev. John Sneyd 1871

One of Ralphy's story books.

The Trinity Aisle in Mavesyn Ridware church showing the crusader tombs that so inspired little Ralphy

Chapter 2
Ralph's Family and Early Childhood

Ralph was a hoarder. Cardboard boxes of documents littered his home and three tin cabin trunks contained the precious and sensitive evidence of his aunt's marriage breakdown and his father's quarrel with his grandfather. The Sneyds were very conscious of their family history.

In the 1920s, when Ashcombe Park was sold, Ralph acquired a real prize, the Sneyd diaries - literally hundreds of them; red, black, green and tan leather-covered diaries, some tooled in gold, some plain, some neatly closed, others bulging with loose sheets and little packets containing the baby-curls of his long dead uncles and aunts. For many years they had stood in neat, chronologically-ordered rows on the shelves of the library at Ashcombe Park. They had been kept by his ancestors, his Great-Grandfather William who died in 1851, eleven years before Ralph was born, his Grandfather and Grandmother Sneyd, his Great-Uncle Ralph, his father and his uncles. There were also some large, bluey-green ones, embossed and bound in cloth, written by his Aunt Susan, Mrs Susanna Ingleby, when she was a girl.

The Sneyds had been an awkward, quarrelsome lot. Ralph never knew his grandfather because the Reverend John Sneyd and Ralph's father, John William, had quarrelled back in the 1850s, over the best way to raise money against the family estate to pay off the debts incurred in a failed copper mining venture in Wales. The case had dragged on and on, but, in 1852 the Reverend John Sneyd could no longer keep his creditors at bay and he was faced with losses of £32,500 [£2.3 million]. John William was thirty, and for the first time in his life he stood up to his father, and pointed out the long term effect it would have on the family if his father sold off the estate. How would he support himself? What about his younger brothers? Did John Sneyd not realise that few gentlemen could actually live on their earnings as clergyman, or farmers, or military men? The Reverend John and his brothers had been subsidised by the Ashcombe estate throughout their lives, living in grand houses, their parents' wealth financing their extravagant lifestyles and growing families. If the estate was sold, John William and his younger brothers and sisters would have had no such support.

John Sneyd was stung to the quick, probably because he knew he was largely to blame. Desperately worried about impending financial disaster and furiously angry, the Reverend Sneyd asserted his right to be the pater familias and made a final, grand, futile gesture. He threw John William out of the house. It was late at night and pouring with rain. John William stumbled through the dark woods to Woodlands, another Sneyd house a few hundred yards away where his Uncle Henry and Aunt Penelope lived. They took him in, sympathised, put him to bed and dried his wet clothes. They all thought it would be over by morning.

But Ralph's father was as stubborn as his grandfather; neither would give way, and both knew the problem was bigger than either of their solutions. John William fled to his sister, Penelope Brodie, in Scotland. In 1852 she was twenty-six, the second wife of John Clerk Brodie of Idvies, and already the mother of three tiny children. The family were wealthy; Idvies was a vast country house in Angus and they also had a fashionable town house in Edinburgh. Aunt Penelope was another relation Ralph would never meet. She was kind to his father but later, when Aunt Susan's marriage failed and she, too, arrived in Edinburgh for an indefinite stay, Penelope lost patience. Not until he was an adult did Ralph visit Scotland and meet his surviving Brodie cousins.

In the end, tactful friends and the ever-resourceful Joseph Challinor, the family solicitor, talked John Sneyd into a compromise solution, mortgaging the estate to them and buying it back a bit at a time while still running it as though it was his own. It was a face-saving solution for John Sneyd, but it also enabled him to continue his quarrel with his son. John William became the scapegoat for all his father's problems - *my faithless son, John William*, he wrote in his diary, coupling him with *those Welsh devils* as the source of all the family misfortunes. Dryden Henry, his second surviving son, inherited the Ashcombe Park estate.

As an old man, gazing at the long-unread diaries of his forbears, Ralph could probably sympathise with his father. He could never have done so when he was young. They were completely unalike: John William, the sportsman, the country squire, obsessed with poachers and happiest up on the moors with a gun in his hand, conventional, conservative, not an original idea in his head; Ralph, bookish, spiritual, artistic, musical, keen to travel, to see new things, explore new ideas, confident and happy in his own eccentricity. No wonder they didn't get on. But nonetheless, Ralph could not have expected to be disinherited of

Basford in favour of his Uncle Gustavus.

Ashcombe Park went out of the family too. Ralph may have dared to hope that his Uncle Dryden would leave it to him - as a confirmed bachelor Dryden Sneyd had no obvious heir and he had always been kind to Ralph. Even when Dryden and John William were at loggerheads over the boundaries between their two estates, Ralph himself had always been a welcome guest at Ashcombe. There were letters as late as 1893 inviting him to visit, to dine, and addressing him warmly as 'old chap'. But when Dryden died, in 1913, he bequeathed Ashcombe and the estate to his cousin, Major-General Thomas William Sneyd.

Ralph must have been bitterly disappointed. Thomas William was already an old man and he died in 1918. His only son, Thomas Humphrey, had been killed in France in 1915. Although he had a baby grand-daughter, Averil, Thomas William would not let a girl inherit. So Evelyn Sneyd, wife of Thomas William's younger brother Henry, purchased the house in 1918. Henry died two years later. Evelyn could not maintain Ashcombe. She wrote to Ralph in 1926: *It is a great grief to me ...that Ashcombe must go as I hoped to save it for my son. Of course it would have passed out of the family in 1918 if I had not bought it, and it is very disappointing to feel I only deferred the evil day. But it is quite impossible on my income to keep it up or live there. The increased cost of living & wages make repairs out of the question & the place is going downhill every year... I have lost many hundreds on it... there was always a deficit when balanced against the rents - on an average about £250* [£8,870] *a year. I am not getting a high price but the relief of getting the drain on my resources finished is very great... Phoebe* [Thomas William's daughter-in-law] *has the pictures which I was obliged to sell to her....*

That was when Ralph acquired the diaries - Evelyn had encouraged him to take family items. She obviously felt she needed to explain herself to him in some detail; Ralph was probably not the only person who expected Dryden to leave Ashcombe to him. But the paintings, his ancestors' portraits, went to Basford.

'Poor Ralph!' said Marion, over coffee one evening, as she opened another tube of Smarties. 'Have you noticed there are never as many orange Smarties as the rest - and they're the best.'

'No, I can't say I have! Why poor Ralph?' Marion was so easily sidetracked!

'I know John William disinherited him....'

'Yes, but we'll have to explain that later.'

'...but I've never really understood why Basford went to Averil?'

We knew Averil Scott-Moncrieff well. By the time we came to write this book she was a very old lady, living in one of the grand houses Ralph had known as a boy - now a nursing home. She still greeted us warmly when we visited her but we were no longer sure that she knew who we were. Her bright smile and aristocratic mannerisms were still intact but she didn't always make sense. But when we had first known her she had been as bright as a button, living in a house full of cats and domestic chaos, plying us with enormous tumblers of gin and wonderful, home-made soups laced with garlic and telling amazingly scurrilous stories about her great-great-uncle, Gustavus Sneyd.

'Well, Averil inheriting was down to Gustavus...' I began, through a mouthful of chocolate.

When he disinherited Ralph, John William bequeathed Basford to his youngest brother, Gustavus. When he died, in 1926, Gustavus could - and probably should - have left it to Ralph. But Ralph was disappointed again when Gustavus left it to his great-great-niece, Averil Sneyd. She was just eleven then, a pretty, wilful, lively and very modern little girl.

'It must have seemed grossly unfair to Ralph,' I said, 'and Susanna would have been heart-broken to see him disinherited.'

Marion had opened another tube of Smarties and was counting the orange ones out. 'Only six; the last tube had eight....!'

I ignored her. 'Of course she left him Fair View, and over £9000 - that would be around £600,000 today. But I don't think Ralph ever got over losing Basford - remember that letter he wrote to Gustavus *from your affectionate but deeply wronged nephew?*'

'But times had changed,' Marion mused, opening yet more Smarties. 'Servants were hard to come by, building work cost more as labourers began to be paid more. Ralph could never have afforded to maintain Basford...'

'...But it didn't stop him wanting to. OK, how many orange ones this time?'

'Five!'

It was the diaries that Evelyn Sneyd had given to Ralph De Tunstall, her great-nephew, that had started our interest in the Sneyds. After Ralph's death the collection, or most of it, was acquired by a book dealer who sold it to another dealer who sold it to Keele University Library. I discovered it there, and as women and historians, Marion and I were particularly interested in the diaries kept by Ralph's Aunt Susan - but our interest soon extended to the rest of the Sneyd dynasty.

Susanna Ingleby was a great diary keeper; in over thirty years she never omitted a single day's entry. Her diaries tell us a great deal about Ralph's early years.

1862 May 3rd: John William & Agnes's son in heir born at Etwall [Agnes's family home] at about 8 o'clock in the morning. John William has taken a house at Armitage for three years at £30 [£1,700] *a year.*

John William seems to have confided his plans to his sister Susan even then. The rest of the day's entry was bland. On the day that Ralph was born his grandfather went to Leek, his grandmother and Aunt Ada went to see the family mine, his Aunts Emily and Susan called at Ashcombe, and his Uncle Gustavus was hit in the face by a cricket ball!

All seemed to be going well. John William went off on manoeuvres with the Yeomanry and Agnes wrote to him there. He replied on May 15th: *I cannot tell you how much pleasure it gave me... to find that my dearest & our brat are going on well... I am very glad to find our brat behaves well & lets you sleep.* But within a week or so Agnes was very ill. John William wrote to his sister.

I am afraid my dearest, dearest Agnes is as ill as she can possibly be... If it is God's will to take my dearest, dearest Wife, will you, dear Susan, be so good as to live with me? It is dear Agnes's wish as well as my own.

Agnes died on June 27th, 1862. Ralph was 8 weeks old.

Susanna Ingleby loved children. Her marriage had broken down largely because she could not accept the celibate lifestyle her homosexual husband wanted because she knew it would deprive her of ever having a family of her own. Agnes's death gave her an undreamed-of second chance. Victorian society accorded a sister housekeeping for her brother very much the same social status as a wife. Out of the blue, Susanna's life had changed for ever.

Ralph was christened on the 8th of July. On the 12th they left Etwall and set off for Rugeley to prepare the house his father had rented. Armitage was a drab little village, overshadowed by huge factories manufacturing sanitary ware; no doubt it was a cheap place to rent - and John William had to watch the pennies. His in-laws were not impressed by his choice. Old Mrs Cotton wrote regularly to Aunt Susan asking for news and photographs of *our dearest*

Ralph and for *a tiny lock of his hair (if he has any to spare)* but she could not refrain from oblique criticism. *We heard that your Brother has some idea of leaving Armitage, if so, I hope you may reside not quite in such an inacceptable place as now,* she wrote in 1863 with a healthy contempt for grammar. The Cottons were always frightful snobs.

It must have been desperately sad for John William to move into what should have been his marital home without his *dearest, dearest Agnes.* But Susanna Ingleby was happy and busy -shopping, measuring for blinds, calling on the new neighbours:

July 21st: John Wm, Mrs Howe, Caroline, baby & I left Mrs Myatt's lodgings in Rugeley and came to Armitage Cottage. Mrs Howe, Caroline & Baby came in Millard's cart.

Ralph wouldn't have been able to remember either of them, of course. Neither stayed long. The first nursemaid he would have remembered was Betsy Leigh who arrived when he was four-and-a-half and stayed until he went away to school. But there had been others - his aunt recorded them all and the wages they were paid.

Susanna Ingleby was always careful and frugal, but even at Armitage Cottage they always had two servants, a cook-housekeeper and a nursemaid. 'Ralphy' was the focus of his aunt's life. At the back of most of her diaries was a record of his height and weight and she recorded all the milestones of his childhood.

Baby began short clothes
Baby was vaccinated by D H Monckton MD
Baby cut his first tooth
Ralphy began to use a knife at meals
Ralphy began knickerbocker suits

But in fact she spent comparatively little time looking after baby Ralphy and when the nursemaid of the moment had one of her very occasional days off, Aunt Susan always noted it: *I looked after Baby all day.* Susanna Ingleby probably saw herself as being rather enterprising in doing even this. Her own mother had had nothing at all to do with her babies after they were weaned. A full day of feeding, changing, bathing, playing, taking for walks and putting to bed was not something most upper class mothers expected to cope with. A caring mother saw her children briefly in the morning and then for an hour or so in the late afternoon before she went off to dress for dinner and the children were put to bed. Well-to-do mothers went away on holiday for weeks or months at a time leaving their children in the more-or-less capable hands of hired nursemaids and nannies.

Ralph actually benefited from the fact that his father and aunt were comparatively poor. John William's income was just £100 [£5,800] a year from two farms that his grandfather had left him; Susanna Ingleby had the same amount annually from her estranged husband and a small but erratically-paid allowance from her father. There was no money to pay a maid to cover the nurse's days off and so Ralphy's aunt looked after him herself.

Aunt Susan took her role very seriously. She bought childcare books and no doubt read them assiduously. Mrs Warren's *How I Managed my Children* was her favourite. Mrs Warren was the Dr Spock of her day, and her book consisted of a series of anecdotes about how she persuaded her children to go to bed on time, to eat foods that she thought good for them, to share their toys, to play nicely and to donate their pocket money to the poor and needy. She stressed the need for a rigid routine, lots of plain, stodgy food, plenty of fresh air and exercise - and vigilance over the activities of nannies and nursemaids. She disapproved of prams and pushchairs - armed with wheeled transport nurses could go far afield on their afternoon walks and take the child to unsuitable places.

Aunt Susan could take no chances with her precious little nephew. She must have been relieved when he reached his first birthday - the first year of life was the most dangerous for the Victorian child.

May 2nd: 1863 Baby's birthday was kept. I called on Mrs Birch and Miss Wilson. Alice and Ada [teenage neighbours] *called and brought a box of letters and a ball for Baby. John William came here from Stafford and brought a water cart for Baby. I gave Baby a box of bricks.*

Birthday presents for children were still something of a novelty in the 1860s. Ralph's father and aunt had celebrated their childhood birthdays with parties and 'feasts' - but presents were a rarity. Attitudes had changed and as an only child Ralphy was much more fortunate. We know from his aunt's diaries that he had a cardboard model of a station and a fort, a toy horse and cart, card games, battledore and shuttlecock, a sword, wooden boats to sail on the canal and lots and lots of books. Improving stories about children who were good and brave. Books about birds and butterflies, plants and toadstools.

Classics like *Uncle Tom's Cabin* and *Grimm's Fairy Tales.* Ralph also took a children's story magazine, *Chatterbox*, which came every month and each year his aunt had the issues bound into volumes. But by modern standards he had few material possessions. Mrs Warren would have approved - children, she believed, were confused by too many playthings.

Ralph and his aunt drew pictures and made scrapbooks which he saved carefully. Indeed, even as an adult he found scrapbooks a useful way of keeping items of interest. They were usually exercise books covered in marbled paper, but sometimes printed books or catalogues were re-used, so that, peeping out behind Ralphy's drawings of houses and factories there would be the text and engravings of a farmers' catalogue or a religious tract. Paper was expensive in the 19th century and Aunt Susan was a penny-pincher. Ralph's childhood scrapbooks show very clearly the paucity of coloured images available in the 1860s, even for a child from a well-to-do family. The most colourful things in them were his papa's cartridge wrappers in bright red and blue that were decorated with pictures of different kinds of game birds.

There were pictures cut from Aunt Susan's magazine *The Ladies' Treasury* - ladies in fashionable costume, a picture of a sewing machine, advertisements. Ralphy probably preferred her gardening catalogues from Suttons of Reading with their bright yellow covers and illustrations of fruit and vegetables and flowers or his father's agricultural papers which had engravings of livestock and farm machinery. They didn't even have Christmas cards when Ralph was little and all their birthday cards and valentines were home-made. Most of the pictures in the scrapbooks were drawings done by Aunt Susan or himself. She drew animals for him - dogs, birds, farm animals and a portrait of his pony Jennetta. Jennetta was given to him the Christmas he was three and was a stout, good-tempered little Shetland. Years later, Ralph would carefully annotate these drawings, saying which of them were his aunt's and which were his own.

Ralph always seems to have enjoyed drawing. His scrapbooks were full of sketches, battle scenes with knights in full armour shooting arrows at each other, bugs and snakes and creepy-crawlies, flywheels and traction engines and pretend machines like Heath Robinson illustrations. Angels in the sky. Armitage cottage with the pottery works behind, dominating the view. At night the kilns glowed a hellish red, and all day, everyday, smuts and coal dust blackened the garden and dirtied the house. Aunt Susan insisted that the right way to learn to draw was by copying pictures out of books and at least some of Ralphy's drawings seem to have been copied from encyclopaedias. He was talented. Even as an eight year old his drawings were well-observed, when he drew his home he drew Armitage Cottage, complete with its bay window. He soon developed a rudimentary understanding of perspective - a childish drawing of a cottage shows it at an angle to the viewer, the garden is full of snakes, the sky is dark with creatures. Ralph does seem to have had a passion for drawing snakes - they feature in numerous illustrations, hanging from trees, entwined round a hapless deer, menacing a tiny bird. Some drawings are rather darker - strange, shaggy yeti-men, figures flying through the sky on winged armchairs, a spider-monster in a living room and a set of scribbles that appear to feature an animal on an operating table!

Dull and pedestrian though they are, Aunt Susan's diaries enable us to reconstruct the happenings in her own and her nephew's early life in great detail. They record trips back 'home' to Leek, taking advantage of the Reverend John Sneyd's absences to visit friends and relations. And there were trips to the seaside. In February 1865, for example, they went to Dover to see Ralph's Grandmamma Cotton and Aunts Bertha and Fanny.

It was probably quite a difficult holiday. There was some trouble between Ralph's father and Uncle Rowland Cotton over some money John William was thought to owe. When poor Agnes was dying many doctors were called to tend her, two even came from London. When John William could not afford to pay them his in-laws had picked up the bills. Agnes had also borrowed money from her sisters to pay for her trousseau and John William had not repaid that loan. None of this had anything to do with Susanna but it probably made for a rather strained visit.

Fairly soon, his father's feud with his in-laws curtailed Ralph's visits to see his grandmother and aunts. John William's endless quarrels frequently made life very difficult for his son and Susanna. Not until he was an adult did Ralph resume contact with the Cottons.

The diaries made regular references to Ralphy's illnesses. Aunt Susan always believed him to be sickly.

May 17th 1864: ...Ralphy was rather poorly and had a rash.

May 18th: ...Ralphy took some grey powders....

October 13th: ...Dr Monkhouse came to see Ralphy and ordered him a bath and powders he has bad spots.

October 14th 1865: ...Ralphy was very sick and poorly.

October 16th: Poor Ralphy was very ill. Dr Monckton came to see him and thought he was beginning scarlet fever....

But he wasn't. A week later he was up and about again and *began to take steel* - a popular tonic. Despite Aunt Susan's worries, few of Ralphy's early childhood illnesses amounted to much. He had measles when he was nine and typhoid fever three years later but he made a full recovery both times.

Victorian parents worried a great deal about health which was entirely understandable. Babies and children died in great numbers. Smallpox vaccination was relatively safe and effective, and by the time Ralph was a child it was compulsory, but diphtheria, typhoid, scarlet fever, measles and whooping cough were all common and all were potential killers. Consumption - tuberculosis - was a spectre that haunted families and of course there were no antibiotics to treat it.

There are numerous photos of little Ralphy - as a tiny baby submerged in a long white gown, as a toddler in a white embroidered frock with a big sash, as a little six year old in a kilt with a velvet jacket and waistcoat, complete with sash and sporran, and as a nine year old, ready for school, in a tweed knickerbocker suit and waistcoat, made for him by Mr Lamb of Derby and teamed with thick socks and stout, well-worn boots.

19th century children's clothes were high maintenance. Babies and toddlers of both sexes wore white cotton dresses that needed careful laundering and ironing and showed every splash of mud and dribble of gravy. A child dressed head to foot in white was demonstrably the object of a good deal of care and effort. Mrs Warren recommended *stout Holland aprons* for play, but Holland is linen and requires careful washing and ironing. There were no easy-care fabrics in the 19th century. Nor were there any truly waterproof ones, at least not until right at the end of the century. Keeping babies changed and dry must have been a nightmare - it is not surprising that Mrs Warren placed a great deal of stress on potty training. Keeping little boys in dresses or kilts made this process slightly easier. Six year old Ralphy wore a kilt to have his picture taken, but for everyday wear at that age he would have worn what his aunt referred to as *high dresses* - wide trousers with a loose smock top or jacket, made in some sort of washable fabric. Convention decreed that these, too, should be a light colour.

Doing the washing for their charges and keeping clothes in good repair by sewing on buttons and mending tears, were part of the nursemaid's duties. Children simply didn't have enough clothes to keep them looking decent from one weekly wash to the next. Armitage was an industrial village with coal dust and mud, grimy streets and unpaved country footpaths. Betsy had her work cut out to keep Master Ralphy looking smart enough to please Mrs Ingleby.

Victorian children were not always well behaved, though mawkish stories like *Archie's First Sixpence* in an SPCK booklet that Aunt Susan gave to Ralph, would suggest they were. The story hinges on the impossibly saintly Archie's attempts to do good with a sixpence his uncle gave him. Ralphy was a religious child, but given sixpence he would undoubtedly have spent it on himself!

Aunt Susan records how naughty Ralphy was on his third birthday when it was too wet for him to play outside with his new wheelbarrow. Such entries are rare so it seems likely that that day he was over-excited. But expectations of children's behaviour were higher than they are today. A pampered only child like Ralphy was probably heard as much as he was seen - in letters to him when he was at school his aunt urged him not to bore people by talking too much - but even at three he would have been taught good manners and how to behave in adult company.

Of course, he would not have encountered any of the food additives current wisdom blames for children's bad behaviour. Most of Ralphy's food was made at home from fresh, local ingredients. And the diet his aunt's childcare books recommended for children was plain and starchy: plenty of milk, but not a great deal of other protein, vegetables (with the goodness boiled out of them) and very little fruit. Fruit was thought to be too acid for childish stomachs. Even in very hot weather, Mrs Warren stressed, no child should have more than two glasses of home-made lemonade a week! Ralphy would have had few sweets and the recipes for cakes, puddings and biscuits that appear in his aunt's cookery book have far less sugar in them than their modern equivalents. By and large, Ralphy's diet did not provide him with an excess of energy with which to be really naughty, and he was encouraged to use the energy he did have to the full. Each day he was taken on long walks and encouraged to play in the fresh air - there was no TV or PlayStation then.

Mrs Warren warned parents to beware of 'over-stimulating' their offspring. Excited children got overheated and silly and then there would be tears before bedtime, Victorian nursemaids and parents were led to believe. A regular routine was seen as the ideal. Susanna Ingleby's diaries do not suggest that Ralphy's regime was particularly exciting, though there were occasional treats. In January 1867, for example, Ralphy was considered old enough to go with his father and Aunty Susan to a party at Hawkesyard, the home of Josiah Spode, the grandson of the potter.

January 10th: Showery. John Wm, Ralphy and I went to the Xmas tree party at Hawkesyard. Ralphy and I returned home about 10 o'clock, John Wm got home at $^1/_2$ past 1. John Wm won a ball and Ralphy a humming top.

Mr Spode gave splendid parties. There would have been a great tree lit by the soft light of dozens of flickering candles, the smell of resin and candle-wax filling the air, the light reflected in dozens of glittering fragile glass baubles. And the candles, guttering and swaying, tilting alarmingly in their tin holders, threatened to set the branches alight - there would have been buckets of water to hand of course. They stayed till way past Ralphy's bedtime then he and his aunt drove home together, down the dark, wet roads, leaving his Papa to drink and listen to the band until the early hours.

That year aunt and nephew seem to have done much more together. She took him for many of his walks and he began to accompany her on many more visits. The messy part of Ralphy's childhood had been left to the nursemaids but by 1867 he was more of a companion to Susanna, a talkative, pretty, precocious little boy whom she was happy to show off to her friends

Soon he was also having regular lessons with his aunt. She taught him to read and write, one of his early exercise books contained his name 'Ralph De Tunstall Sneyd' (the 'De' always had a capital D) written on page after page in large, rounded, copperplate script. He learnt simple sums, and on walks he was encouraged to collect specimens for the study of natural history: tadpoles, birds' eggs, snail shells, pebbles, flowers, grasses, leaves and, above all, toadstools. Ralph was fascinated by toadstools and as quite a small boy one of his presents from his Aunt Emily was a tiny book of illustrations of different sorts of fungi.

Aunt Susan read to him and he learnt the rudiments of geography and history, the names of capital cities, major rivers, towns, mountain ranges, deserts and seas, the dates of battles and the names of kings. Aunt Susan liked facts and Victorian teachers set much store by rote learning. Ralph was always fascinated by foreign climes and travelled extensively as an adult, and his imagination was fired by things mediaeval, by the Arthurian legends and tales of chivalry. These ideas were fixed in his head by a happy coincidence; within a mile or two of Armitage lie the Ridwares, the hamlets of Mavesyn, Pipe, Hill and Hamstall Ridware. Little Ralphy was often taken to Mavesyn Ridware church as a treat, to something called the 'Trinity Aisle.'

'Do you remember we went there on our very first trip to Armitage?' Marion asked.

I nodded. It was back in 1994, the first time we went to Staffordshire together. We had been curious to know why Ralphy liked that church so much.

'As soon as we walked in we saw them, standing like a row of giant stone playing cards, but not aces, queens or kings, these were knights, and they were Ralphy-sized! That's why Susanna took him there.'

'Have you ever seen any other crusader tombs like those?' I asked.

'Never!'

No doubt Ralphy's aunt told him stories of the knights of old and, in his vivid imagination, he saw himself amongst them, riding into battle...

There were other places to visit, season by season. In the spring they went to the daffodil fields and to see the flowers as they came out in the woods and fields around. Armitage may have been an industrial village but the countryside was not far away. Growing daffodils to sell by the bunch in the local towns seems to have been a Victorian practice. Year by year, whether she was living in Cheddleton or Oakamoor, Armitage or Abbots Bromley, Susanna Ingleby *went to the daffodil fields*.

In 1867 Ralphy joined his papa and Aunty Susan at Tixall Lodge for Christmas. Tixall Lodge was the gatehouse and all that remained of Tixall Park, a great, ivy-covered, stone-built 16th century property. Their friends, Mr and Mrs Mayne, rented it. Even then Ralph seems to have spent most of his time with Betsy and the servants, though he did go to church with the family and walk in the park on Christmas Day. They were back home for New Year and his aunt and papa seem to have had a high old time, staying over at Hawkesyard and playing 'Ghosts' each evening. There was a lot of visiting and entertaining, but it was grown-up stuff. The only thing laid on for Ralphy was a visit to Armitage Lodge where kind Mrs Birch arranged for him to play with a zoetrope, a drum-like affair with slits round the rim. You put strips of drawings inside, spun it, looked through the slits and the pictures seemed to move. To a little boy it must have seemed quite magical - a galloping horse or a clown tumbling over and over and over again.

In March 1868 Ralph had his first real encounter with death. Mrs Spode at Hawkesyard died after a short illness. Aunty Susan took Ralphy to watch her funeral procession, fourteen black carriages, the horses all with black plumes, men in top hats and white gloves walking slowly behind the hearse, heads bowed. Ralph had known of other deaths - uncles, cousins, cousins' children - but they were not people he knew well, people he had seen regularly for as long as he could remember. Death, for a little Victorian child, was something you had to get used to; you would encounter it often. Aunt Susan and Ralphy did not go to the funeral but they watched from a discreet distance, standing in a nearby field, no doubt with Aunty Susan talking of heaven and angels and harps....

Ralphy was growing up. His aunt's next few diaries recorded a lot of 'firsts'. He learnt to paint, had his first ride *by the side of a horse*, his first baby tooth came out, he had his curls cut off. His aunt made a new friend, a Mr Palmer, who, in fact, hoped to be rather more than just a friend. From late in 1869 Mr Palmer was an almost daily visitor. He showered Susanna with presents and gave Ralph a tortoise and a host of curiosities for his collection. At the age of seven Ralphy had progressed from collecting natural history specimens. He was now collecting coins, archaeological bits and pieces, anything else friends and neighbours were kind enough to give him. His father and aunt thought it a pleasantly educational hobby for a little boy.

Life changed completely for them all in the autumn of 1870. Armitage Cottage was damp, there were problems with the drains - sometimes the smell was so unbearable that they all had to decamp upstairs. Their landlord was unable, or unwilling, to do anything about it and John William had decided there was no alternative but to move. He rented a house in Abbots Bromley. *September 27th 1870: Lea Fields, rent £45* [£2,600]. *We expected Aston's vans at six o'clock but they did not come till nine, we left Armitage Cottage about four o'clock, the vans did not arrive here, Lea Fields, until half past seven. We had to unpack by candlelight.*

Seven year old Ralph probably thought it was all quite an adventure. No doubt he missed Armitage where he had lived all his life. The Birches at Armitage Lodge, the Wilsons at the Rectory, Mr Spode at Hawkesyard, Mr Palmer, the Cluttons and a whole host of other people made up his world. Many of them would be his friends for the rest of their lives - Mrs Birch was still sending him Christmas presents when he was eighteen. Of course, today Armitage is only a few minutes away from Abbots Bromley by car, but in 1870, for a family without a carriage, it was just too far to visit for the day.

New friends had to be found.

For Ralphy, this was a great novelty. His childhood in Armitage had been a lonely one, spent largely with adults. But his aunt's friend, Harriet Pickering, lived in Abbots Bromley. Her husband was Lord Bagot's land agent - and her two children, Katie and Eddie, were much the same age as Ralph. The three became friends and for a few months Ralphy saw them regularly. But barely had he had time to settle into Abbots Bromley than his life was turned upside down again.

January 26th: Fine. John Wm took Ralphy to Miss Cranes' School, Boxwood House, Leamington....

'When do you think they told him he was going away to school?'

'Probably not very early - Mrs Warren said it wasn't a good idea to let children get upset about things they couldn't avoid.'

'What surprises me is that they didn't visit him - Leamington wasn't that far away.'

'They were probably told it would unsettle him. After all, well into the second half of the 20th century parents were kept away from children in hospital. It was probably the same at boarding schools.'

Contact with Ralphy was by weekly letter - and for a little boy for whom reading and writing were still chores, it was a most inadequate means of communication. The effect it had on him lasted a lifetime.

One of Ralphy's drawings.

Chapter 3
Ralph goes to the Miss Cranes

George Eliot, Disraeli, Dickens and Darwin attended various small schools for short spells in their childhood. None went to public school. None went to university. A rigid school syllabus and cramming for examinations might well have cramped their style, imagination and individual development. Fortunately for us, and for them, they went to schools which were not curricula and examination dominated. And so did Ralph.

In January 1871 - three months before his ninth birthday - Ralphy moved on from his privileged, if somewhat isolated, childhood and went to school. The one chosen by his father for his allegedly delicate son was in a genteel town house in Leamington run by six spinster sisters - the Miss Cranes. It had been recommended by Mrs Challinor, wife of the Sneyd family solicitor in Leek, as being entirely suitable for Ralph. Her son Edward was already there.

Ralph would go to three more small private schools. Two were run by vicars in their own homes, each augmenting his tiny stipend by taking a handful of paying pupils. Only one was what we would today recognise as a prep school. What occurred behind the closed doors of these smaller schools - both before and after the Education Acts - is not documented anywhere at all. No inspection was necessary. No official records exist. It is only through the letters and diaries written by children who went to these schools that we can get some idea of what went on.

Ralphy's letters tell us, as they told his aunt and father, something of what he studied at school - though not nearly as much as we would like. What they do reveal, with crystal clarity, is Ralphy's development as an individual and the growth of his lifelong obsession with collecting. His voice comes through loud and clear from the very first letter.

Boxwood House   February 2nd.
My Dear Auntty,
I aM happy and well at school. I hope you and Papa are quite well and going on well. There are 6 Miss Cranes and more than 20 boys I must write more next time love to all
*   I remain   Your affectionaet Mephew   RDT Sneyde* [e crossed out]
*   P.S. I am sorry My Rabbit is dead.*

March 9th 1871
My dear Aunty
The rain is fast here today and we cannot go out. I hope you and papa are quite
well. I have a little cold. I very often draw. Miss Caroline kindly took us to
see a stuffed crocodile, it was a very small one. I am glad all my pets are well.
*   My best love to you and Papa...*

Like most children, Ralphy lived in the present. He did not say where he saw the stuffed crocodile. Perhaps in a travelling show. Many such shows with 'curiosities' still toured the country in caravans and trailers which stopped for a day or two in each town. Wombwell's was the most famous - one of their trailers was pulled by an elephant. One can imagine the effect that must have had in a town before the age of cinema and television. An elephant in the street! Such an excitement! But for Ralph, seeing the little stuffed crocodile had been a disappointment. With his vivid imagination he was probably expecting a huge, scaly beast!

Susanna must have been desperate to know more about his life at school. What did he have for breakfast?. Did they have morning prayers - as they did at home? How much time did he spend on reading and writing and arithmetic? Did the Misses Cranes have time to stimulate him in the wonders of nature and science as she had done?

'I just don't know which ones to leave out!' I sighed, one day as we pored over a mountain of letters. 'It's like eavesdropping on a conversation between them.'

'That's the problem - but although reading hundreds of Susanna and Ralphy's letters may be gripping for you, it will make a pretty tedious book.'

'Really? I think it's fascinating. She tells him the news from home, but she also copies out snippets from newspapers that she thinks might interest him. Look at this - *I suppose you have heard that the war is over in Spain, and Don Carlos was to arrive in England last Friday. England is nearly always ready to receive those who are cast out by their own country.* And just look what she got back!'

May 4th 1871
my dear Aunty,
Thank you for your letter, and the nice book you were so kind to send me on
my Birthday. Aount Emily sent me tnelve stamps, Miss Crane exchanged them
for a shilling, and I have bought a magnete with it, and it attracts well.

'Well, he was only nine!'

'But Eddie Pickering managed to write proper letters home and he was much the same age. Look at this':

My dear Ralph,

I miss you very much. How do you like school. I have bought some marbles and wish you were here to have a game with me. That large hole you saw has been filled up. We have a little calf. How do you get on with latin. I have been a long time in writing to you, but I have been very busy. Katie has had a cold... after you went I went on the Ice on Thompsons pits, the boys and I had a slide across. I often see your black dog and he seems very sensible... On Saturday a deer ran into our garden pursued by some hounds and a lot of men rode over the rye. William ran out and shut the gate going into the field to stop them coming into our garden.   They got off their horses and threatened to horsewhip him. They made a great mess in our garden.

I am, your loving friend

T E Pickering

Apparently, when he went away to school it was Ralphy who decided that all his letters should be kept. Year by year his aunt stitched them together in books, each with a brown-paper cover. We found them all carefully stored in a little wooden box with a sliding lid.

'They're charming', said Pam, 'because of the misspellings and the odd way he juxtaposes things as much as anything. And yes, they do show how his interests were developing. But you lose such a lot when you only quote extracts...'

We had toyed with the idea of publishing Ralphy's letters in a separate book - *My Dear Aunty* was the working title. Pam still felt this would be better than overloading this chapter with them - but she could see I was going to take a lot of convincing - I thought they were wonderful.   Hopefully the compromise we managed works.

Ralph was at his first school for almost six months without coming home, something today we would think of as intolerable for such a young child. But it was the norm, something you just had to put up with, and Ralphy seems to have coped very well.

Just before his first holiday Susanna had a nasty fall and hurt her leg badly. Since she was not well Ralphy spent quite a lot of time that first holiday with his father and his friend Eddie Pickering - riding and shooting. The time must have passed all too quickly and at the beginning of August Susanna recorded in her diary, *August 3. John William took Ralphy to Rugeley to meet the Miss Cranes who took him back to school.*

Bonod hose
Orgugt 5th 1871
My dear Aunty
I have arrived saftly at school. I hope your knee is better today there is a new boy come. Is Papa quite well now I hope the pets are qwite well I am going to slep in the upper room I hope I shall fine you quite well
I remain yourr
Affectionatlly nephew
R DE T Sneyd

Ralph seemed to have forgotten practically everything he ever knew. Susanna and his father must have been even more worried when they heard from the Miss Cranes that he was not saying his prayers properly and that he seemed to have forgotten all the arithmetic he had learnt in his first six months with them. As usual it was Susanna who wrote the long letter in reply and we get the first indication of the 'carrot and stick' technique, the bribes and nagging that she was to use throughout his schooldays.

Lea Fields
August 7th 1871
My dearest Ralphy,

I was very glad to hear you had arrived at school alright. I thought it very kind of the Miss Cranes letting you write so soon... I hope you will have as pleasant companions in your bedroom as you had last half year... I hope you will be a good boy, and work very hard at your lessons, you know I was very sorry you should have been obliged to be kept to the first 2 rules in sums, because if you pay attention you are not backward at figures and I do hope you will say the church catechism without one mistake, as you can easily do that, and mind you say your prayers slowly, as it is impossible to think of what you are saying when you seem to get them over as soon as possible, do not let Miss Crane have to tell you once about being too quick over them. I was pleased with the way you have got on with nearly all your studies and I think the Miss Cranes have taken great pains with you. If you work hard till Xmas I will give you a book called 'Flowers of the Fields'. I think it is as easy to understand as any book on botany. It has about half as many pictures as there are pages and is a 7 shilling [£20] book. Did you remember to tell the Miss Cranes that I had made your old suit of clothes large enough for you and that I wished you to wear them until they are too shabby with an old collar buttoned onto the jacket as they are not large enough to button onto your shirt. In the two suits that are alike, the set which has been worn the most has a large C on them and the other has B.

....I was glad to hear that you often play cricket as I shall like you to get to play well, but I think you must all have got very hot over it as lately it has been difficult to keep cool... The thunder and lightening were very bad in North Staffordshire last Thursday, here the sky was so black about 10 o'clock that it was difficult to see to sew. A church was struck at Stone and a person who was near said the flash was like a red hot bar which left a strong sulphurous smell behind and in that town and elsewhere the shops had to be lighted at 10 o'clock in the morning...

Ralph replied:

They have been putting down new gas pipes and they nearly stopped up the road. We have seen three dragonflies... Miss Crane has given me a book called 'The first steps in General Knowledge, on the Starry Heavens'... We have fine Kite flying.

Susanna's next letter to her nephew added something else to the bribes and nagging - unfavourable comparison of his progress with that of other children. She was on a visit to relatives - Alecks Fraser was Ralph's second cousin.

We see very little of Alecks, he has his breakfast before we come down as he has to be at school which is a mile off by 9 o'clock. He comes home for dinner but he has to start off to school at a 1/2 past 1 and does not come here again until nearly 6 o'clock, and after that he has to prepare his lessons for the next day. He is a very good boy and although a 1/2 of a year younger than you are he has a watch of his own and he never has to be told everything about time but starts off alone. If you are a good boy and work hard at school you may have a book and it may cost 7s 6d [£21]....

Ralphy did not work hard - but he got the book! Much to Susanna's annoyance one of Ralphy's letters contained the news that he had taken himself off to the dentist - without any reference to his father or aunt. She wrote back and expressed surprise that he should have incurred them in expense without checking with them first. Ralph was unabashed.

....it was a first tooth I had taken out, to make room for the second tooth which would have grown twisted if the first tooth had not been taken out. We saw the comet the other evening which was very beautiful, and some meteors, and some very beautiful stars.

Nov. 16th
Thank Papa for his kind letter. I should like to have seen the things in the museum. [John William had been to Lichfield] *I hope your chilblains are better. I have seen 8 shooting stars ...It is just five weeks to the holidays. They are on the 21st of December. We had a half holiday on Tuesday and the boys acted a Chararde, the word was Portrait it was Frank Barber's birthday. I have bought a telescope for two shillings* [£6]. *it is a very good one....*

Before Christmas he also wrote home about a Latin primer - so even though he couldn't write English properly he was struggling with Latin.

On 30th January 1872 John William took Ralphy back to school in Leamington and the letters started again. Perhaps to interest him more in numbers Susanna recounted to him information she had read about a new exhibit, an elephant, at the South Kensington Museum in London.

....from the tip of his tail to the end of his trunk he measures 11 feet and 3 inches and the circumference of his trunk at the base is 4 feet and 4 inches... the texture of the hide is a study in itself, it can only be compared with the bark of a tree broken up and intersected by myriads of deep channels....

She told him about a new law that had been passed about shooting elephants for sport *...there have been so many shot lately that it is feared that there will not be enough left for the war purposes in India....*

In her next letter Ralph received the first intimation that he was to move house again. High above Abbots Bromley, Lea Fields was exposed to all the wind and rain, it was cold, draughty and damp - no wonder that Susanna suffered chilblains and colds for months on end *...we shall likely not stay here a half a year longer as this house is out of repair and we cannot get the owner to do anything....*

May 2nd
We do not forget that tomorrow is your birthday and I write to send you our best wishes for your health and happiness. When you left home I said I would not send you a present on your birthday as I had given you so many things, but as I have bought a book on Fossils I must let you have it; at the end I have

gummed an account of the Fossil Man found at Mentone. Uncle Tom and most of his family were there for a good many months and found many curious fossils there... have you noticed Euston Place in Leamington? I stayed two months there at No. 2 in 1860, two years before I began to look after you. I am glad you are pleased with the piece of white marble, it was well you told us you had found it on a stone heap ...Your wheat is very much higher than any other about here. Catherine [the maid] *wishes you many happy returns of tomorrow. Your Papa joins me in kind love,*

May 6th
My dearest Ralphy,

I was very glad to hear yesterday that you were well enough to sit up... [There had been an outbreak of measles at school] *I think it shows you have very good nursing... I am glad you are being a good boy and that you think it rather jolly to be poorly and to be so attended to; you must give as little trouble as possible....*

'Susanna would have been beside herself with worry,' I said. I've got this book, William Buchan's *New Domestic Medicine*, at home, published in the 19th century, and it gives a stomach-churning description of the complications of measles. Do you think we can quote some of it...?'

'I don't think there's room really. Children went blind or deaf, or died, of course - but measles is still a serious disease today, and anyway Ralphy wasn't very ill - so I don't think we need to go to that length.'

I was disappointed.

Susanna soon had something much worse to worry about. In June 1872 she and John William were summoned to Cheddleton. Their father had had a stroke and appeared to be dying. The Reverend John Sneyd called everyone to his bedside and had his solicitor, Mr Joseph Challinor, read out his will. Ashcombe Park and all the lands and farms attached to it - many of them still mortgaged - were to go to Dryden Henry, John William's younger brother. All John William was to have was his father's silver - silver that had been given to John Sneyd by embarrassed brother magistrates when he had been forced to resign from the Bench for abusing his position. John Sneyd had hated it - it was a reminder of his public humiliation, of one of the few times when he did not get his own way. Silver was for traitors - Judas had received silver. No-one at the bedside could miss the symbolism of John Sneyd's final, vindictive act towards his eldest son.

John William had been unwell for several years and he never recovered from this final insult - he became more reclusive and bad-tempered than ever. Maybe, when he came home that summer, Ralph at last learnt the details of the dreadful quarrel between his father and grandfather. But back at school that autumn, all he could think about was his collection. His last words to his aunt as they parted were that she wasn't to move any of his books or treasures so that he would know exactly where everything was when he got back for the Christmas holidays.

August 12th, Lea Fields

I hope by this time you have settled down again... I shall like to know if you have the same bedroom and the same boys in your room. I hope you will work very hard at your lessons, it will please me very much to hear you are getting on well, try to keep your eyes looking at your slate all the time you are doing your sums, I think you will do them as easily as any other boy as it is in the early parts you make the stupid mistake, with letting your thoughts wander; and take care and say the church Catechism without any mistakes, it ought to be as easy to say it in class as alone... I feel sure the Miss Cranes will let someone cut your nails when they get too long as I have been so sorry to see you have begun to bite them; did you remember to take your best gloves out of your pocket of the suit you were travelling in: you must remember to wear the short old braces with your trousers, as they are full long... I have put all our treasures carefully away. I know exactly where they all are. Your books I have left out as you placed them.

August 15th

Thank you for your nice letter... Last Monday afternoon Miss M.A. Crane kindly took us to see Blondin, he did many wonderful things on the tightrope. I like school very much....

A letter from his father was a rare event - John William seldom wrote.

Lea Fields
September 10th.
My dear little boy
....I was much pleased to receive your letter on my return home from Sir John Crewe's last Friday. I enjoyed it very much and had famous sport. Jesse was very good and was much admired. He was always anxious to mark and in famous spirits. Young Mr Crewe caught several Camberwell Beauty Butterflies

on the heather. They are very beautiful, it is about 83 years since many of them have been seen in England, perhaps you may have seen them in your walks. There is a nice account of them in the Butterfly book you have left out at home, so most likely there is an account of them in the book you took back to school. They are a rich purplish brown with a pale straw coloured exterior border within which is a line of black with a row of beautiful blue spots upon it. They are very large... Aunty sends her thanks for your letter. We hope you will be careful about cleaning your teeth, very likely the great quantity of iron and quinine you have taken has done them harm. I am glad you like your drawing lessons.

September 12th Leamington
Thank Papa for his letter and for the nice account he gave me, I am glad he enjoyed himself. I bought a printed sheet of flags and a sheet of crests of all the Nations, the flags cost one shilling [£3] and the crests one shilling and sixpence [£4].
I hope all the pets are quite well, give my rabbits plenty of food please. Last Tuesday evening we all sat up till after ten o'clock to see some beautiful fireworks....

Susanna replied:

....I am glad to hear you have been able to get a sheet of flags and crests, and also that you showed them to me as I had rather intended to order them for you. There have lately been several Red Admiral butterflies in the kitchen garden so your Papa has caught 3 for you as he thought you would be pleased with them. I keep them in your glass box and they will not get damaged. I think they are as handsome as any English butterfly, they look very large and gay when they are flying about... the rabbit has plenty to eat and is as tame as possible. About a week ago about 12 people came here and danced in the Hobby Horse show. It is an old performance which used to take place in this town 3 times a year and then the money gained went to some charity, one boy rides a wooden horse and several men carry horns which ought to have the arms of the chief families of the place painted on them, but now the men keep for themselves all the money they get. The horns are kept in the tower of the church. [She is describing the Abbots Bromley Horn Dance].

September 12th
...we have had a sudden change to cold weather, as soon as your hands feel very cold please ask one of the Miss Cranes to be so kind as to get a pair of mittens for you, like you had last winter, so as to keep the chilblains off for as long as possible...

October 3rd.

My dear Aunty,

Thank you for your nice letter. Last Michaelmas day being on Sunday, we went to Warwick on Monday for our Michaelmas holiday. We went to the castle and saw all the pictures. There was a table inlaid with presious stones, worth ten thousand pounds [£546,000]. *We saw a great deal of Armour. There was a picture of Charles the first on horseback....*

October 24th

....When the Miss Landers [from Armitage] *came to Leamington they gave me a book on eggs and nests. They also gave me a cake and when I left them they filled my pockets full of apples and pears. I am glad the pets are well and that there are a great many frogs, toads and lizards about the conservatory. Miss C Crane gave me the gauntlets so I have not had any Chilblains. I am very sorry that you are suffering from them already....*

November 12th Lea Fields

....I see from the Stafford papers that there was another Hippopotamus born in London on the 5th of November. It is to be called Guy Fawkes, the other soon died, the mother not allowing anyone near enough to feed it, and the papers say that a family in Yorkshire have a tortoise which they can tell by the rings on its shell to be two hundred years old. It has been in the family for a hundred years. All your pets are quite well. Katie went for a ride on Jennetta last Friday....

November 19th Lea Fields

....We have just received our annual present of a pork pie from Mrs Nixon, I wish you were here to have some of it. She also sent a little piece of her daughter's wedding cake. I am keeping a little piece for you. I wonder if the Miss Cranes tell you about things which we hear from the papers, there has been another dreadful fire in America and a dreadful hurricane which destroyed a town in Sicily and left about 1,000 people without a house and about 1,000 more with very little left. About 32 people were killed and 20 more seriously hurt. Lately there seem to have been so many accidents. I think I mentioned to you that there is to be a large middle class girl's school in the town. £1,500 [£82,000] *has been given for it.*

November 12th Leamington

The holidays will begin on the 19th of December. Our examination will be going on next week, so perhaps I shall not be able to write to you. The other day we saw two beautiful silver cups in a shop window. I saw an eclipse of the moon on the morning of the 15th did you see it? I think I shall travel with Kenny as far as Armitage

November 26th Lea Fields
We shall be very much pleased to have you home again on the 19th... I hope you will try to be very good at the examinations, and please the Miss Cranes. It was very kind of them to let you see the eclipse of the moon. You seem always to see all the wonderful things at Leamington and we miss them here. My Almanac gave the wrong day...

December 5th
My dear Aunty,
Thank you for your nice letter. Miss Crane kindly had a man to show us a good magic Lanthorn on Tuesday. There were a great many Photographs some of which were of Litchfield Cathedral We saw Photographs of clusters of stars. When we had seen them, we were shown the different look of colours by the common gas and by the lime light. Miss Crane sends her love to you and is sorry she has not been able to answer your kind letter yet but she will do so in a day or so.

Ralphy came home for his holidays on 19th December and Susanna recorded in her diary *Ralphy 4 feet 8$^1/2$ inches*. Then:
Xmas Day. Damp. John William and Ralphy went to church in the morning. I stayed at home because of my chilblains. John William gave Ralphy two copy books. I gave him Common objects of the Country, Richmond Gale [a second cousin] *sent him a book about volcanoes, Mary Hand, Dora and Betsy sent cards. Catherine gave mittens and a card... Ralphy gave me a kettle holder.*

Ralphy was growing up. Soon he would no longer be her baby but an independent young man. But she still had a few years of pasting things in his scrapbooks with him, reading to him, sharing his passion for collecting and helping him to arrange his treasures and doubtless it was she who had to calm John William down when they received another rather large doctor's bill that Ralphy had run up the term before without any reference to them at all.

February 11th 1873 Lea Fields
I was pleased to hear you are pretty well again. I suppose that you are still wearing the mittens that Catherine gave you, as soon as you do not require the flannel for your chest you can use it for washing with, but wear it as long as

you like this cold weather; we like to be told if you are poorly enough to require a Doctor as we were surprised to see £1 5s [£68] for medical attention and 6s [£16] for wine last half year you never having mentioned the slightest illness. My chilblains are better but I still can't sew at present. I had to stay in bed two mornings as I could not dress myself and two more mornings for a very bad headache. It is a great wonder for me to be shut up and require waiting on. The Blithfield poison case is in all the papers The Gamekeeper drank cyanide by mistake when he came in thirsty from shooting. Dr Morrell says he drank enough potassium cyanide to kill 40 men... Your Aunt Emily says the snow in London is so bad that the snow ploughs had to be used twice in Oxford Street and in that street alone 300 carts were employed to cart the snow away... Your poor Grandpapa has caught a cold and has to keep to his bed....

Ralph was nearly eleven and in his aunt's eyes he could still be very silly and inconsiderate, as this next letter shows. She was extremely cross.

February 18th 1873 Lea Fields

Thank you for your letter and your Papa and Catherine join me in many thanks for the very pretty Valentines you sent us. Catherine was surprised that you remembered her surname. Yours was the only valentine she got on the right day, but she had 4 the next day. I thought you were considering that as you wrote to me that would serve instead of a Valentine as mine did not come until the 15th, owing to the stamp being put on the back of the letter; I suppose you or some other boy had put it there for 'fun', but it was no good there. I sent the envelope to Rugely to enquire if the 2d was charged there as there was a nasty tempered man there and I could see from the postmarks that he had kept the Valentine a day in Rugeley but the answer I got was that the 2d was charged at Leamington and the delay was not explained, but it was the way of the post master to delay any letter for a day that is not quite right.

'That's odd isn't it? Not at all what we think valentines are for now.'

'Ralphy always sent valentines to the maids and Aunty Susan, and they sent them to him. I think it was a family custom more than a general one - in one of his letters he says that the other boys didn't receive them.'

'How embarrassing!'

February 20th. 1873 Leamington

....I am sorry I put the stamp on the wrong side of the envelope. I am glad your chilblains are better... This is a very foggy morning. We have had some nice

walks lately... My Chilblains are nearly well. With love to you all
  Believe me,
  Your affectionate nephew Ralph, De, T, Sneyd.
P.S. I am so sorry That Grand Papa is dead. Miss Crane has just told me. I
thank you for the black neck tie.

John Sneyd survived his stroke by eight months. He went to London and consulted Sir William Gull, the royal physician, but then he had another and died. His death was recorded as a 'PS' in Ralphy's letter. Perhaps it was a more fitting memorial than he realised - and certainly it chalks up the position that the Reverend Sneyd held in his life. Nonetheless, Ralphy would have been expected to wear his black necktie for several weeks to mourn the grandfather he had never met.

He was fortunate in being a boy - mourning dress for women and girls was much more burdensome. Susanna had written poignantly in her diary when she learnt of her father's death *February 22nd 1873. I put away my coloured dresses...* She would have to wear black for a full year. She also had to tell everyone the white lie that John William was *too unwell* to attend their father's funeral.

February 25th 1873 Lea Fields
I knew you would be sorry to hear of your poor Grandpapa's death, he was buried in Cheddleton yesterday, a great many of our relations were there and the tenants but your Papa had too bad a cough and cold to leave this house. Mr Joseph Challinor joined in the hounds at Loxley on Saturday and as they ran this way he called here, he told us he had taken you a short walk and he thought you seemed well. I hope he did not make you another present as he has given you so much... My very bad chilblains are healing but I have some fresh ones. I am afraid this weather will make them worse. Mr John Sleigh has sent some foreign stamps for you. Work hard at your lessons and do not look about when you are doing your sums.

'It's interesting isn't it,' I mused to Pam, 'just how many people gave Ralph things - coins, stamps, things for his collections, money and cakes and oranges. It wasn't just Susanna. Why? Were they sorry for him or did he have a sort of charm that made people want to give him things? Presents flowed towards him as if drawn by a magnet!'

'Charm with a capital 'C' would be my guess,' she laughed.

Mrs Mayne was so kind as to come and see me on Tuesday, and she is going to invite me to go and see her in Leamington and she was so kind as to send me a box with some oranges and a cake...

Mrs Birch who has been staying in Leamington kindly asked me to take tea with her last Monday ...yesterday she came to wish me goodbye and brought me some cake.

Susanna sent news of other gifts:

....You will be very much pleased to hear that your Aunt Emily has given you a Queen Elizabeth shilling which was found under the roots of a large tree which stood opposite the gates. It is rather discoloured but the work on it is quite sharp. Your uncle Dryden has given you two small Roman coins, they are bright and quite sharp. They were found in the ground and given to your poor Grandpapa ...there is an account of them which I have packed up... Now mind you work hard. Your Papa and I have quite settled for you to go to Mr Walsh's at Midsummer

'Mr Walsh's school was only a stone's throw from the Miss Cranes you know,' Pam informed me one day as we were trying to get the book into some sort of order.

'How do you know that?'

'I looked at a map! I also had a session with the 1871 Leamington census returns one day. Fascinating, there were fifteen boys living at the Miss Cranes' and thirty-nine at Mr Walsh's. The boys at the Miss Cranes' were mainly local and they ranged in age from seven to ten - though there was one twelve year old. If Ralph was right in saying there were twenty boys at the school they may also have had some day boys. At Mr Walsh's, there were boys from as far away as Ireland, India and the East Indies, and they were older - ten to thirteen.'

'So perhaps that's why John William wanted to move Ralphy - so that he would be with some older boys?'

Pam's thorough academic approach had born fruit again.

Lea Fields
April 22nd 1873
Your Papa thanks you for your letter, the French money that your Papa got in London are two 'Dix Centimes'. They are just the size of our pennies. They have the head of Napoleon the 3rd on one side and the eagle on the other.

One is dated 1854 and the other 1855, if you had not cared for such things he would most likely have parted with them in London - so many foreigners come there. I have put them with your coins. Prince and Princess Christian came to stay with Lord and Lady Shrewsbury at Ingestre last Tuesday. They were grandly received at Stafford and after that they wished not to be made a fuss with, they saw the country round Ingestre on Wednesday and on Thursday went to Alton and on Friday came to Blithfield. We heard they would come and see the trees in Bagot's Park, so we went to the Goat Lodge to see them and 7 of the young Lowes and the Blurtons were there. After we had waited a little while the Princess and Lady Bagot came up in an open carriage and when just opposite to us Lady Bagot stopped her carriage while she spoke to Mr Turner, the Park keeper, who wore the same green coat as he wore on October 24th 1832 when he escorted the Duchess of Kent and our Queen, who was then Princess Victoria as they passed through the park... The Princess bowed to all our party. Your Papa and I walked in the park and we twice more saw the Princess and afterwards the Prince and Lord Shrewsbury and three other gentlemen... 5 pairs of boots were given to the Princess at Stafford, that town being famed for its boots. Eddie Pickering's Papa took him to London to see the sights in his Easter Holidays, he liked the Zoological gardens better than anything. Perhaps we may have a chance of taking you there before too long... I hope you are always good when you are out visiting. You must work very hard at your lessons now.

The summer of 1873 was to be a time of upheaval for Ralph's father and aunt and they were to spend much of it in London. For years John William had suffered from a throat complaint that made it difficult to talk. Now, in London, he would undergo expensive, invasive and painful electric shock treatment from a Dr Morrell Mackenzie - originally from Stafford. It was called 'galvanism' and was all the rage. They stayed in London for several weeks and Susanna wrote interesting letters to her little nephew. She was enjoying herself:

Your Papa has begun to be Galvanised... and afterwards we by underground railway went to Kensington... we took a two hour drive in the park with your cousin Ellen Kynnersley and saw the Princess of Wales. I saw her well. Today we are going to dine at Mrs John Sleigh's and on Saturday we are invited to play croquet at Mrs Antrobus's.

Dr Mackenzie says your Papa's throat is better, but I cannot hear that his voice has improved at all... Last Wednesday we spent at Crystal Palace and on Thursday we went to Westminster Abbey, Friday we spent at the South Kensington Museums and on Saturday we went to a croquet party at Mrs Antrobus's, and on Sunday we went to church at Highgate and dined at Mrs John Sleigh's... today we dine at Mr Hunt's and drive out in his carriage in the park afterwards ...and we have other invitations to dine out so we are very gay and enjoying ourselves. We very much wish you were here with us....

Leamington

Thank you very much, for your nice letter. I am glad that Dr Mackenzie says that Papa's throat is better, I hope at the end of the week, he will be well enough, to return home. Our Holidays begin, on the 20th of this month, when I shall be very glad, to see you, and Papa, I am very glad that you, and Papa have been to so many parties, and seen so many places. I have a set of Avoirdupois Weights and 16 Coins.

London

We have been seeing most of the grand sights in London and have enjoyed our stay here, but money goes very quickly in Drs fees and we must get home as soon as we can... we should have enjoyed ourselves still more if you had been here with us. Your Aunt Ada's husband gave us tickets to the Zoological gardens last Saturday as that is the day that the band plays. If you come here we shall of course take you there... I am glad you are pleased with your weights and coins.

Whilst they were in London the Reverend Charles Ingleby, Susanna's estranged husband, died. He was just fifty-one. Susanna was still wearing black for her father - but now she had to go into even deeper mourning with more crepe and a widow's cap. Ralphy would not have thought this odd - women of his aunt's generation were in mourning much of the time. What he did not know was that this death was to matter to him very materially, for it at last made Susanna an independent person with control over her own money. Married women at that date had no legal right to invest and Susanna had had to rely on the family solicitor to manage her money for her; as a widow she could act for herself. She invested in stocks and shares - mainly in the new Canadian railways - and Ralph, although he had no idea of it at this time, had his future assured by her good management and wise provision.

When Ralphy's term ended he joined his aunt and father in London, for John William was still having treatment from Dr Mackenzie. They visited the zoo, the museum, the Tower of London, Westminster Abbey, Madame Tussauds - it must have been thrilling for a country child. On the 28th of June they returned to Abbots Bromley. John William had had 40 visits to Dr Mackenzie and was still no better.

Ralphy spent the rest of his summer holiday arranging his coin and stamp collections, helped by his ever-doting aunt who was busy making special trays for his coins, and in riding his pony and collecting butterflies and birds' eggs. He visited his friends Katie and Eddie Pickering and shot at archery targets with them, so despite his bad report he had obviously still been given the bow his aunt had promised him as a reward. Susanna proudly recorded that *Ralphy shot best!*

He helped with the local hay harvest and called, with his aunt, on relatives and people in the village. All too soon the holiday was at an end. Ralphy was to start his new school in Leamington with the Reverend Walsh. John William and Susanna were to return to London where poor John William was to resume the painful treatment with Dr Mackenzie. They must have waited eagerly for Ralphy's first letter - but when it came the spelling was terrible and even the year on it was wrong!

A drawing Susanna did for Ralphy.

Chapter 4
Ralph changes School

Waterloo House,
Waterloo Street,
Leamington August 20th 1872
My dear Aunty,
I hope you arived in London quite safely. We all take cair of our deskes and we write when we like. I hope Papas throat is better. I supose you have not bought the cabenet yet. there are 4 Masters at this school counting Mr Walsh. After evening prairs the boys say thare prairs to them selves. I have been driling today. I should like to know very much how you got on in London....
Yours Affectionately
Ralph, De, T, Sneyd.

Ralph's spelling was truly appalling, even for a ten year old! Both Pam and I were used to students who couldn't spell, who spelt phonetically or were dyslexic, who confused 'were' and 'where', 'there' and 'their', 'door' and 'droo', who put double letters where there should be single ones and vice versa. But Ralph's spelling didn't conform to any recognisable pattern. Over the years we had often talked about getting an educational psychologist to look at his letters. I also wanted someone to analyse his drawings - as a former art teacher I recognised Ralph's talent but thought that some of his work was quite disturbing.

Now we were actually writing the book we decided it was time to act. Pam emailed the Education Department at Leicester University. As we had hoped, they suggested two of their own staff, Professor Cooper and Dr Merry, and offered us an appointment. Unfortunately, it was on the day I was setting off for a long holiday in Thailand - so Pam went to see them on her own.

'Had an amazing morning,' she emailed smugly a day or two later, 'you missed a treat!'

Professor Cooper and Dr Merry had obviously allocated an hour for her visit, but in fact she stayed for almost three, with one or other of the two men popping out for fifteen or twenty minutes at a time to see clients, then breezing back in saying, 'Now, tell me what have I missed?'

Dr Merry was the specialist in interpreting children's artwork. He confirmed what we already knew, which was that Ralphy was quite exceptionally gifted artistically, but he did not see any real problems coming through in the drawings. He pointed out that the house surrounded by snakes and creepy crawlies was not, as we had interpreted it, under threat, the creatures were not drawn or positioned in a menacing way and some of them were actually smiling! He saw no problem with Ralph's interest in snakes either. 'After all,' he said, 'they make nice shapes!' The angels-in-arm-chairs he thought odd but could ascribe no particular meaning to them. It was all slightly disappointing.

But they were both fascinated by Ralph's history and thought that his family relationships were at the root of many of his problems. The Sneyds, they decided, were all pretty dysfunctional. Both John William and Susanna, they opined, were deeply damaged by their experiences. That damage was probably compounded because their contemporaries saw a broken marriage and a quarrel with your father as shameful. They had to conceal their experiences, bottle up the hurt.

The result was that they were neither of them secure enough to parent little Ralphy very successfully. Professor Cooper diagnosed an 'affective disorder'. Ralph was insecure because he was never really sure that he was loved. He was spoilt and smothered as a child and then shipped away to school for six whole months with no visits. He must have felt confused and rejected though in fact he adjusted quite well. But then there were three changes of school in quick succession - two of them because he seems to have failed to meet the standards required of him. His aunt's letters became increasingly unkind and rejecting and his father stopped writing altogether. Ralph must have been very hurt and unhappy.

He was naturally dreamy. Many of his letters home from school would have been checked before he sent them - and if they were full of mistakes he would have had to copy them out again. Maybe more than once. He would have got bored and made silly errors. Some of his mistakes can only be explained in the context of this sort of careless copying - 'lought' for 'bought', 'Bonood' for 'Boxwood', and so on. We hadn't thought of that - but it made sense.

There was more. Ralph, they thought, had mixed feelings about writing home. So many letters provoked outbursts of criticism that he would have been nervous and tense. And, as we had noticed ourselves, Susanna was inconsistent, she sent out mixed messages - she forbade him to collect and then acquired specimens for him, she promised him rewards for good work but doled them out however dreadful his report was, she fussed about his health but grumbled when he took himself to see a doctor. He didn't know where he was with her. Every letter contained criticism, there was always a sting in the tail, cropping up where he least expected it.

Ralph was a lonely, sensitive little boy and his aunt had made him very dependent on her. But then he was sent away to school, abandoned and rejected. Subconsciously, the psychologists thought, he could not stop worrying about home and his relationship with his aunt - to the extent that he could never immerse himself whole-heartedly in his studies. His handwriting remained childish and he made childish spelling mistakes. It was not deliberate but nor was it entirely accidental - when he made mistakes she criticised him but at least she stayed in touch. If he stopped making mistakes maybe even that contact would cease. He was a long-distance version of the child who is so desperate for attention that he would rather be beaten than ignored.

And at the same time, Aunt Susan was using Ralph to satisfy her own desperate need to be loved and respected. Her birth family had shipped her off to be brought up by her aunt. The man she married proved, very quickly, that he did not love her and had wanted a wife only as a respectable cover for his homosexuality. She had never done anything to displease her father, but when, with his blessing, she went to live with John William, he all but disowned her.

Many of her siblings died. She lost contact with her brother, Dryden, when he and John William quarrelled. Her sister, Emily, was always argumentative and judgemental and her youngest brother, Gustavus, let her down time and time again. She needed Ralphy to love her, he was almost all she had.

They were unhealthily inter-dependent. As Ralph grew older and asserted his independence his aunt panicked and sent him cruel, infantilising letters: make yourself agreeable... people don't really like you, they are just being kind... don't talk too much... eat what you are given... don't miss the train or get out at the wrong station. It is not surprising that he chose to prove himself in ways that excluded her. And the more he struggled, the tighter she pulled the net - it was a destructive downward spiral that damaged them both.

The move to Mr Walsh's was not a success. A few weeks into the term Ralph wrote home:

We get up at a $^1/_2$ past 7 have breakfast at 8 and begin lessons at $^1/_2$ past and *go out at 12, dinner at ¹/2 past 1 and begin work again at ¹/2 past 3, tea at ¹/2 past 5 and lessons at ¹/2 past 6 and have prayers and go to bed at 8. We have for breakfast bacon, ham, brawn, rolled beef and some of the boys have Australian beef which they bring themselves. We have square blocks of bread some of the largest being 4 inches and coffee in mugs, - for dinner we generally have mutton, beef, veal, ham, pork and sometimes hash and curry and large treacle or jam tarts. We began our table napkins last Sunday week; at tea we have cups for tea - we play an hour in between dinner and work, there is a large gymnasium with tan on the ground so if the boys fall from the ladders they may not hurt themselves. I like school very much; the 4th class boys go out with Miss Scott to buy grub every Saturday.*

There was hardly a mistake in the long letter from which this extract is taken, and it is hard to believe that a boy who the week before had had trouble with words like 'care', 'desks', 'arrived' and 'prayers' could suddenly spell 'gymnasium', 'Australian' and 'brawn'! He must have copied it word for word.

Lea Fields

Your Papa and I were very much pleased to receive your long letter and now quite understand how a great part of your time is spent and am very glad you have so much good food to eat, it does not sound as if you require to shop for yourselves on Saturday. You will remember that you have very bad teeth, so do not make them worse with eating sweets but buy something useful if you are in a great hurry to spend your money... Your Papa and I returned home last Friday. I do not think his voice is any stronger, he has gone to bed early as he could not speak comfortably... after church on Sunday your Uncle and Cousin Carry and I went to the Chase to see the fighting and had very good places, we all intend to go again tomorrow to see the musket fighting and on Thursday we hope to see the marching. We were not able to go to Crystal Palace but in Oxford Street I bought a cabinet for 30 shillings [£81] and have been thinking that if I hear at Christmas that you have worked hard at your new school and have hardly any fines and been as good as possible I will give you the extra 12 shillings [£32] so that this handsome cabinet can be yours, but if you have not worked hard up to Xmas I will give you another chance of having it next year, and if you do not attain it then your 18 shillings [£48] will be returned to you. Next time I write I will send you a couple of sketches of it and the size etc.

Susanna was bargaining with Ralphy. He in his turn sent letters home telling her about things he thought might interest her - cricket and football matches against Rugby School and a circus with performing dogs.

But towards the end of term things deteriorated and Ralphy's last two letters were short, scruffy and ill-written - even his food had got worse. Susanna and John William must have despaired.

Leamington
I hope all the pets are quite well It is only 3 weeks and 6 days to the holodays. I shall be very glad when the holidays come. We have sausiges for dinner every Tuesday. I have soup every second day for lunch, and poridge every other night for supper. The holidays begin on the 18th. We have no examinations hear. I send a few crests and a stamp, please to put them with my others.

Whether Mr Walsh did not want Ralphy back, or whether John William decided that the school was doing him no good, or not keeping a careful enough check on his spending, or whether it was too expensive, we don't know. All we do know is that Ralphy did not return to Mr Walsh. After only one term there he was uprooted yet again and sent to another new school.

It is tempting to imagine the conversation around the breakfast table at Lea Fields before Ralphy came home that Christmas, with John William growling, 'He still can't spell, and his last two letters could have been written by an un-schooled idiot of seven! It's time he had some real discipline. Small school I think - run by a clergyman - he needs to be kept hard at it. I'm fed up with this namby-pamby approach. The boy is soft - and you are keeping him that way!'

Susanna probably twisted her napkin in her fingers realising that the awful thing was that most of what John William was saying was true. Ralphy's improvement, in spite of her urging and bribing, was pitifully small. He seemed to be interested only in his collection of curiosities and, even though he was prepared to read widely about those, he would not apply himself to his school subjects.

And so it was decided. After a dull Christmas - his aunt and father were again far from well - on January 27th Ralphy was packed off to a small school at Hockerton in Nottinghamshire, a tiny hamlet deep in the country. It was run by the Reverend F.G. Mills who claimed to teach Latin, English, arithmetic and Christian studies - and most importantly, Mr Mills was a 'gentleman', not just a paid teacher, as Susanna was at pains to point out to Ralphy.

Three pages showing some of Ralphy's childhood drawings.

Ralph as a schoolboy
in 1871

The Miss Cranes' school
in Leamington,
Boxwood House,
Beauchamp Square,
which Ralphy attended
between 1870 and 1873.

Mr Walsh's, Waterloo Place in Leamington. Ralphy attended for one term in 1873

Ralphy's drawing of Hockerton

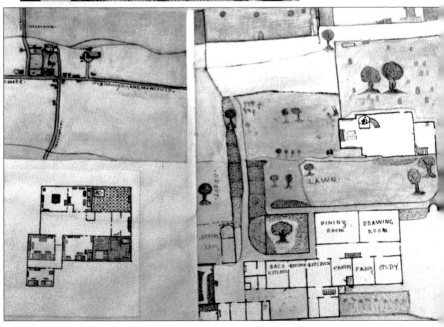

James Cornish - who travelled abroad
with Ralph in 1880.

Charles Cornish, Vicar of Debenham
1860-1883, father of James and Vaughan
and Ralph's teacher for six years.

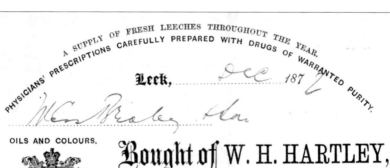

Debenham Vicarage where Ralphy went to school from1874 to 1881.
The photos of Debenham and the Cornishes are courtesy of the The Debenham
History Society, from *James Cornish's Debenham.*

Old Debenham.

Basford Hall in the 19th century and below, showing the arch
above which Ralphy had his museum.

Pam and Marion researching at Basford, al fresco.

Joyce Shenton and Pam sifting through Ralph's trunks.

Chapter 5
Ralphy's Treasures

Most boys collect things. But Ralph went further; his collection would become a mania whilst he was at school, and afterwards. If he couldn't compete academically then he would shine in his own way. What he collected, or bought, or swapped, dominated his letters and his thoughts.

When Susanna Ingleby encouraged her little nephew to learn the names of the flowers and trees and birds and toadstools they came across on their walks, she simply thought she was encouraging an interest in natural history and widening his vocabulary. Taking samples home was a natural extension of the process. Soon he was acquiring birds' eggs - his aunt blew them for him, piercing the ends with a big needle, wiggling it about inside the egg to break up the yolk and then blowing, long and hard, through one of the holes until the liquid came out of the other. It was a delicate job, a tiny empty egg was very fragile for a small boy to handle, and to begin with little Ralphy probably simply did not have enough puff to blow an egg clean.

She found that making lists of his collections was a good exercise to help him with his writing. *Fossils 20, Petrefactious shale 4* eight year old Ralphy wrote in his best rounded script, filling page after page in an exercise book with lists of his pebbles and shells and various *remains.*

By 1873, he was beginning to take his collecting very seriously and it features more and more in his aunt's diaries. He caught butterflies and gassed them in jars. *Crushed laurel leaves to kill butterflies* Susanna Ingleby noted in the back of that year's diary, ever willing to help her beloved nephew.

July 19th Showery. We all three walked in the warren. Ralphy took his butterfly catchers, he found a wood pigeon's nest & went to ask Mr Pickering if he might have the eggs ....

Later that year, she was *lining a cabinet for Ralphy* to keep his collections in. He was only doing what other little boys did, she reasoned, he'd grow out of it soon enough, but meanwhile she could use his interest to teach him to be neat and well-organised.

Aged ten, writing home about a school trip to Warwick, Ralphy reported at unusual length on a visit to the museum:

We saw stuffed fishes and birds and skeletons of birds and fossils, and extinct animals, the largest of which was the skeleton of a great fossil Elk. Then we went to see the punch bowl and sword of Guy, Earl of Warwick and many other curiosities I will tell you about when we meet again ...

At this stage he did not have much money to spend and he was probably not allowed to go out by himself, so his opportunities for collecting specimens were limited, but his family helped him.

April 13th 1875 ... I heard from your cousin Carry today, she is keeping some old French Republican coins for you ...

April 27th 1874 ...Your Papa found a water-hen's nest so low down in the bank that when there was rain it would have been in the water, so he brought it up here. Mr Bloor has blown two eggs for you...

In 1874, Susanna and John William were preparing to move back to Basford, the home they had been brought up in. There was a lot to do. The house was in a poor state of repair and they had little money to spare. They hired a man and four vans and a trussel to move all their things for them. Everything had to be packed very carefully, china especially, as the roads were very rutted and things would be jolted about on the journey. Susanna recorded that she packed up all *dear Ralphy's treasures as carefully as I could* and she tried to label everything clearly. There were people in the village to see and say goodbye to, plants from the garden to pot up - so much to do. She and John William had also been to London several times to order new furniture from Maples. They finally left Abbots Bromley on March 31st. On the long slow journey Susanna sat in the wagonette - with the dog! The house was in a worse state than they had imagined, the roof was leaking, the chimneys had not been swept for ages and in consequence everything was sooty and needed decorating. John William at once started proceedings against his cousin, who had been living there, for not maintaining the place properly. But it was an exciting time. There was so much more room than they had had at Armitage or Lea Fields and Ralphy was to have a big room all to himself. There would be plenty of space for all his collections...

Mr Mills had no more success with Ralphy than Mr Walsh had had, but Susanna and John William were too busy to notice. Basford was still in chaos when Ralph returned home for the Easter holidays. If Mr Mills had given him a bad report, his father and aunt were in no mood to do anything about it.

But a few weeks into his second term at Hockerton, Ralph was sent home *poorly and sick*. He had typhoid fever. The doctors called twice a day and counted his pulse which was alarmingly high. The new-fangled medical thermometers were cumbersome and inaccurate, so the good doctors of Leek relied on the tried and tested method of measuring the pulse rate. Aunt Susan recorded every visit and every reading in her diary, and she, Aunt Emily Jane, the housemaids and family friends took it in turns to nurse the little boy day and night - wiping his fevered body with cool wet cloths repeatedly to bring his fever down. Even John William sat up with him one night to give Susanna some rest.

It was an anxious time. Ralph was desperately ill for weeks and afterwards he was left weak, hardly able to walk out of doors. He went to Wales in September to convalesce but soon relapsed. It was not until April 1875, almost a year later, that he was able to return to Mr Mills.

Hockerton Rectory April 10th 1875
I hope Papa arrived home quiet safely. I have got the old day nursry for my bed room now, my hed is neir the wall. all 3 of the servants are new ones. all the same boys are here. They have not ben reeding French History since I have been away so I shall begin again where I left off. My garden is now a wilderness. Have I got any coins yet... I have been working hard getting the plaster off the church. I went up to the frunt dore how are all the pets. Please draw me a sketch of the tadploes. Please tell me if you have got any coins for me...

Ralph was now less than a month away from his thirteenth birthday and his father and aunt must have been horrified when they read this illiterate letter. They may also have had serious doubts about what was going on in the school - though Susanna's reply does not suggest she questioned Mr Mills about his use of the boys as unpaid labourers in his church.

...The getting the plaster off the church must be very dirty work. I should not like to see you in such a mess. Mind you work hard at your lessons and get on with your sums and Latin... The tadpoles are coming on very well in the conservatory. Their heads are getting rounder every day. They are like this now [Susanna did a careful drawing] *There are about 40 of them and they play about in the basin...*

Nonetheless, in September John William decided to send his son to yet another school, this time very much further from home, in Debenham on the Norfolk/Suffolk border. That it was run by the Reverend Cornish, who was interested in natural history and archaeology, and himself an avid collector, may have influenced John William - perhaps he thought Ralph would study harder under someone who shared his enthusiasms.

Chapter 6
Ralph goes to Debenham

On the morning of September 24th 1875, John William and Ralph left Basford Hall early for the journey to Debenham. Ralph was now thirteen and very tall for his age. They travelled by train from Cheddleton to St Pancras Station, then took a fly, a horse-drawn cab, through the choked, smelly, smoky, noisy cobblestone streets of London to Liverpool Street Station. They pushed their way through the crowded platforms - men in top hats and ladies in voluminous skirts - and climbed up into a carriage on the train to Suffolk. Trains at that time were not very comfortable unless you could afford to travel first class - which Ralph and John William could not. Toilet facilities were scanty - it would be a good many years before all trains had corridors and toilets which were easy to get at. In 1875 Midland Railways were the first to include upholstered seats for third class carriages - most seats were wooden and hard.

Soon they would be out of London and speeding through the countryside, smoke streaming past them depositing sooty smuts on the windows of the swaying carriages. Finally they would arrive at Ipswich. From there another journey of about twelve miles by fly would take them to Debenham, another new school and another set of boys to get to know. The journey would have taken at least twelve hours, and Ralph was to make it six times a year.

The villages of Witnesham, Framsden and Helmingham through which they passed on the way to Debenham would have been very different to those he was familiar with. For the first time he would see the pretty Suffolk plaster pargetting on the village cottages - flowers, leaves and delicate scrollwork running across under the eaves, down the sides of the doors - and pastel-coloured lime washes on the walls. These softly-coloured streets would become familiar over the coming years as Ralph was to stay at Debenham until he was almost nineteen. The countryside around Armitage where he spent his first eight years was flat, but it was nowhere near as flat as the countryside he now saw - windmills everywhere, in fields and in streets, stark silhouettes against the sky.

Ralph's letters from Debenham were not written in the neat copperplate which he was obviously made to use at Hockerton, and are in consequence much longer. Though the spelling, punctuation and use of capital letters was still as erratic as ever, they were quite neatly written, and the first letter revealed that Ralph had found a soul mate.

Debenham. September 26th 1875

My dear aunty,

I hope you will take care of yourself I hope Papa arrived home quite safely. This is a very nice house... Vaugne [Cornish] *has about as good a collection as I have, he has given me 4 sharks teath and 2 coins one of witch is a coin of Constantin the Great. This is a great place for finding fossils. There is a kind of fossil called a sea eye which is very common about here. I hope all the pets are quite well give my love to Papa*

Beleive me

Yor afeconate nephew

Ralph de Tunstale Sneyd

A few days later he was asking his aunt to ... *send all my best duplicats please put them in a small box and pad them with cotton wool and they will come for 2 pence. I have a very good change with Quaghne he sais he cannot wait till cristmas ...*

In return he sent her a *peace of lace bark from Jamaica. It is very prity...* Aunt Susan's concerns grew. She did as Ralph asked, stitching the coins carefully into little bags, but admonished him to work hard at his lessons.

Do not think of anything else except them and try and do as well as the other boys, never mind thinking about coins, I am not fond of boys changing things as they know nothing about the value of them and when once that sort of thing is begun they do not know when to stop.

'She'd always encouraged him before,' said Marion. 'I suppose she suddenly saw his hobby getting out of hand - he seemed to be getting obsessed...'

'I think she was jealous. She'd always helped with his collections - all that pasting of things in scrapbooks and lining drawers and blowing eggs! She was a bit of a control freak, she didn't like him doing things without her say so ...And, of course, Ralph ignored her!'

October 24th, 1875 ... I [gave] *all of them except the queen Anne shilling and the American cent and the 3 phennings for a beautiful white sea egg that Vaugn valued at about 18d* [£4]. *I got the other coins changed for a splendid electrolipe of an old great seal. I have bought a pair of Chineas slippers for 2s....*

There are a great many very old pieces of pipes about here some of them about the date of Queen Elizabeth I have got a good many of them. Mr Cornish says the pipes that we find are undoubtably old ones as they are very thick and chiney he has seen a good many in the Salsbery Museom.

I am afraid there is not much fur [fear] *of me bringing home many colections, I cant get foscils for love or money? The girls produce no more. The men at the brick kilns do not dig in the summer for clay and so do not find any & I do not get any on the stone heaps because the boys who get the stones of the land when they find foscils ceep them.*

The girls Ralph referred to were local girls who worked in the brick factory. It was their tedious job to pick out stones and other impurities from the clay before it was used for bricks, and they had discovered that the young gentlemen from Mr Cornish's school would pay a penny or two for any fossils that they found.

Mr Cornish seems to have given his boys a good deal of freedom to go shopping in the village or wandering around the countryside when they were not actually doing lessons. We guessed Ralph probably also had rather more pocket money than he had had in Leamington and Hockerton.   But paradoxically, now that he could indulge his passion for collecting, his aunt decided that it was a bad thing.

Nonetheless, back at Basford, donations to Ralph's museum continued to arrive, and Aunt Susan's letters sent out very mixed messages. He was to concentrate on his lessons and forget about collecting. But then she acquired a *readshand* for him - we decided this meant 'redshank' - and persuaded Captain Colvile to dismantle one of his walls to retrieve a large fossil Ralph wanted. In June 1876 Cousin Beatrice Fraser ... *was so kind as to bring you ... an Emu's egg, and a queer shaped piece of wood which is used in Australia for throwing at birds, and three Australian peach stones, they are so prettily marked that they are often worn as necklaces...*

Frustrated at not being able to see his new treasures Ralph wrote for more details - although he'd obviously already looked them up as he knew the emu's egg would be dark green and that the piece of wood for throwing at birds was called a boomerang. A few months later more objects were offered as a bribe for good work.

... if you get on with your lessons your Papa will let you have a few bones that were found at the Water House in some limestone rocks, the best parts were

sent to the Manchester Museum, these your Papa has are quite small, they were a Mammoth and an Irish Elk ...

Ralph himself went on acquiring things - polished stones, stamps, another sea egg, bits of old clay pipes, fossils from the clay-pits, a pen knife made *from a little piece of the Royal George* - and his rivalry with Vaughan Cornish continued. *Vaughan has not got nearly such a lot of nice things as I have* he reported smugly in September 1876 at the beginning of his second year at Debenham.

By Christmas 1876 he needed another new display cabinet and some of his things were being stored in the housekeeper's room. In February 1877 he wrote home about buying coins from an advertisement in *Exchange and Mart*. His aunt disapproved - *You must not get into debt buying coins or I shall be very angry with you...* she grumbled. It sounds from her letter as if he had already run up debts buying in this way before. She also voiced her fears about his unsupervised correspondence; *I hope you spell the words all right in your letters about them, I hope Mrs Cornish knows you are getting them and will see that all is right ...* Ralph was fifteen but Aunt Susan could not allow him to pursue an innocent hobby without nagging.

Ralph wrote back, explaining very sensibly that he got his coins on approval and that the man was selling them very cheaply - but Aunt Susan had already written a letter to Mrs Cornish about the matter. Mrs Cornish had had more than enough of Mrs Ingleby's interference and replied that Ralph would not, in future, be allowed to purchase any more coins by post. As so often happened in his childhood, the people around him created unnecessary obstacles to perfectly ordinary activities.

There are a very pleasing varity of creatures in this river here, there are neuts, horse leaches, cadicis, minows and many other things ... When I get home I shall have to look at the natural history of Belmont for I am in a hurry to see them more particularly as Mrs Cornish has put a stop to my reading hir books on the subject, and partly because she thinks some of the things are ugly, in fact I think that none of the family care very much for natural history... he wrote in the spring of 1877. Ralph had eight weeks to wait before he would be able to look them up. It must have been unbearably frustrating.

His passion for cadises lasted for weeks and his aunt was treated to several letters describing the curious things out of which the ones in the local river had made their shells - needless to say, he'd collected a number of them.

I do not think these things stop me attending to my lessons as I only get them on half holidays he parried when she criticised him, but Aunt Susan believed, like the Cornishes, that the time had come to wean Ralph away from collecting. *I do not care about you bringing any curiosities home as I want your thoughts on your lessons* she wrote, rather unkindly, later that term. He took no notice and sent her a long letter, complete with diagrams, about the best way to blow and keep birds' eggs! *The best way to blow eggs is the way they blow them in the shops - with one hole, they do it with an instrument.* Ralph drew diagrams and expounded at length. His aunt was incensed and in her reply she berated him cruelly and accused him of being *dreadfully stupid* - and as for birds eggs, well: *You know I do not care at all for eggs & I suppose I shall never blow another, but I must say those I did for you are nearly as good as any you have, I should think it is much easier to get them really clean when blown from end to end & the best collections I have seen are in bran. I am not at all fond of wool.*

'She really was stung by his letter, wasn't she?' I said. 'He'd been told that it was best to blow eggs across rather than from end to end, hiding the holes in the spots if the egg was patterned, and to keep them on cotton wool, not bran, to avoid mites - and she's taking it as a personal slight!'

'Well, she'd blown his eggs from end to end and bought the bran to keep them in...!'

Susanna, we concluded, really was being rather petulant. However, Ralph was equally unwilling to let the matter rest, and though in his next letter he assured his aunt he was doing extra work before breakfast and giving his *thorts* to his lessons, he could not resist explaining further about the egg blowing and the disadvantages of bran! His informant was James Cornish *who has a very good collection and manages to keep them very nice and clean.* Of course, keeping Ralph's eggs clean was yet another job that fell to Aunt Susan. They were prone to insect infestation and had to be checked regularly. If mites were found, the eggs had to be washed and some might have to be thrown away. Aunt Susan reported from time to time to Ralph that she had been to see that his eggs were all right, though being Aunt Susan she could not resist making him feel guilty about it. *I will see* [the eggs] *again when I can walk that far. I have been in bed nearly a week as I have had so much pain ...* she wrote on one occasion.

Correspondence about the collections continued until Ralph left school.

His aunt scolded him roundly for asking their friends, the Hutchinsons, to bring him items back from their holiday in Egypt. 'Asking for things' was a cardinal sin in her book. But she did not tell any of their relations and friends that Ralph was to be discouraged from collecting and so gifts kept coming. Over in Norfolk, Cousins Mary and Elizabeth Nelson gave him amber and jet and boxes of shells and a bottle containing two seahorses, a centipede and two scorpions in spirits! This introduced Ralph to a new and particularly unpleasant way of storing specimens. Soon there was correspondence with his aunt about *putting animals in spirits* and a hilarious letter from her about how the cook pickled a slow worm for him.

I answered two letters whilst Mrs Bloor was washing the Slow Worm, she cut off the parts you did not like & rolled it up & put it in a French Mustard bottle & we put the spirits on it, it looks very well, the sore part has broken out a little again. Mrs Bloor was very kind in doing it so nicely for you... she seems to be getting quite fond of such things... I put camphor on the things you named and have sealed up the bottles with the animals in, because I found the corks very damp, you had put the seahorses etc. etc. very badly in the spirits, I have made them all hang apart...

Creatures in spirits needed a lot of maintenance and could become very smelly. With Ralph away at school the task of caring for them fell to the long-suffering Mrs Bloor, supervised by Aunt Susan. *I saw Mrs Bloor tie down some of your animals with new bladders. I hope you will never get any more nasty smelly things...* she wrote in February 1880. But he did, and a year later she was again complaining.

I hope you have not been buying a lot of rubbish, you must remember we cannot have any more things here that smell bad, the cupboard your bottles are in has to be kept on purpose for them as they cause everything to smell bad & that used to be a useful cupboard for Elizabeth for her sewing.

But in her next letter she was telling him that she had asked his Aunt Emily to *call at Hartley's* [the chemist's] *in Leek & ask if the bottles ought to be filled with spirit to keep animals well.*

'Why didn't she put the wretched things in one of the outhouses?' we wondered. It seemed most unfair to us that the maids should not only be deprived of their cupboard but should also have to live with the smell that emanated from it!

Samuel Harrison was the gardener, and he also helped Ralph. He fancied himself as an amateur taxidermist: *I took the squirrel, water wagtail, bat & snake down to the Bath House one day last week. Harrison will get a case made for them which will stand on your painted cabinet in the housekeeper's room...* Aunt Susan reported.

'Lucky old housekeeper!'

'Well, they didn't have a housekeeper, did they - I guess it was Mrs Bloor's, and I suppose she shared it with the maid.'

'And the cupboard full of bad smells?'

'Lovely!'

We giggled as we amused ourselves by imagining conversations between Susanna and Mrs Bloor. 'What's that in your basket, Ma'am? 'Oh, just a squirrel, and a water wagtail.' 'Right y'ar, Ma'am!' And what Mrs Bloor said to Mr Harrison didn't bear thinking about!

Over the next few years Harrison received various instructions from the young master - in one memorable letter he was requested to *stuff the hedgehog & clean Linda's skull*! Linda was the family dog, a St Bernard who had been poisoned. Aunt Susan had the rest of her made into a rug! It cost a shilling and was made up by a tailor in Leek.

We do not know whether Harrison cleaned the skull but we know he didn't stuff the hedgehog. *I fancy that animal would be rather a trouble to do,* explained Aunt Susan with uncharacteristic reasonableness!

Ralph's collections were a sore trial to the entire household. After a while he began to collect weapons - swords, javelins and the like. Ralph hung them on the walls and the staff had to keep them polished. Checking on Ralph's 'treasures' was Aunt Susan's job, and though she never reported any damage, she frequently told him that it was unbearably hot in the stable block where many of his collections were kept.

'Would that have done any harm?' asked Marion.

'Very probably - depends what he had up there. If it got very hot it would probably also have got very cold - and most of the organic specimens would have suffered from temperature fluctuations. And we don't know what the standard of Harrison's taxidermy was...' I guessed that a lot of Ralph's early specimens deteriorated pretty quickly.

Chapter 7
Getting to know the Cornishes

Pam and I travelled to Debenham on a drowsy summer afternoon to try and see the house where Ralph had gone to school. We couldn't find it. We browsed round the church where Ralph worshipped each Sunday and asked one of the ladies who was arranging flowers if she knew where the old vicarage was.

'Oh, that caught fire and burnt down in the 1920s,' she said. Another lady joined in. 'Wasn't there a book published a few years back about the Reverend Cornish by the local history society? I think it was based on something his son wrote, they used to sell copies of it at the shop just up the road from here.'

We hurried to the tiny shop. Crammed with packets of biscuits, tins of soup and fish, papers, postcards, potatoes, ice-cream, soap-powder and floor-mops, it didn't look like the sort of shop you'd find a history book in - but we asked anyway. The lady behind the counter rummaged in a pile of books and papers on the floor, 'I thought we had just one copy left.' We held our breaths. 'Yes, I thought so,' she said, straightening up and smiling, 'The very last one.'

'Ralphy wants us to write his story,' said Pam happily as we stood outside in the street that Ralph knew so well. Over tea in a local café we looked at it. There in front of us was the kindly face of the Reverend Cornish, calmly reading, and we were at once transported back into Ralph's time through the words of James Cornish:

Part of the house was old but many rooms had been tacked on so that it was fairly large. Many of the ceilings were very low, and at some of the doors my father had to stoop so as not to knock his head on the lintel. The structure was chiefly a timber frame with intervals filled with lath and plaster - a very flammable method of building and by no means warm in winter. Illumination in winter was difficult. Lamps were little used, for colza [rape seed] *oil lamps were tiresome to work, and the paraffin lamps invented in the 1860s were ill-made and apt to explode and take fire, so candles were generally used ...they were not cheap and we had no money to burn or waste ...we spent the winter evenings in semi-darkness ...and our mother read aloud ...the Waverley Novels, Captain Marryat's First Masterman Ready, and The Children of the New Forest ...and poetry too, The Lays of Ancient Rome, the Lay of the Last*

*Minstrel ...we caught the swing and rush of the lines and learnt them by heart.
...nothing can make Latin Grammar attractive and French we hated, but all
the more informal education we absorbed eagerly.   Our father would pick up
a Livy and translate a passage about Hannibal crossing the Alps, or show us
an old atlas on which the marches of Alexander were traced, and tell us of the
Persian Wars, of Marathon and Salamis.*

James went on to recall the many hours they spent in nature study:

*....Our first interest was in collecting fossils, for Geology was perhaps the most
popular science then, and a cabinet of mineral specimens, and shelves on which
fossils were displayed, were part of the furnishing of many houses in the
country... Vaughan ...had his own special interest which was astronomy. Two
large globes stood in our dining room, one terrestrial the other celestial, and
the latter he studied with enthusiasm ...night after night he would go star-gazing
and learn the constellations and the chief stars... When I was about ten* [in
1870] *my father began to take a few pupils to educate with us, for the income
from the living of Debenham was small. Good preparatory schools then were
very scarce, and he soon had several offers of boys... now the villagers
possessed a new interest for we kept things alive with cricket and football.*

In his letters Ralph often wrote about such games, *Yesterday we plaid in
a crickit match, On our side we had some boys out of the vilage & we played
against some of the new school whom we beat by 1 inings.*

James went on to describe smallpox and typhoid fever in the parish. Both
illnesses were potentially fatal. The Reverend Cornish nursed sick people who
had no one else, staying up night after night.   Parishioners did not forget such
selflessness in their *tall, stalwart, impetuous and generous* vicar. But it was
Mrs Cornish who was instrumental in ridding the parish of the scourge of
typhoid. Mr Cornish had demanded, and got, a government enquiry which pin-
pointed the cause to particularly bad drainage at one end of a row of cottages.
He ranted and raved but to no avail. Then Mrs Cornish went to see the owner.
Quietly but firmly she spoke to him of the many cases of typhoid in the village,
described poignantly the deaths and suffering.   Her gentle approach had the
desired effect; proper drainage was installed and the typhoid cases stopped.

James described his mother as *small and slight, quiet, self-controlled and
wise. I have not met any woman who excelled her in intellectual capacity...*
Small wonder then, that she had problems with wayward Ralph and his
pedantic, interfering aunt.

We found a picture of Mr Cornish's vicarage in the book - a graceful old house at the end of a circular drive. Ralph shared a room with Vaughan Cornish when he first arrived, then had a room to himself right at the top of the house. He was also sufficiently close to his Norfolk relatives to be able to spend weekends and occasional holidays at Barton Bendish with his Great-Uncle John Holley and his wife. Childless themselves, they welcomed Ralph and his school friends to their home and let them ride horses wildly in the grounds.

The letters between Ralph and his aunt for the next two years paint a vivid picture of their lives. In them the tiniest deviation from the normal boredom of daily routine was eagerly grasped and recorded. Susanna told her nephew every detail of local life:

Last night there was a penny reading in Cheddleton. Elizabeth [the housemaid] *went to it with the young Tudors, Lizzie Tudor sang.*

Early on Friday morning there was a fire at Cheddleton Paper Mill. It burnt down the engine room and the damage was estimated at between £300 and £400. [£17-23,000]

I have been to a very large School Feast today at Mr Boucher's, [he was the vicar of Cheddleton and the feast would have been for the local school children] *there was a service at the church first & then dinner & then tea & after tea there were splendid swings & Mr Boucher turned over in them like we see at the Circuses.*

The black Jubilee Singers are performing in Leek. Everybody is very much pleased with them, they have sung before the Queen. They will most likely remain a year in Great Britain. Seven of the singers were born slaves, they give the money they get to a college in America for freed slaves, they got £10,000 [£576,000] *when they were here before in Great Britain...*

Mr Sleigh gave a very large Picnic party at Sharpcliffe last Saturday, your Papa was at it, he is pretty well better now... Your Papa sends thanks for your letter but as he never writes when he can help it, I write as usual.

You would have liked to have been at Rudyard last Monday week, Captain Webb who swam across the English Channel was there, he began with going up a ladder 26 feet high & from it plunging headlong into the water, he then swam about 300 yards & showed off a few tricks while in the water, there was also a Mr Beckwith, and a son & daughter who were said to spring about in the water in a wonderful way & a Mr Bibbers; a little boy Beckwith jumped 16 feet down into the waves but you will have to read an account of it when you come home, your Papa would have gone to see it, if he had not been poorly the day before, there were about 20,000 people there, several boys swam races & one man swam a race with a dog & the dog won. Your Papa is pretty well again now.

Ralph was careless and absent-minded. The trait was established in his boyhood and was to last all his life. He lost things. Forgot why he was going somewhere or left things behind. Susanna always worried that he would lose his luggage - even though she spelt out for him in great detail exactly how to care for it, and how to get it moved from station to station. She harangued him to little effect; Ralph and his baggage were not infrequently parted! *Mrs C thinks the luggage may come tomather, she has provided me with a night shirt and a brush and comb,* he wrote in 1879. Susanna had sent Staffordshire oatcakes with him for the Cornishes to try on that particular occasion and knowing that he had lost his trunk she must have worried about them. Ralph's letter, when it came, was hardly diplomatic.

The oatcakes were rather stale when they came but we got through 5$^1/2$ of them. The others were thrown away by mistake thinking that we should not want them. I think we had all but one hot buttered. Mrs Cornish thought they were like a sort of leather flavered with butter and gruil, I have got the tooth brush and nail brush all right but I have not found the two hats.

It must have been infuriating for his aunt - and as if that wasn't enough there was the vexing question of his clothes.

I cannot understand how you have grown so very much in height & width in one term or how your coat can have got wrong in the collar but I hope now your clothes will do until the holidays....

I hope you have not required your second pair of common gloves, I will mend them and send them next week....

I think your trousers can be made to do until the holidays. I am sending a piece like them, if the best pair is not worn at the bottom they can be let down there...

Ralph replied:

I have had the older and erlier pair of my trousers that are alike altered by having a piece put on the bottom of the legs to make them longer, & I have also had my jacket let out & lowered at the neck.

I have to wear my best trousers now because Mrs Cornish thinks both the others are too tight. I will take great cair of them. I neaver climb treas now.

Although there were shops which sold ready-made clothes, most garments were still made at home or by local tailors or dressmakers. Ralph growing out of his clothes whilst away from home posed a real problem. He must have been uncomfortable and perhaps embarrassed, but Susanna was a penny-pincher and did not want to waste money before seeing the problem for herself. She seemed immune to his discomfort and Mrs Cornish's advice.

Susanna sent endless news of other boys who were doing better than Ralph:

The young Fraser is such a good boy that his master says it is 6 years since he had so good a pupil....

The young Bouchers get on so very well Herbert has a 1st class and Charlie has won his 3rd scholarship....

Knowing of Ralph's interest in fungi, she passed on a recipe to him:

I heard from cousin Mary a few days ago. She mentioned she has seen some more of the spiky Fungus 'Clavaria Vermiculata' and she heard they are very good boiled in bundles like asparagus and eaten with butter and parsley and onion and salt and pepper, but she fancies that the dressing would hide the flavour of the fungus.

It was unlikely that Mrs Cornish would cook for him, but it was something to write about. There was so little real news. She always told him about the pets. *Mrs Bloor's canary got out of its cage a week ago and Lily caught it and bit it so it died. Jesse has been rather poorly but he is better now, Lily and the rabbit are well* and there was also news of tadpoles, frogs, toads, hedgehogs, and a tame robin *which is very troublesome in coming into the house.* She told him about badgers and moles that had been caught. Ralph wrote back at once and asked her to get the gardener to bury them so that he could have their skulls when he came home - and he told her of the pets they had at Debenham. *The boys have just caught a young hedgehog they are keeping it as a pet, they feed it on bread and milk.*

Astronomical happenings were of interest to them both and they exchanged news of their sightings with genuine pleasure.

....have you ever seen a luner rainbow I saw one one night not long ago it was just round the moon and the colours were light and duskey yelow, duskey brown and duskey green. It was very curious.... wrote Ralph.

I wonder if you are looking out for falling stars, your Aunt Emily in her late walk from Leek has seen several; tonight is generally considered a good night for them, but the Stafford paper says that the best time is in the very early hours of the morning & to look East as the best group is in the constellation Leo, another group will be on the 27th in the constellation Andromeda, the nights the Stafford paper mentions are November 13th, 14th, 15th, 24th, 25th, & 27th but the paper says that for 5 or 6 weeks there will be a chance of seeing them... I shall look out tonight. I got up in the middle of last night, but I could not see anything & was afraid of catching cold & having chilblains replied Susanna.

She suffered terribly from chilblains. They lasted longer and longer each year, preventing her from going out, from sewing and even at times from getting dressed because her fingers were sore and bleeding. Then there was the rheumatism that confined her to bed in the cold, damp, empty house and the neuralgia and headaches. Some serious forms of rheumatism are associated with chilblains, and perhaps that is what she suffered from. Basford Hall is high on a hill overlooking a valley where the Churnet flows and the soil is heavy clay. At almost any time of the year, the fields round the house are waterlogged - cows up to their hocks in squelchy mud stare mournfully at you as you drive up to the house. No wonder that Susanna and John William suffered so much from the cold and damp.

But the first part of her letters, after the initial *My dearest Ralphy, Thank you for your letter* was always the nagging - week after week after week.

You must read your letters over before you send them then you would know that you have written 'nise' for 'nice' and 'ireland' instead of 'Ireland'....

You must work very hard at your lessons this term, you are so very backward in everything....

I cannot understand how you can be so stupid as not to know the rule of three yet....

Mr Cornish wrote to your Papa last week and said he found you very backward in everything and that he thought sums were the thing you could do the best. I said I always think you did things nearly as well before you ever went to any schools....

Ralph sent home any tiny bit of praise he received - and it was scant indeed for there was little to commend in his school work.

Mr Cornish thought I got on very well with my Livy. I shall get on well with my leasons this turm I hope I shall get some curicsilis [curiosities] *this turm....*

I am glad you liked my last letter. I do not generaly find much to say, as we are very quiet here. I am giving more of my thorts to my leasons I am going to do some more leasons in the mornings I did a page of copeing out before breakfast yestoday, I quite understand that it is very emportant to know French when one goes on the Continent. Do you think I had better learn German next term. I suppose you could get through Germany with French much better than with English.

We only learn a little of what he was studying at school. There seemed to be no particular timetable. The Reverend Cornish had only a very few boys in his 'school': his own sons Vaughan and James, Ralph and his cousin Richmond Gale and one or two other boys, some from excellent families. *The other* [new] *boy is called Manners the son of Lord John Manners the Post Master General,* wrote Ralphy one term. Susanna would have been pleased at the company her nephew was keeping. The Cornish boys and young Manners were being prepared for university - Greek and Latin were mandatory entry subjects then and since they were learning them Ralph went to the lessons as well. At least he was then able to write home to his aunt, *we have started seaser...* and doubtless she was thrilled to be able to tell her relations that 'Ralph has started to read Caesar in Latin'. He was to attempt Greek as well!

Ralph's spelling and punctuation remained as bad as ever and he was very careless, often putting the wrong address on the top of the letter and sometimes the wrong year as well as the wrong date! I spent many frustrating hours shuffling the letters about to get them in the correct order. The only way to do it was by looking at questions and finding the answers. Sometimes Susanna corrected the dates - eventually even she seems to have given up! Ralph's frequent references to coming home, counting the weeks and days until the next holiday, show that, much as Susanna scolded him at home, he much preferred to be there than at school. *It is only 7 weaks till I come home, It is a month and two days till the holidays, It is less than 3 weaks till I come back.*

It is tempting to quote all the letters; they read like a novel with Susanna and Ralph the main characters, each absorbed in their own world. As time went on we can sense growing irritation on both sides. All Susanna wanted was that her nephew be a well-mannered, ordinary boy and grow up into a country gentleman like his father, grandfather and uncles - a staunch and unquestioning member of the Church of England, respected and conventional. But Ralph was never ordinary.

He told his aunt of things they did outside of lessons - carefully choosing things he thought would please her.

I enjoyed myself at Uncle John's very much. On the 1st day we went out riding and had a splendid galop Uncle John let us shoot and he loded I killed 2 hedgte sparrows I had the 1st kooked for dinner I like shooting very much. Uncle John gave me 5 shillings [£14] *I gave the groom one.*

On Tuesday we went to an African panerama chiefly about Doctor Livingstone, the pictures were very small, after the panerama we were shown how things looked by different lights. The man dressed up some boys in coloured things, and throu some powder on a little fire and thay turned different colours. On Wednesday we had a collection for the Indian famine, a very excenrtic man preached.

On Wednesday we all went in a fly to a place called Monelsoam [probably Mendlesham] *to a Misionary meating there two People spoke one of them very well indeed he told us a great many things about India which I will tell you about when I get home, in the evening we sat down to a large supper party, we got home somewhere about 11 0'clock yesterday a gentleman came here for tea and dinner and he went to baith with us....*

One of Susanna's real pleasures in life was her garden. Her letters detail its progress: when she and Harrison were potting things up for the winter, when they were putting out the brightly-coloured bedding plants in the circular bed in front of Basford, when they picked their first fruit and vegetables. Ralph may have genuinely been interested - or he may have written about his garden at Debenham because he knew it would please his aunt. He asked her to send him hemlock seeds and wrote enthusiastically:

The things in the garden are growing very well there are a great many strawberries which Mrs Cornish lets us have for tea, we have them all mashed up on a plate with milk and plenty of sugar, we nearly always now have a dish made of lettice and milk and brown sugar we make it ourselves on our plates. I like it very much.

Gardening does seem to have been an activity they could share.

Ralph certainly had what we would see now as some unusual interests for a 15 year old. *I hope they will save the fighting dragons in Ipstones church and that they will be restored,* he wrote home in a letter. That summer Ipstones church was reopened after restoration and the dragons were indeed salvaged and set into the south wall. They are the remains of an early Norman tympanum, Celtic in style.

Perhaps Ralph though his aunt would be pleased that he had joined in enthusiastically with the latest craze the boys at Debenham had embraced in the summer of 1876 - stilts! He told her some weeks later:

I have lirnt to walk on stilts I have bought a pair for myself for 2 shillings [£6] *I went a mile and a half on a pair that was lent me. I have subscribed a shilling to get some fireworks on Guy Fox day.*

But if the stilts had seemed to be a good idea they were also to lead to Ralph writing one of his longest letters ever to his aunt.

Thank you very much for your kind letter and for letting me have the monney I wanted it will come in very usefully, particulary as I have to pay half the cost of a shop window that was broken but wich I had nothing to do with, and this is the whole history of the thing all the boys were going down the street to do shopping buying sweats, Grissell and Knox were on stilts as was Richmond but he was not supposed to be walking with us the first shop we went to was the bakers were Grissell left his stilts because he did not care to go all the way on them then we went to the grocers I putting my stilts down on the ground, but Hamish put his leaning on the posts on the side of the door after I had been in the shop about a minute I went out to look at some potid meat tins there were in the right hand window. I had been staying there for about a minute quite still when I heard a crash behind me and looking round I saw that Hamishes stilt had gone through one of the pains of the shop window. It had been placed at the top of a slanted post like this [Ralph included a sketch here] *I think I was a yard of the post when the stilt fell and was standing quite still so it was not me that nocked it down. But as I was the only one outside I got the blame. We of course had to get a pain of glass directly and luckilly the price was not more than 2s 6d.* [£7] *I should not have to have paid anything if I had not had my stilts with me, as a rule had been made without my knowledge and certainly not been rigorusly observed by any of us! some of the boys were going to make a subscription but Mrs Cornish soon put a stop to that, but as it was such a small sum it does not much matter.*

At other times he seemed to go out of his way to irritate her:

Debenham January 23rd. 1876
My dear Arty tarts,
I arived at school all right we got into a gards van for part of the way. I have

got all my things safe. Den is not coming to this schol again all the others are coming. An organ grinder came here today with a monkey. My stilts at home are twice the weight of these. I have made some very good changes of foscills....

Not unreasonably, she was incensed, but not by the silly nickname.

My dear Ralph,

We were pleased to get your letter yesterday and to hear that you had arrived at school safely, but we were very sorry that you went in the Guard's van as you ought to have known that after your Papa had taken the great trouble in putting you into a comfortable carriage that you ought to have remained there until you arrived at Ipswich, instead of getting out and going to the Guard's van which is not a 'Lawful place' to travel in besides being very draughty, and you know what a great deal of money has been spent to try and keep you in better health ...but I hope that until you are older and travel alone that you will remain where you are placed and all your life travel in the parts of the train proper for passengers and not with the servants of the train who are paid to give up all their time to the working of the train and not talking to boys. I am sure your Papa would not have walked a good deal in the rain to get a beetle for you if he had known that you were in the guards van, but perhaps he will let you have it if you try not to do foolish things again...

With no link between one carriage and another Ralph must have got out of his carriage, run along the platform and jumped into the guard's van. A big adventure no doubt, and further evidence of a wilful and individualistic streak in him which was to become more and more apparent as he grew older.

Susanna's last letter of 1877 spelt out in detail how Ralph was to arrange his luggage, what labels he was to put on his cases, how he would recognize each station and so on. Given that he was now fifteen it did all seem a bit excessive: *...be very quiet in the train & do little talking, you will be at Derby at 3.15 & there Harrison will meet you,* she concluded. Another year had ended. Susanna might have expected the following one to be much the same: infuriatingly careless errors in Ralph's letters, worry about his school work, more lost boxes and bags - and endless additions to his collections. There was all that - but there was to be a new dimension as well that she could not possibly have foreseen.

Chapter 8
Catholicism: the Prelude

Debenham December 1st 1878

My dear Aunty,

Thank you for your two nice letters. I think nobody was able to see the meteors on the 23rd of last month... on Wednesday last we went to a wild beast show it was a small but good one there was a Gnu, & a Tasmanian devel, a white Yak, a clouded Tiger etc etc I want very much to go to Cheadle in the holleydays, to see the Catholic Cathedral. I mite take something to eat on the way. I should like to get there on Christmas Eve when something was going on.

Ralph wrote that letter to his aunt when he was sixteen and it was the first intimation that Susanna had that he was interested in the Catholic Church. At that stage neither of them could have foreseen just how far he would pursue his interest and the devastating consequences it would have.

Ralph's grandfather, the Reverend John Sneyd, had been an Anglican clergyman, a middle-of-the-road churchman who distrusted both the Evangelical and Anglo-Catholic branches of his church. It had never occurred to Susanna to question her father's views. She was a devout Anglican and had first taken Ralphy to church in Armitage when he was five years old; thereafter he had attended church regularly both from home and from school.

The church he now wanted to see, St Giles' Roman Catholic Church in Cheadle, was designed by A.W.N. Pugin for the Earl of Shrewsbury. It was probably his finest work. Pugin is considered by many to be the foremost British architect and designer of the 19th century, his best known work, of course, being the Palace of Westminster. He was a man of extraordinary talent, and managed to achieve more in his short life than most do in a normal life-span. He died aged 39 and as well as being a nationally renowned architect he had married three times and fathered eight children!

The Catholic Emancipation Act had only become law in 1829. Within living memory, for Ralph's father and aunt, Catholicism had been a banned religion. As young adults they had seen its resurgence and the opposition that provoked. Their domineering father, like many of his generation, viewed Roman Catholicism with deep suspicion. Travelling in Paris in 1859 he commented in his diary that the people went ...*to church in the morning and committed all manner of wickedness in the afternoon!* To strict Protestants, the gaiety and holiday atmosphere of the Continental Sunday continued to shock well into the 20th century. Sunday was a day for church and sober, pious activities. The idea that church was a part of everyday life, that you could attend a service and then go out and enjoy yourself by having a meal, playing games or singing and dancing was anathema. For the Reverend John and his ilk pleasure was suspect at best; on a Sunday it was unthinkable!

Catholicism was certainly associated with Continental attitudes by the English, but it was also the religion of Irish labourers, the men who cut the canals, laid the railways and did seasonal work on English farms, and who were feared for their fighting and their drunkenness and, like gypsies, were the chief suspects when things went missing. But on high days and holidays, when they were not too overhung and when there was a Catholic church in the vicinity, they would dress in their battered, tattered, colourful Sunday best and go to Mass, trailing their wives and children in their wake. What sort of religion could it be, wondered the respectable Anglicans through whose neighbourhoods the itinerant Irish passed, that would embrace such families?

Anglicanism was much less tolerant of poverty. Servants and working class people were expected to go to church, indeed in many cases their jobs depended on their strict attendance. But poor people were only welcome in most Anglican churches if they dressed respectably and sat at the back. The Catholic Church did not make such distinctions. Indeed, the distraught mother of one 19th century convert to Catholicism, a young Irishman called George Tyrrell (later a well-known theologian), wrote of her mortification that *a son of mine could go to mass with the cook!*

Anglicans had a long list of other concerns about Roman Catholicism. The Reverend Charles Kingsley (author of *The Water Babies*), who was vehemently anti-Catholic, wrote that Catholic priests were actually taught to tell lies! He also claimed that celibacy weakened and emasculated men so the priests were usually also poor physical specimens. His views were extreme, but many saw priestly celibacy as unnatural and perverted. In the eyes of married Anglican clergy like Ralph's grandfather it was something that could not possibly be God's will - and to prove it, the Reverend John Sneyd married twice and had fourteen children.

Many argued, as Luther had done three-and-a-half centuries earlier, that Catholics offered up their prayers to God in a language they did not understand. Catholic priests were thought to be too powerful. It was nothing short of blasphemy that a priest could represent God and absolve people from their sins. Mariolatry - the veneration of the Virgin Mary as the Queen of Heaven - was another concern. Protestants believed that she was worshipped as a goddess and this was idolatry. If a Catholic married outside the church their spouse was expected to convert and their children had to be brought up in the faith. To worried Protestants, this was a way for Rome to extend her influence and widen her congregation - and indeed, between 1800 and 1850, Britain's Catholic population increased from around 100,000 to over a million - though largely as a result of immigration rather than conversion.

But while Ralph's family thought Catholicism was evil and dangerous, he was not alone in his interest. In the latter part of the 19th century and the first half of the 20th, many intellectuals found themselves drawn to the Church of Rome. John Ruskin, the great 19th century writer and critic, was sympathetic to the Church and amongst the converts were Augustus Pugin, Gerard Manley Hopkins and Oscar Wilde.

It is difficult for us in the 21st century to imagine just how vitriolic anti-Catholicism was in Victorian England. And given the opposition they faced it is difficult, in our godless age, to imagine why so many people were so anxious to convert to the Church of Rome. Gerard Manley Hopkins summed up the feelings of many converts in his poem *To seem the stranger*.

> *To seem the stranger lies my lot, my life*
> *Amongst strangers. Father and Mother dear,*
> *Brothers and sisters are in Christ not near*
> *And He my peace, my parting, sword and strife.*

Susanna's reply, back in 1878, to Ralph's request to visit Cheadle was not unexpected. She said no. But Ralph was not to be deflected. Unbeknownst to his aunt he had already been to see the Catholic priest in Leek, and that Christmas, when he was thought to be with friends, he took the train to Alton to visit the Catholic community there. But it would be some time before Susanna learnt about that, and as usual, 'Dear Aunty' eventually gave in to her demanding nephew. During the Easter holiday of 1879 she took Ralph to Cheadle. She had no idea what she was unleashing.

On walking into St Giles' for the first time Ralph must have been overwhelmed - as we were the first time we saw it. We had decided to go over to Cheadle to see for ourselves what had tempted Ralph to make such an audacious request. Neither of us was prepared for what we saw - virtually every part of the church is decorated. From the floor to the ceiling the stonework is painted, the walls are decorated with painted tiles and rich patterns, inlaid tiles cover the floor, the rood screen is of brass and gilded wood. The reds, golds and brilliant blues and greens vie for attention against wonderful wood and metal carvings. The very building seems to sing with joy and light and Ralph must have been similarly impressed, probably even more so since it would have had so much religious significance for him. But Susanna hated St Giles, for her it was over-decorated, garish, and heathen - and she told her nephew so in no uncertain terms.

We also felt we had to see Alton, see where Ralph had met the priests, see where, later, he was to send his children to school. So we set out from Leek on a glorious autumn day in October 2004, avoiding the theme park, and driving through country lanes, past lakes attached to the estate and through the pretty village, to the castle high above it.

'Have you noticed, said Pam, as we arrived at the gates, 'we haven't got lost once, not once, since we started on the Ralphy book - not even when we went to that caravan park somewhere out in the sticks on the other side of Newcastle. And yet think of the hundreds of times we were lost when we were researching Susanna!'

I thought for a moment. It was true. Completely true.

'Why,' I asked, 'do you think that is?'

'Well, I've been giving it some thought and how's this for a hypothesis? Susanna always told Ralph exactly where to go, which train to get, what to look for on the station. Do you remember one letter when she said to him, I think he must have been about seventeen or eighteen at the time, something like, *You'll know when you get there as there is a big glass roof.* And that was Stoke station which he'd been to hundreds of times before! How about it wasn't Ralph who was hopeless at finding his way about, it was Susanna - and she projected all her own worries on to him?'

Far from being totally useless as Susanna seemed to believe, when the need arose Ralph was completely competent. He had no difficulty sorting out train timetables from Leek to Alton or getting from Leek to Cotton to see the priests at St Wilfrid's College.

We drove through the castle gates into a small car park. The trees were turning to their full autumnal colours - and Alton Castle was before us. It is unbelievably beautiful. When Ralph arrived he must have thought he had found the medieval castle of his dreams. The short journey by train from Cheddleton through deeply wooded valleys must have added to the excitement of his clandestine visit. How nervous the young Ralph must have been. He would have arrived at the lovely little station deep in the valley below the castle. From there he would have climbed the narrow path up the steep wooded hillside - then suddenly he would have seen the magnificence of the castle, turreted and with a tiled roof patterned in green and gold like a Russian palace.

Cromwell had destroyed the original castle in the Civil War - but the Shrewsburys never gave up the old faith and in the late 1830s, when it was legal to do so, the 16th Earl decided that he wanted to re-establish a Catholic centre at Alton. He engaged Pugin to design and build it for him - a complex of buildings including a monastery, school, hospital, library and chapel. The buildings form three sides of a quadrangle, the castle, somewhat apart, forms the fourth. Pugin used a beautiful, deep pink stone for most of the buildings and planted cedar trees between them. After the Earl died, the school was taken over by the Sisters of Mercy in 1855 and the presbytery became their convent. Now it is a thriving school again, and a residential centre for Catholic children, offering outdoor activities and spiritual guidance.

The coldness of life at home, the dreariness of school, the growing separation from his father - all that must have dissolved as Ralph arrived at Alton:

> *I seek Alveton's castle high,*
> *Whose towers seem to pierce the sky.*
> *Long may that noble castle stand*
> *A glory to my fatherland*
> (*The Land of the Dark Pine Tree*)

he wrote in 1886, using the old name for Alton. It was his 'Fairy-Land', the place of all his dreams. It was also his undoing.

We went into the chapel that Ralph would have known so well, small, friendly and with beautiful pictures of the Virgin. It had been harvest festival time and the church was decorated with fruit and flowers; children from the school had painted pictures and made several small scenes of delightful straw animals - rabbits having a picnic, donkeys in big hats. We walked in the shade under the cedars, and across the grass. Separated from the castle and the chapel by lawns is the priests' house, its back to the castle and facing the village. We looked up through the gate in the wall and followed, in our imaginations, the brick path to the humble dwelling where the priests still live.

'Ralph would have walked up there,' we said to each other, feeling a little closer to him. He later recorded that the priests were very kind to him and gave him tea and cake. After the first successful visit it was inevitable that he would go again. And again.

Perhaps he became careless. Perhaps, in the small-town society in which he lived where everyone knew what everyone else was doing, it was inevitable that the untruths he told to cover his tracks would be exposed. It was Mr Challinor, the family lawyer, who told Susanna and John William about Ralph's visits to Alton. They were furious. From their point of view Ralph had behaved completely disgracefully *and* he had lied to them. And all in pursuit of a religion which they saw as completely evil.

John William stormed over to Alton to see the priests and let them know how totally opposed he and Susanna were to his son having anything to do with the 'Romanish faith' as he called it. He insisted that they must have no further contact with Ralph. Susanna was almost beside herself with anger and frustration. She launched off an angry fusillade of letters to friends and relatives telling them how evil and untrustworthy Ralph had become.

He was basically a sensitive young man. It pained him that his family would not even listen to his point of view. Conversations - such as there were - ended in tears. But since they would not listen to his arguments, and feeling that he was no longer a child, there was no other course to take but to defy his father and aunt and follow what he felt was his true path. They seem to have managed the situation extremely badly. The surest way to push a youngster towards something is to forbid it! The more his father and aunt ranted and railed, the more determined Ralph became, and as far as the priests were concerned, they were only doing their duty to God in teaching him. The priests at Cotton told him very firmly that he should not join the Church without his father's knowledge, but nonetheless, he went to both Alton and Cotton again and again. Perhaps he was ashamed that he had to lie about it - but at the time there seemed to be no other way of getting the instruction he so desperately wanted. 1879 was a difficult year, but worse was to come.

By midsummer Ralph was certain he wanted to become a Catholic. He started talking about it at school to Mr Cornish and his fellow pupils - it was as badly received there as at home. In the tin trunks we found letter after letter from his aunt; letters railing against what she saw as his stupidity and wickedness, cruel letters, threatening letters.

June 18th 1879 ...I am not at all surprised that Mr & Mrs Cornish do not understand you when all your relations are so much astonished at your having thought of the Romanish faith... I hoped you had given up all that folly... you have not the slightest power to change your religion before you are 21 and I hope that before that your brains will be able to understand what is right...

July 9th 1879 ...I hope you will before long know how very wicked it is to disobey a parent, and it is worse in your case because of you being an only child, and your Papa a widower, & how you could like to follow directions from a priest who to obey caused you to tell so many LIES is perfect madness...

October 8th 1879 ....I will not help you forward in anything until I find you have given up, forever, all your Romanish folly, and not a penny of mine will help you....

But the more she berated him the more intense and obstinate became his desire. He felt he had to follow what he believed to be the true faith. Things got so bad that towards the end of 1879 Ralph must have decided to try to do as John William and Susanna asked. He was being pulled in two by what he believed to be the true religion on the one hand, and knowing that he was causing deep distress to those whom he loved on the other.

Debenham September 28th 1879
....I am sorry that I went to the Roman Catholic Chapel in Leek. I wont go there again without you want me to....

October 11th ...I hope I shall not cause you any more trouble again. I will not do anything you do not like me to do & I will not let my thoughts dwell on any disputed questions of religion & when I come home will be able to help you & do good in the place....

No doubt heaving a sigh of relief, Susanna replied:

Basford Hall October 20th.
....I am glad you are giving up your Romanish fooleries, of course when you are at home you must go to Cheddleton Church... so I hope I shall never hear any more about Romans, your foolishness has surprised everyone. Try your very best to attend to what is said in Church and say your prayers properly out of the books I gave you & then perhaps you will get to know what is right.

After Easter you will go somewhere to learn farming or something as an idle man is a plague to everybody. We cannot let you sit in the kitchen when you are at home.

Debenham October 31st
I have no objection to going to learn farming after Easter provided that I am not long away from home. When I am away I am in a perpetual state of nervousness for fear something should be going wrong. It appears to me that you have had some exaggerated tales told you about me but I hope you do not believe all you hear. But I hope you will never more have cause to find falt with me for I am going to remain in the English Church. I have bought 3 fossil sea eggs and an old javelin.

Basford Hall November 2nd.
Thank you for your letter. I am very glad to hear that you have at last come to your senses about the Romans. I cannot think how you could ever fancy that their teaching which led to such <u>lying & deceit</u> could be right, but now you must pray to be kept in the right way & trust to your relations & friends to tell you who to make new friends & not go after strangers who will only get what little money you have from you. Work very hard at all your lessons so that you will get knowledge to be of use in the world, try to please Mr & Mrs Cornish... are you cutting your nails properly and not biting them?

The onslaught against the Catholic Church was unremitting, despite Ralph's promise to remain in the Anglican fold. No wonder he was biting his nails! But the pull of the Catholic faith - or the kindness of the priests - was just too strong for him.

During the Christmas holidays Ralph tried his best to be a comfort to his aunt, but it was a cold and cheerless home and he spent a great deal of time away from it visiting and dining with people in Leek. He was probably pleased to get back to school and enjoy the company of James Cornish. Perhaps he felt that things would be a little less strained at home if James was with him for the Easter holiday of 1880 and he wrote to his aunt to ask if he might invite him. Her reply was dismissive.

We cannot have Mr James Cornish at Easter. I keep very poorly and even your coming home for a few weeks is as full much as I have the strength for, I think it very thoughtless of you wishing to have a friend here when we are both so very far from well.

So the Easter holiday followed much the same pattern as the Christmas one. Ralph was eighteen that May - but still Susanna arranged for her sister Emily Jane to go with him as far as London on his return to school on May 4th, the day after his birthday, which seems to have been a miserable affair with no celebration of any kind. How galling that must have been for him. Back at school he wrote - with more than customary care - this letter home.

May 30th Debenham
My Dear Aunty,
Thank you for your letter. I am very sorry that my wish to become a member of what I believe to be the true Church, should cause you so much trouble, but do what I can I am unable to bring myself to believe in some protestants doctrines... and I think you will allow that it is useless to profess to hold opinions which one does not believe in, besides if I did become a member of the Church of Rome, the principal thing I should have to do would be to go to Mass every Sunday and only my nearest relations need know about it. Of cause I should never think of joining the Catholic Church without your knowledge... I do not now bow or cross myself in Debenham Church... Mrs Cornish wishes me to go see some friends of hers in Germany in the summer.

He would spend the summer of 1880 travelling with James Cornish. Perhaps his family hoped that James, who was just a few years older than Ralph and planning to become a clergyman, would talk Ralph out of his fixation with Catholicism. They had also decided to keep him at school for a while longer; they probably thought that he had proved himself to be too immature to be let out into the real world just yet - learning farming was put on hold. But Ralph had made his decision, even though he knew it would be some time before he could realise his ambition.

> *My Mother Church I'll sing to thee!*
> *I long for thy true liberty;*
> *Thy perfect freedom I would see...*
> *Where are the knights of chivalry?*
> *Who, long ago, did fight for thee;*
> *Why come they not to set Thee free?*
> *(My Mother, The Church)*

he wrote romantically. But in a letter to his aunt he explained himself calmly and sensibly without making any false promises.

...The Matron at Cotton was not the person who gave me the wine, but the priests gave me wine and biscuits. They were very agreeable and said themselves that they did not wish to kidnap me into the Church of Rome but that they wished to give me time to think before I took so important a step as that of changing my religion, they strongly advised me to tell my Father my wish to become a member of the Catholic Church, perhaps with travelling I may get more settled in my oppinions one way or another.

Then in his next letter he reverted to his usual more erratic spelling and kept to entirely safe topics,

June 20th Debenham
Thank you for your letter and for sending the post office order. I hope you are better. Gordon has hired a trisical which he lets us use now and then he keeps hens and ducks.
    In haste,

John William was driven to distraction by his wayward son. He had kept Ralph at school for as long as possible but the boy would have to leave sometime. University was out of the question and Ralph showed no interest at all in learning anything that might provide him with a career and an income - so they would have to have him back at Basford. But with the Catholic problem still unresolved it was unthinkable - whatever would people say? So John William issued an ultimatum: join the Catholic Church and you will never be allowed home again.

As to a career, John William had decided that Ralph was to go to Mr Broughton at Wortley to learn farming. John William notified Ralph of his decision. Susanna sent him a prayer book. Ralph ignored them both.

June 27th Debenham
I have bought some more curiosities. I think I shall want new collars as what I have are getting rather tight. I have had the toothache lately, and the doctor has siringed my ears. I have no objection to learning farming but I thought that idea was blown over.

For a while it looked as if Ralph would give in. He was desperate to leave school and maybe he hoped that if he promised to remain an Anglican he might be allowed home for good.

July 11th Debenham
Thank you for your letter, I think I forgot to wish you many happy returns of

your birthday, I do so now... I hope you are better. I hope to stay at home after Xmas. As you so much do not want me to leave the Church of England I think I will not leave it. I cannot think what ever you mean about my not reading to you. I always read whenever I was wanted to do so. I have a bad headache so excuse my short letter.

At some point he must again have promised to stay in the Church of England but perhaps he asked whether he might occasionally be allowed to go to Mass in Leek. Susanna replied, rather ungraciously, making it clear that he was to be kept on a very short leash.

I am glad you are giving up your Romanish fooleries, of course when you are at home you must go to Cheddleton Church, if you did not go there alone someone would be appointed to take you there & where ever you are of course you will have to go to church with the family you are placed with, so I hope I shall never hear any more about Romans, your foolishness has surprised everyone.

Perhaps it was that at this point that Ralph realised she would never forgive him for his interest in Rome, and she was never going to treat him as an adult. He might as well be hung for a sheep as for a lamb!

The priests' house at Alton which Ralph visited.

Chapter 9
Ralph goes Abroad

Nearly everyone goes abroad these days, think how very dreadful it will be if you cannot speak French, Aunt Susan nagged in 1877 in an attempt to make Ralph concentrate on his lessons. She herself had only been abroad twice, on a year long family excursion to Belgium and Germany in 1858-9, and for a short honeymoon in France in 1860. As far as we know Ralph's father never went further afield than Ireland - but increasingly their family and friends were holidaying on the Continent.

The 'grand tour' had been part of the education of young gentlemen in the 18th century. At best it broadened their horizons and gave them a glimpse of what the Greek and Roman civilisations had left behind helping them make sense of the Greek and Latin that formed such a large part of the curriculum at their public schools. At worst it allowed them to sow their wild oats as far away from home as possible. But the French Revolution, followed by the Napoleonic Wars and other nationalistic uprisings, made much of Europe unsafe for travellers for some years and the practice tended to die out.

Young gentlemen of Ralph De Tunstall Sneyd's generation were more likely to be sent to do their growing-up in the outposts of the British Empire than in Europe. A spell in the colonies - as a farmer, explorer, administrator or soldier - had come to be seen as a more useful experience for the sons of gentlemen than a prolonged holiday in southern Europe. But their sisters were still often sent to schools on the Continent to perfect their French, German or Italian. It was also common practice to employ foreign governesses - Ralph's Aunt Ada was taught at different times by Madame Cambray and Fraulein Gogol.

In 1845 Thomas Cook of Leicester set up his travel business. He had begun modestly enough in 1841, organising train trips for local Temperance societies - he was secretary of the Leicester branch. His first solo venture was a 'Cook's Tour' to Liverpool. Soon he was chartering trains to take people from all parts of the British Isles to see the Great Exhibition at Crystal Palace, and within a decade he was taking parties of respectable English tourists on continental tours. By 1880 most of Europe was politically stable and attracted increasing numbers of Britons - among them James Cornish and young Ralph

De Tunstall Sneyd, with tickets in their pockets from the firm Ralph described as *Kook's*.

In 1880 a trip abroad was more adventurous than it is today. There were guide books but people were much less knowledgeable about the art, architecture, scenery, wildlife, food and customs they were likely to encounter than we are today, with our diet of television travel programmes. Eighteen year old Ralph must have been very excited and apprehensive when he set off with James.

They would be away for two months. At the end of July they sailed to Antwerp. They went on to Brussels, via the battlefield at Waterloo, across Germany to Frankfurt and Dresden and back to Coblenz and Cologne. They sailed down the Rhine to Heidelberg and made a short detour into Switzerland before returning overland via Strasbourg, Paris and Rouen.

Susanna had given Ralph a copy of Bradshaw's Railway Map of Europe, a sturdy, linen-backed sheet showing just how far the rail network had spread by 1880. Ralph carefully inked in his itinerary to show her when he got home. This was much the same route that Susanna had taken with her father, stepmother and sisters back in 1858, only she had done it much more slowly, spending six weeks in Brussels and staying for five months at Heidelberg. Her letters are full of instructions to Ralph about reading his guidebook to make sure he didn't miss anything of importance and scoldings about what she saw as his unwillingness to improve his French and German.

I am glad you were... able to enjoy seeing Antwerp you do not mention Ruben's pictures and the pulpit in the cathedral but I hope you noticed them I am glad you saw Waterloo... the same woman kept the museum when we were there 22 years ago perhaps you remember that I gathered blue flowers like you sent. Mine are good still.

I was most thankful to be allowed to have German lessons from a lady when I was at Heidelberg. I am afraid you would have liked to spend your time in idleness instead of as I did get up as soon as it was light to be able to work longer

But Ralph and James were not in the least idle - in fact they were indefatigable sightseers. They went to churches and cathedrals, castles and palaces, zoos and museums, exhibitions and concerts and circuses. They went for long walks, climbed mountains and swam in lakes - much to Aunt Susan's consternation. She was terrified they would fall or drown. Ralph bought pots and swords, picked fungi and collected frogs and insects which he preserved in spirits bought en route as he needed them. *There are a great many different frogs about here*, he wrote from Wittenburg. *I have put some in spirits among others a green tree frog. I have one alive with me too.*

'Imagine how much stuff he must have had to carry home...!'

'You must include that letter about the caterpillar,' said Marion. 'It always reminds me of Simon!' Marion's son shared Ralph De Tunstall's passion for creepy-crawlies.

I thumbed through the pile of transcripts. 'This one?' I asked '- *at Heidelberg on a Friday morning we found a great goat moth caterpillar walking across the road I put it away into my pocket handkerchief & that in my pocket to keep it safe, we then went to the chemist to get some spirits for it and some other insects but when we arrived there we only found one grasshopper on Monday morning, However, James saw the creature coming out of the rim of my coat just under my chin.'*

'Doesn't it conjure up a wonderful picture!'

'It's a good thing James Cornish knew Ralph so well!'

Ralph was having the time of his life. He wrote long descriptive letters home, picking out things that surprised him for special mention - flocks of flying cranes, cattle being fed on green maize stalks, the taste of frogs' legs. He described scenery and pictures, holy relics and circus acts. He told his aunt which church services he had attended - and when they had been to Mass he was careful to stress that it was only because there was no suitable English church available. His interest in Catholicism was still a very sore subject back at Basford.

In Cologne he made a discovery in the museum there - the Durer drawing on which he believed *Fougue* based *Sintram and his Companions* - Friedrich Heinrich Karl La Motte Fouque's *Sintram* was a tale of a knightly quest for the Holy Grail. Clearly young Ralph Sneyd was already something of an expert on the subject.

Susanna Ingleby could not resist commenting on her nephew's spelling - *you always spell cathedral 'cathedrial' and you use 'heer' for both hear and here* she grumbled, carefully correcting words and place names to show him later. But even she had to admit that these letters were much better written and spelt than the ones he had sent her from school.

For all his aunt's criticisms, Ralph seems to have got a lot more out of his first trip abroad than she did from hers. He was fascinated by everything he saw and this first excursion with James whetted his appetite for travel. It must have been hard for him to settle down to his lessons again when they returned to

Debenham in October.

He finally left Mr Cornish's at Easter 1881, just a few weeks short of his nineteenth birthday. To begin with he tried hard to please his pernickety aunt and cantankerous father. He took his turn at reading family prayers. He helped around the grounds, gardening, digging and tidying the yard. He dutifully ran errands, visited relations and took responsibility for a number of old ladies to whom he used to go and read.

In early May 1881 his cousin, Henry Bamford, came to stay and Aunt Susan paid for the two of them to have a walking holiday in Dovedale. Ralph was restless and she was anxious to keep him occupied. They were away four nights, staying in hotels, and *the outing for the two cost £3 15s* [£230] she recorded in her diary. Perhaps she hoped Henry would be a steadying influence. He was four years older than Ralph, the youngest child of her late sister, Harriet Bamford, and he was soon to be ordained - just the young man to steer Ralph away from what, at the time, his aunt hoped was just a flirtation with popery.

But that summer Aunt Susan had more pressing things on her mind than Ralph. Her youngest brother, Ralph's Uncle Gustavus, vicar of Chastleton in Oxfordshire, had got himself into serious trouble. He was accused of fathering a child with a teenage kitchen maid whose family lived in the next parish. Susanna contacted the Sneyd family solicitor, Mr Joseph Challinor, and despatched him to Chastleton to find the girl's family and pay them to keep quiet. And Ralph's Aunt Emily hurried over to Chastleton to be a respectable female presence at their brother's side.

Their actions in 1881 would only postpone the crisis. Within a couple of years Gustavus Sneyd's angry parishioners would force the Bishop of Oxford to take action, and the Reverend Sneyd would be the subject of a Consistory Court hearing. Shortly after that he would be declared bankrupt. Nonetheless, by keeping his nerve, insisting he was the injured party, and by making a tactical marriage to Chrystobel Harris, the niece of Miss Whitmore Jones of Chastleton House, somehow Gustavus Sneyd managed to hang on to his parish.

It was when *the Gustavus business* (as Susanna cryptically referred to it in her diary) was at its height that Ralph had been despatched to Mr Broughton's to learn farming. The last thing Ralph De Tunstall Sneyd wanted in the summer of 1881 was to spend yet more time away from home. Storage crates from Lees the cratemaker in Leek had arrived at Basford. He had ordered new display cabinets and he wanted to spend time working on his collections, deciding what to show and what to put away. He had no desire to be a farmer - but the arrangements had been made so he had no choice in the matter. Or had he? *Mr Broughton says you seem to take no interest in what is going on, only caring for your own pleasures & queer tastes. Mrs Broughton thinks you backward and careless with your music...* Aunt Susan scolded in a letter on July 19th. Within a few weeks things had got worse and Ralph's father was summoned to Wortley. On August 16th John William Sneyd arrived back at Basford with a relieved, but probably rather shame-faced Ralph in tow. Did Ralph deliberately set out to annoy Mr Broughton so much that he would be sent home? We shall never know for certain.

Free at last from the constraints of Debenham Vicarage and Mr Broughton's farm, in the late summer of 1881 Ralph really began to enjoy himself He could work on his collections to his heart's content up in the rooms over the archway and carriage house. They had originally been tack-rooms and, in his grandparents' day, accommodation for the grooms and outdoor servants. But times had changed. John William Sneyd did not keep a carriage, he had no horses and his only outdoor servant was Samuel Harrison, the gardener, who lived at the bottom of the hill in the Bath House complex.

The Hall and outbuildings were in a state of decline. No grooms now lived above the carriage house, there was no tack in the space over the archway. Aunt Susan decided it was the perfect place for Ralph to keep his collections. There was a fireplace so he could be warm, the space was separate from the house, he had his own, lockable, front door - and it was away from his father's disapproving eyes. Over the years John William Sneyd had become increasingly irritated by his son's collecting habit. What had been an amusing hobby for a small boy he saw as an aberration in a grown man. From time to time anger overcame him when he saw his son spending hour after hour doing heaven-only-knew-what up in his *museum*, entertaining friends there, getting the already-overworked maids to take up coal for his fire and trays of tea for his visitors. On at least one occasion John William had snapped and taken away the key to the museum. Aunt Susan smoothed everything over, of course, and John William relented, grudgingly. But resentment of the museum as a symbol of his son's oddity continued to simmer. John William Sneyd disliked oddity in any form. He didn't understand it and he didn't want to.

Aunt Susan tried harder, but she too often lost patience with her charming but stubborn nephew. Shortly after his return from Mr Broughton's he moved bedrooms - it looks as if he was being given a larger room to accommodate his growing collection of books. Susanna's diary entries scarcely conceal her irritation that she and the maids had to do most of the work. *I patched up the paper in Ralph's new room. Ralph helped a <u>little</u>*

Ralph's circle of friends was widening. Mr (later Sir) Thomas Wardle was beginning to take an interest in the tall, artistic young man. Thomas Wardle was rich and influential. He was knighted for his services to the silk industry and he had many contacts in the design world, but his lasting claim to fame is that he was William Morris's dye-master, working with him to recreate the natural plant dyes that featured in Morris's textiles. One day Mr Wardle gave Ralph a tour of his dye-house. His aunt recorded despairingly *Ralph went to Mr Wardles's dyehouse & helped with the dying & made a great mess on his hands.* To Susanna Ingleby, her nephew would always be a naughty small boy!

Increasingly, Ralph was staying away from Basford Hall. He seems to have been a welcome guest at the Challinors - both they and the Wardles had sons of Ralph's age with whom he had been at school in Leamington. His aunt's friends, Mrs Cruso and old Mrs Nixon, also enjoyed his company and he spent many nights away from home staying with one or other of these households in Leek. Ralph's interest in Catholicism hung like a black shadow over his relationship with his father and aunt. It coloured their reaction to everything he did and they nagged him incessantly. It was a long walk from Leek to Basford Hall and when all that awaited him there was carping and complaints and a cold, damp bedroom, Ralph found staying in other peoples' houses much more pleasant.

As time went on he faced more and more disapproval at home and it was by no means all deserved. Ralph was a sore disappointment to his family in many ways and John William Sneyd seems to have given up on him quite early. He hated letter writing, so he seldom wrote to Ralph when he was away at school - it was all left to Aunt Susan. Even when Ralph was at home for the holidays, father and son seem to have spent very little time in each other's company. John William's passion in life was shooting, but although Aunt Susan spent £9 [£560] on a gun for Ralph's Christmas present in 1879 John William did not take his son out on the moors with him. Nor did he teach him about estate management as his own father and grandfather had taught him.

John William was a bitter, disappointed man. Deprived of the Ashcombe estate he took little interest in Basford - unless by chance his younger brother Dryden appeared to be trespassing on his boundaries. That aroused John William Sneyd to fury, followed swiftly, and often unsuccessfully, by legal proceedings. Poachers taking fish from his stretch of the river also infuriated him. But he seems to have left his tenant farmers very much to themselves - *...as you know, your Papa does not like farming* Susanna had written to Ralph when he first suggested a career in agriculture. Ralph was thus never encouraged to feel he had any stake in the Basford estate.

He was also constantly told that he should *do good in the place*. John William Sneyd had been an officer in the Yeomanry. But by the time Ralph was a young man the Yeomanry had almost lost its role to the civil police and the regular troops - and in any case, Ralph did not have the temperament to enjoy playing at soldiers. Nonetheless, desperate to find something for him to do, as late as 1885 his father and aunt tried to persuade him to join up. In April he lunched with Captain Heath and the Volunteers but clearly, what he saw did not encourage him. Later that year his father bestirred himself to visit their neighbour, Captain Colvile, to see what he thought about Ralph joining the Guards. Fortunately, Captain Colvile seems to have known Ralph well enough to explain that it was an extremely bad idea.

The Sneyds were all magistrates and it seems odd that John William made no attempt whatsoever to get his son appointed to the Bench. Ralph may have rejected his father's lifestyle - but then John William had done little to make it attractive to him.

Aunt Susan would almost certainly have liked Ralph to become a clergyman like his grandfather and uncle. Ralph was deeply religious, even as a child, so it would have been an obvious career, but his lack of academic achievement made it impossible.

In fact, none of the roles Ralph's family would have liked him to take up would have made much difference to his actual income. Magistrates were largely unpaid, so were Yeomanry officers - even officers in the regular army subsidised themselves to a considerable degree, buying their commissions and paying for their own uniforms, horses and equipment. Clerical stipends were small - most country livings were worth less than £200 [£12,000] a year out of which paltry sum many clergy also paid a curate. In those days most Anglican clergyman still had private incomes. Even farming, in the later years of the 19th century, was uneconomic. Whatever he had done, Ralph, like his father and uncles and aunts and cousins, would have relied on family money to fund his activities.

So, secure in the knowledge that, however much Aunt Susan grumbled, there would be money to support him, Ralph cheerfully evaded his family's attempts to find him what they considered suitable employment. What he wanted to do - as he had told his aunt in one of his last letters home from school - was *to go in hard for collecting things*. To study the natural world, antiquities and religion seemed to Ralph to be a perfectly good use of his time.

In 1881 Aunt Susan was fifty and John William Sneyd was fifty-nine. They had both had unusually unfortunate lives, neither enjoyed good health and both had become self-righteous, judgemental and pessimistic. Living in their childhood home they were reminded on a daily basis of just how much their lives had changed; the house was cold and dilapidated, they relied on the services of a drunken, opinionated cook and a series of young, scatty, dim-witted maidservants, they ate frugal meals, they had few visitors and even fewer invitations. They were introspective, lonely, bored and uncomfortable.

It was a depressing home for a teenager and they were depressing company. Susanna Ingleby went to church, busied herself with charity work and spent time with her sister Emily, her aunt and her cousins who sympathised with her and reinforced her opinions. John William retreated into his silent, self-pitying world and did very little. Ralph was their scapegoat. For their benefit as much as his, a scheme was hatched with old Aunt Mary up at Belmont to send Ralph abroad again.

Early in April 1882 Ralph set out for Australia. He sailed on the *Marmaric* from London, via Plymouth, across the Bay of Biscay, down the Spanish and Portuguese coasts, skirting West Africa, putting in at the Cape and then sailing across the Indian Ocean to make landfall in Western Australia. The *Marmaric* then sailed along the south coast of Australia to Williamstown (now a suburb of Melbourne) on the promontory at the mouth of the River Yarra where Ralph disembarked. There were only seven other travellers on the voyage *one of them a lady* - the *Marmaric* seems to have been a cargo ship that also took a few paying passengers. Ralph didn't actually work his passage but he was expected to help. *We get plenty of exercise hauling ropes and emptying buckets,* he told his aunt in a letter.

Ralph's letters home from Australia in 1882 are notable for their descriptions of wildlife. On the voyage Ralph and his fellow travellers had little to do and they seem to have spent a good deal of time enticing birds on board their ship - mutton birds, cape pigeons, mollyhawks, petrels, Mother Carey's chickens, even albatrosses. Sometimes they shot them, sometimes they let them go. Ralph records skinning a *Mother carry's chicken* he caught himself, and the ship's cook seems to have run a profitable sidcline in preparing the birds the passengers brought down. Ralph was not alone in his collecting of natural history specimens. The wildlife he saw on that trip was unlike anything he was used to in Europe, but his aunt was probably not much the wiser after reading Ralph's lengthy description of the birds he saw off the coast of Africa.

There is a large Albertros with the back, underside and head white, but the upper side of the wing dark coloured, besides a brown albertros with a lighter underside. There is a molleyhawk with the upper side of the wings of a dark grey or nearly black colour... there are also molleyhawks of a dark brown colour

The meticulous description of the different colour schemes of the various white, grey, black and brown seabirds went on for pages and was repeated in letter after letter!

Aunt Susan hoped the sea air would improve Ralph's health. It is unlikely that the *Marmaric* was a very big ship and they crossed some extremely rough seas in the Bay of Biscay and around Cape Horn - fortunately Ralph was a good sailor. Because the voyage was the main purpose of the trip Ralph spent a disappointingly short time actually in Australia - barely two months. He was the paying guest of Mr William Fish, a friend of a friend of his great-aunt, Mary Sneyd-Kynnersley. Mr Fish lived at a place called Malvern, then about five miles out of Melbourne, and charged £2 [£120] a week for board, lodging and washing.

Ralph found plenty to entertain him. He explored Melbourne and all the major sights there, he went to St Kilda and picked up catfish on the beach, he went shooting with Mr Fish and made expeditions into the bush on his own. It is to be hoped that Mr Fish warned him of the dangers of Australia's wildlife - cautious, over-protective Aunt Susan would have been horrified had she realised her precious nephew had risked encountering funnel-web spiders and copper-head snakes! Australia is a huge country and Ralph could only see a very little of it - but he did his best. He made expeditions eastwards to Sale in Gippsland and the lakes, north to Euchuca, then at the end of the railway line, and west to the gold-mining town of Ballarat. He visited his great-aunt's friends, the Smiths, at Kew, now a suburb of Melbourne but then very isolated.

In Melbourne Ralph was fascinated by the Chinese workers who had come in their hundreds to work as labourers in the new country; he visited their *josh houses* (temples) and watched them eat rice and fish with chopsticks. There were no Chinese restaurants in Britain in 1882 - seeing chopsticks in use was a great novelty. But he was equally fascinated by everyday things. *The hedges around Malvern are usually made of a species of acacia,* he told his aunt shortly after he arrived in Australia. *I have seen 2 or 3 distinct kinds of acacia but the sort which the hedges are made of is generally very prickly, it has a pretty yellow flower, then there are blue, red, white and peppermint gums, wattles, etc, etc*

He did a great deal of shooting and found himself a taxidermist in Melbourne to prepare his specimens. *I have got several curiosities*, he told his aunt, shortly before leaving Australia ...*I have a gigantic kangaroo about as large as myself it is a male, also a young native bear, two common opossums, a black and white native cat, a bandicoot, a flying fox, a platabus* [platypus]*, a small flying squirrel, a Lyor bird, a laughing jackass, etc., stuffed very well...*

'Note the 'etc'!'

'It's a miracle he got them all home! Just imagine arriving back at Basford with that lot!'

Marion looked thoughtful. 'Seriously, though - he was pretty good at looking after himself, wasn't he? It must have taken a lot of organisation to get all that lot stuffed and ready to take home in the short time he had available.'

We felt that Susanna underestimated Ralph. When he wanted to do something or go somewhere he was extremely competent. He was only careless and forgetful when he was bored.

Despite all his extra baggage, Ralph travelled home rather more comfortably than he had gone out - on a steamer, the *Indus* - and by a rather more exciting route. They docked at Columbo in Ceylon (Sri Lanka) and were there for two weeks. Ralph and his fellow passengers visited the sights - lakes and gardens, a cinnamon plantation, *Black Town, Cochin China etc.* Ralph then took a train, by himself, to Kandy, which is in the north of the island, and visited one of the most holy Buddhist Temples - the Temple of the Tooth, where a tooth, which reputedly belonged to the Lord Buddha, is held in a golden casket. He put up at a hotel and hired a carriage to take him round the Buddhist and Tamil temples, doubtless entranced by the spectacular mountain scenery and colourful local markets.

From Ceylon the *Indus* sailed to Aden. Ralph records visiting the military installations and the bazaar. They sailed up the Red Sea, stopping in Egypt, then passing through the Suez Canal into the Mediterranean. They stopped in Suez and Ralph hired himself a donkey and rode off to the bazaar to look for specimens for his collection. They docked in Malta and again Ralph landed to explore. They then sailed close to the North African coast, through the straits of Gibraltar and up the Iberian coast, sometimes close enough to have a good view of the towns they passed, and finally landed in Plymouth on November 16th.

Ralph had been away for eight months and had visited four continents.

Chapter 10
Ralph becomes a Catholic

Queen of Heaven! Ever fair,
Robed in white, and blest for ever,
Crowned with stars beyond compare!
Guide us over death's dark river;
Guide us to thy kingdom where
We no more from thee shall sever.
(Queen of Heaven)

Ralph eventually established with his aunt and father that, although he would go to church with them, he would also sometimes attend Mass if he wished to. He started to make friends with Catholics in Leek, but for another two years he remained in a religious limbo. It was stressful, and, as we shall see, Ralph's health suffered. But he knew what he wanted, it was just a matter of biding his time.

Ralph's childhood had been full of secrets, silences and feuds, with many questions he was not expected to ask. There were so many close relatives who for some reason or other he was never allowed to meet, or with whom contact ceased abruptly and without explanation. As a young adult he seems to have been determined to confront his past head-on, to meet the people who had been strangers for so long, to hear their points of view and decide for himself who was friend and who was foe. His aunt watched unhappily, and perhaps rather enviously, as Ralph rediscovered his family and made new friends. Her loyalties were with John William, his battles were hers, even if, as they got older, she was less and less certain that he was always right. She was a woman - men made the rules.

Ralph was aided in his quest by the arrival, sometime in 1884, of his father's cousin and his wife at Lightoaks, Oakamoor. *Tom and Charlotte* as they appear in Aunt Susan's diaries were Major-General Thomas William Sneyd and his haughty wife, Charlotte. Thomas William was the eldest son of Thomas Sneyd, brother to Ralph's grandfather, the Reverend John Sneyd. Thomas Sneyd the elder had moved to Devon back in the 1850s - some said to escape his overbearing elder brother, John - but he died in 1883 and his son decided to return to his home county. Ralph and his aunt were frequent visitors to Lightoaks - for Ralph it was a convenient place to break his journey between home and the Roman Catholic community at Alton.

Aunt Susan had been close to Tom and his siblings when they were young and visits to Lightoaks enabled her to catch up with them again for Tom and Charlotte were great entertainers. Members of the family who had not set foot in Staffordshire for years were happy to go to Oakamoor, and at Lightoaks Ralph met numerous relatives who up until then had just been names. Little did Ralph De Tunstall know then that convivial 'Uncle' Thomas William and his little boy would finally deprive him of both Ashcombe Park and Basford Hall as his father's and his Uncle Dryden's heirs.

'Aunt' Charlotte cannot have been very impressed by young Ralph. Thirty years later, politely entertaining him at Woodlands, she would hiss 'Don't let him kiss you!' in her little granddaughter's ear, and contemptuously dismiss his stories as so much rubbish. Little Averil never understood the prohibition especially as, unlike some members of her family, Cousin Ralph was not at all threatening and his travel tales were fascinating!

In May he was twenty-one.

May 3rd 1883: Wet in the morning but fine afterwards. Elizabeth had dinner with the servants here. The little Harrisons and the little Cordons had tea. I dined at Tattons with Harrison, Shaw, Critchlow, Steel, Copstick, Corden, Harrison, Tudor Jn (his father being ill) Clowes Sen., Clowes Jn., Turner Sen., Turner Jn. & Tatton. This made 14. The wives of 10 of the tenants had tea with Miss Turner, Miss Tatton, Lizzie Tudor and Mrs Ratcliffe, after which I showed most of the party my curiosities & we finished up with drinking healths, fireworks & songs. There was a good bonfire. [then, in Susanna Ingleby's hand] *Aunty gave the dinner and the tea.*

Aunt Susan was determined to force him to acknowledge her contribution. At this stage she still regularly looked through his diaries and corrected his spelling - small wonder that Ralph was never very keen on diary-keeping! As was customary, the tenants, employees and selected neighbours of the Basford estate had been invited to celebrate the coming-of-age of the young master. Similar but rather grander ceremonies had heralded many Sneyd ancestors attaining their majority, although the guided tour of Ralph's museum added an individual note to the proceedings.

For Ralph, the important thing was that he was, at last, recognised in law as an adult who could make up his own mind in matters of religion. He had been visiting priests for years and discussing theological matters. Now he could take instruction and prepare himself thoroughly for the great step he was planning.

He probably went to the priests in Leek, but as Susanna's diary for 1883 is missing we cannot be sure. We had often wondered where Ralph was accepted into the Catholic Church - Susanna could not bring herself to record something so painful. Then, as so often happened, a chance reading when looking for something else gave us the key.

Whilst researching Ralph's interest in Theosophy, I read a diary that he kept about a visit to his relatives in London. Since he wrote so little, when Ralph did write anything down in his diary it meant it was important. I read the entry, *I went to Brompton Oratory*. Yes, of course, Brompton Oratory, that huge, ornate, powerful church in the Brompton Road. That evening I typed www.bromptonoratory into my computer. The Oratory site came up: pictures, the history - and most usefully, an email address for enquiries.

'I've had a small triumph, oh Most Learned One,' I emailed Pam a few days later. 'Want to know where Ralph was accepted into the church?'

'Of course!'

I had been lucky. Ralph's diary had given the date when he attended the Oratory - I contacted the archivist there and asked if they had a register of people accepted into the church, and if so, was there someone called Ralph De Tunstall Sneyd? The answer was more than I could have hoped for. Not only had the archivist found Ralph's date of acceptance he had also, very thoughtfully, scanned and sent a copy of the original entry. I sent Pam the details.

'We should have realised, being Ralph, that if he was going to do something as momentous as this he'd have chosen the equivalent of Westminster Abbey to do it in!' I wrote

'Excellent. A whole tube of Smarties!' came the response.

May 20th 1884 was a date Ralph would remember for the rest of his life. He had been in London for about two weeks staying with some of his relatives - his Uncle and Aunt Palliser. Susanna knew he was with them of course - but what she did not know was what he had in mind. He did all the usual things in London with his aunt and uncle - art galleries, concerts and so on - but his main reason for being there was that he had decided, once and for all, no matter what it cost, that he would become a Catholic.

On May 11th, after attending church with his aunt and uncle in the morning, he went to the Oratory in Brompton Road for the evening service. The Oratory had been finished earlier that year and it was considered to be the most imposing Catholic church in London - a vast building with side chapels and vaulted ceilings - somewhat austere inside at that time, as photos show, as the elaborately decorated ceiling and wall panels had still to be put in place. After the service Ralph made contact with one of the priests, Father Sebastian Bowden, and asked him to accept him into the Catholic Church.

It is scarcely possible to imagine with what trepidation he took that step knowing what the repercussions would be at home. Since Ralph was obviously fully prepared, and since he was taking this momentous step all by himself, Father Bowden - a man with a wide experience of life and men, having been an officer in the Scots Guards before he became a priest - agreed to conduct the ceremony in nine days time and to stand sponsor for Ralph.

I arranged to visit the Oratory in the late autumn of 2004 and on arrival made my way to the priest's house in a tree-shaded courtyard next to the church. The Oxford blue door opened when I pressed the bell and I told the gentleman receptionist I had come to see Father Lang. Within a few moments he arrived. A small, quiet, dark-haired young man, he led me to a small visitor's room. Black and white lithographs showing the gruesome death agonies of several saints filled the walls. I was glad they were not in colour. A statue of St Francis stood under the most unpleasant - smiling calmly - and in the corner an ancient radiator gurgled. Father Lang indicated a chair and, smiling diffidently, handed me a small booklet he had looked out, knowing that it would be useful for our research. It was a copy of the actual ceremony of Ralph's initiation. Nothing could have been more illuminating. Leading the way he took me by a side door into the Oratory and pointed out where various parts of the ceremony would have taken place and indicated books in the Oratory bookshop that had pictures in that would be useful to us. As quietly as he had approached me at the priests' house he was gone, almost before I had time to thank him properly. He had been invaluable.

When Ralph had made the final arrangements for his acceptance into the church with Father Bowden, he heeded the advice given to him by the priests at Cotton. On May 16th he wrote to his father and informed him of his intention.

On Tuesday May 20th he was accepted into the Roman Catholic Church. There was no one else present in that huge church, no one else being received at the same time. First Father Bowden took Ralph into the little baptismal chapel near the rear of the church and there baptised him - pouring the holy water on his head - Rudolphus Georgius Maria De Tunstall Sneyd. Ralph had taken St George and St Mary as his patron saints. Slowly they would then have walked to a side chapel and there, vested in a simple surplice with a purple stole, with his back to the altar, Father Bowden would have addressed Ralph who was kneeling before him. First he exhorted him to thank God from the bottom of his heart that he had been granted the gift of Faith and to prove his gratitude by making good use of it. Ralph would certainly fulfil that promise. That initial exhortation over, the priest turned and knelt before the altar and started the actual ceremony, with the well-known verses: *Veni Creator Spiritus,* Come O Creator, Spirit blest.

Father Bowden had gone through the service with Ralph beforehand to make sure that he knew exactly what he was saying and accepting. He recited the seven verses then said, *Emitte Spiritum tuum et creabuntur* - Send forth thy spirit and all things shall be created afresh, and Ralph responded with all his heart, *Et renovabis faciem terrar* - And thou shalt renew the face of the earth.

Then Father Bowden covered his head and prayed for Ralph, asking God to grant him wisdom and accept the consolation that faith brings. Kneeling before him Ralph placed his right hand on the book of the Holy Gospels and recited the Profession of Faith,

'I Rudolphus Georgius Maria De Tunstall Sneyd, holding in my hand God's holy gospels, and enlightened by divine grace, publicly declare that I accept the Faith which is taught by the Catholic, Apostolic, and Roman Church. I believe that Church to be the one true Church which Jesus Christ set up here on earth; to which I make my submission with all my heart...'

Finally, after more prayers, with his head still covered, Father Bowden placed his hand on Ralph's head and said, 'With the authority of the Apostolic See I loosen the bond which has bound you, and restore you to the Sacraments of the Church and to the unity and fellowship of the faithful...'

Ralph was a Roman Catholic. He had made his choice and it would affect everything in his life that followed. He may have been ecstatic but he knew his family would be devastated. That evening he wrote the difficult letter that he knew would distress his aunt so much. The following day he made his First Communion in the Oratory - having breakfast afterwards with the priests in their house next door

- then left London for Oxfordshire.

Ralph would not go home for some considerable time. After some days at Childrey with Mr Cornish who had moved there from Debenham, he went to Chastleton to stay with his Uncle Gustavus. Given that they were both Church of England clergyman, Ralph received a warmer welcome from them both than he could reasonably have expected. Meanwhile Susanna was writing to his uncle - and he wrote back - nasty, spiteful letters, mocking Ralph and his beliefs: *....he considered you very foolish & hardly a Christian, & certainly not one if you were as bad as you talked. I cannot think how you like to be so wicked, the Romans are quite wicked enough,* Aunt Susan reported. Sly to the end, Gustavus was quite capable of giving his nephew a roof over his head whilst at the same time stabbing him in the back.

Susanna wrote to Ralph too. She was angry, sad, upset - and irrational. She wrote furious letters telling him to stay away - that she and John William were happier and better off without him. Then the next would arrive asking when he expected to be home, nagging him, *Don't stay when you are not wanted. Be sure to do everything you are asked to do,* the sort of letters she had written when he was a child. With failing health and a limited social life, Ralph had become the focus of her life and she was desperately dependent on him. She had been the guiding influence in his life but in forsaking the Anglican Church she felt he had forsaken her and all she believed in so deeply. It was incomprehensible. It was heart-breaking.

Ralph went to stay with other friends and relations, but eventually on the 26th July, after almost three months away, he went back to Basford to face the music. His aunt welcomed him home, but his father was ominously silent.

Ralph was now a young man with a mind and will of his own, confident and completely capable of making his own arrangements. He made it quite clear that on Sundays he would be going to Leek to attend Mass, and Susanna - for all her blustering - was so pleased to have him in the house again that just a day or two after his return she even went across to Alton with him to a bazaar run by the Sisters of Mercy to raise money for the poor. One of the nuns showed her over the convent.

Susanna would gradually become accustomed to Ralph going to the Catholic church in Leek and making new friends although she could never fully accept it.

Catholicism had prospered in Leek in the 19th century. The town's first Catholic chapel was established in 1828. A new church was built in 1860, and a small convent and school were set up the same year. This was largely due to the efforts of Father Anderson who came to the town in the late 1850s and stayed for almost thirty years. Ralph must surely have known him for he went to the priest's house in Leek on innumerable occasions.

He was succeeded in June 1884 by Father Sperling who would become a great friend of Ralph's. The young priest's father offered to build a new presbytery but his son declined this and said what he would really like was a new church. His father at once purchased the land on which St Mary's now stands for £400 [£25,000]. Plans for the new church were drawn up, and money was raised within the parish by donations, including a shilling a week from Ralph Sneyd. This pledge caused endless trouble up at Basford Hall! The magnificent new church was opened on May 12th 1887. Ralph attended the opening and Susanna, a martyr to the end, wrote in her diary on that day, *I just got up to start Ralph off to see the new Roman Chapel opened, he went to a service at 11.30 and 6.30. I was in bed all day with a sick headache.*

1887 saw Ralph at the centre of Catholic Leek, joyous in his new church. Over the years he would celebrate his joy in poem after poem.

> *Star of Ocean, gleaming bright,*
> *I will love thee evermore!*
> *Lead, oh lead me, by thy light,*
> *Lead me to the distant shore.*
> > (*Star of Ocean, Gleaming Bright*)

> *I dreamt I looked into the starlit sky,*
> *And thoughts of Mother Church did come to me:*
> *Unlimited by time and space so high,*
> *With no Beginning and no End - so free.*
> > (*The Church Our Mother*)

> *O Blessed Lady! born to save!*
> *Whose feet the crystal waters lave:*
> *All hail to Thee, O queen of light,*
> *Protect us from the powers of night!*
> > (*Mother of Joy*)

It would be several years before he fully appreciated just how dramatically the summer of 1884 would change the course of his entire life.

Chapter 11
The Lull before the Storm

Leek in the 1880s and 90s was a prosperous little place with a strong cultural life. The silk mills were flourishing, there was a thriving market that drew farmers and their wives from miles around, and every six weeks there was a cattle market that served most of the county and beyond. Leek had a theatre and a race course, successful sports clubs, a busy station with good rail links to London and Manchester, its own gasworks and a cottage hospital built in 1870. The wealth of the town can still be seen in the quality of many of the houses.

Joshua Nicholson was one of the town's most prominent businessmen and he endowed the Nicholson Institute which opened in October 1884 and was a typically Victorian provincial establishment, housing a library - free to those who lived within six miles of the town - a newsroom, a museum and art gallery and a school of art. A technical school was added a few years later. The Institute was opened by one of the most important men in the world of art and design in the 1880s - Sir Philip Cunliff-Owen of the South Kensington Museum. Visitors came from all over the world; from Japan, India, America, Canada and from Lyons, centre of the French silk industry.   No doubt businessmen coming to Leek to buy silk were encouraged by their hosts to visit.   Perhaps even more interesting was the way the trustees invited prominent figures to attend their early Annual General Meetings. In 1899, for example, Lord Kitchener, Mark Twain and Keir Hardie were the invited guests! Leek was no provincial backwater. As a member of the local gentry, on the day of the opening Ralph recorded,

...[I] *walked in a Grand Procession to that building and saw it opened. I then lunched with all the grand people at the town hall, after which I had tea with Mr Bermingham to hear the speeches but we were a little late...*

Perhaps Mr Bermingham sneaked him in, for Ralph is not on the list of 'local gentlemen' invited to the banquet to stuff themselves with turtle and mock turtle soup, oysters, venison, pressed and spiced beef, three cuts of lamb, veal, ham, tongue, boar's head in aspic, peacock, turkey, game, lobster salad, champagne jellies, trifle, tipsy cake, English grapes, pineapples and pomegranates - all provided by Henry Swift, landlord of the Red Lion.

'That's still there, and we've never had a meal there, have we?' asked Marion.

'No, we haven't, but I doubt whether they have turtle soup and peacock on the menu today!'

'They might have kangaroo and ostrich, though!'

It was an impressive ceremony and Ralph would, over the years, make as good use of the Nicholson Institute as anyone else in the town.

George Bermingham was one of Ralph's new friends. The Berminghams were mill owners and prominent local Catholics. George was a foundation manager of the Catholic elementary school and a member of the Leek Board of Guardians. Like many of Ralph's contacts at this period, Mr Bermingham and his family were not part of the Sneyd family social circle. Leek was a small place and nearly everybody recognised nearly everybody else - but that did not mean they acknowledged each other. Mr Hamshaw, Mr Hartley, Mr Jones and his wife and sons, Mr Jeremiah Beardmore of Bucknall, the Godwins, the Gibsons, the Tittertons and Mr Tansley were all part of Ralph's new circle. They did not all meet with Susanna's approval - many of them were tradesmen. Mr Jones was a gunsmith in Leek, his wife worked as a dressmaker and Thomas, the eldest of his two sons, worked in a warehouse. Mr Hartley kept the chemist's shop in the Market Place. William Tansley was a joiner's apprentice and the Tittertons were farmers at Crow Holt in Cheddleton - she used to buy cheese from them! In her diary Aunt Susan often called her nephew's friends by their surnames alone - 'Hartley' or 'Tansley' without the 'Mr' that would have denoted that she saw them as her social equals.

Susanna Ingleby's diaries are tedious in the extreme and it is only through such subtle linguistic shifts that we can discern her disapproval of Ralph's burgeoning social circle. Her diaries are dry and factual. She had a gift for understatement - in the throes of a violently abusive marriage she only allowed herself to write *Very unhappy* once, when things were at their rock-bottom worst. And in thirty years worth of diaries there are fewer than a dozen comments that have any emotional content. So when, on September 1st 1884, she wrote *Ralph made such a fuss about his things that I would not speak to him*, it is probably fair to assume that she is recording a row of epic proportions. He had agreed to pay a shilling [£3] a week towards the building of St Mary's Catholic Church in Leek and Susanna must have been furious about him spending her money to support a creed she detested. His 'fuss' just added fuel to the flames. It would be several weeks before poor Ralph could put a foot right.

September 3rd: ....Ralph would smoke at Mrs Cooper's so I left him....

September 9th: ....Ralph went over to Ipstones & hired a room at 1s a week to put his things in.... I got John Wm to say Ralph might keep his things here. I was ill in the night.

September 16th: ....I began to help Ralph with his room but as he was so wilful I left him.

Clearly John William was equally irked by his son, but the wretched curiosities were the focus of his anger. This again seems to have been more than an ordinary disagreement. It was, Susanna Ingleby tells us, a wet day. Ralph hiked four steep miles up to Ipstones, knocked on doors and negotiated the hire of what was probably a disused outbuilding. In an isolated village at that time a shilling was a lot of money for an empty room. The shilling, of course, would have come out of Aunt Susan's purse, but it was probably the shame of people knowing that her brother and nephew were quarrelling that motivated her to use her diplomatic skills on John William.

Many Victorians were collectors - which makes it hard to see why Ralph's family objected so vehemently to his curiosities. In Leek, his friend, Hartley, collected coins and Thomas Wardle had a collection of Indian artefacts and other items. Indeed, Ralph acquired two of his most dramatic exhibits from Mr Wardle - a pair of 17 foot long basalt columns from the Giants' Causeway. Thomas Wardle had them shipped over from Ireland to his country home, Swainsley Hall. Ralph later had them taken up to Fair View and put them on his lawn.

Ralph travelled a lot, and he collected specimens as he went. Unfortunately we have a much less consistent account of what they were than we have in his letters home from school. In the later letters Ralph's purchases tend to be described simply as *curiosities* (Ralph) or *foolish rubbish* (Aunt Susan)! But we get occasional, tantalising glimpses. In October 1882 Ralph spent some time staying in Bristol with Mr Palmer, his aunt's old friend from Armitage. A little while after he left, Susanna Ingleby received this rather curious letter: *I suppose by this time Ralph has returned to his nursery. I hope the lady's stomach he left Bristol with was not damaged during his travels ...*

'Nursery! Was he implying Ralph still behaved like a little boy or that Susanna still treated him as one?' Marion exclaimed.

I didn't know, but Ralph's taste in curiosities seemed to be getting stranger! Mr Palmer went on to tell Susanna that he had been approached by a *dealer in antiquities* enquiring whether the *tall young man* was still interested in the suit of armour! We thought Susanna would surely have mentioned it if he had bought one of those - but we couldn't be sure. Ralph was said to have owned two suits of armour - we had been told that they were eventually sold to the Three Horseshoes at Blackshaw.

Three years later Ralph stayed with Mr Palmer again. Bristol seems to have had good antique shops. He wrote home, *I have also bought a young alligator for 8/6* [£28]*, besides a small crucifix & 2 statuetts. Can you please send me a little more money as I am very short of cash...* His aunt must have been furious!

We also know that at some point the Nelson family gave him *a handkerchief of Charles II*. It was a cherished possession and was still hanging on a screen in what had been Ralph's study some 90 years later.

When he travelled to Orkney, Shetland and Norway we know Ralph bought geological specimens and an Orkney spinning wheel and many other things besides. He sketched some of them to illustrate a pamphlet he produced about his travels. He bought a lot of things in Iceland in 1891. According to Joyce Shenton, he spent all his money on specimens on that trip and could not afford a cabin for his homeward journey - so he slept on deck! In Australia, as we have seen, he shot a whole range of birds and animals and had them stuffed by a Melbourne taxidermist. In Ceylon he bought *curiosities and a sword* - we know because he managed to mislay them in transit and they were the subject of a good deal of correspondence.

Perhaps it wasn't the objects Ralph's family resented but the amount of bother, and expense, they caused.

Susanna might smooth over the quarrels between her brother and his son, but she herself was an expert, consciously or unconsciously, at emotional blackmail. If Ralph upset her, she took to her bed. And she had no compunction about blaming him for her illnesses. For example, on his way to Mr Broughton's in late June 1881, he and his friend Mr Faulkner, the curate at Ipstones, who had gone to see him off, had been entrusted with posting two letters for Aunt Susan, one of which appears to have been to her doctor asking for more medicine. They forgot.

Why did you not see that Mr Faulkner posted the two letters at the station? They would then have been alright & in lots of time, you heard me say both the letters were very particular & they both missed the post. I was very ill in the evening, I could not lie down in bed but sat in your rocking chair for about an hour & sent Harrison to ask Dr Somerville to come... let this be a warning to you to do exactly what you are told I wonder Mr Faulkner... did not take the letters to Leek, but you were as bad as he was, you knew I had written for the dr she raged in her first letter to him at Wortley. In Susanna Ingleby's world there was no such thing as making a mistake.

It is difficult not to sympathise with Ralph at this period in his life; he was desperately trying to be his own person but still being treated as a disobedient child - and he was dependent on his aunt for every penny he spent. Susanna Ingleby and her sisters had had a small financial allowance from their father by the time they were twenty-one so that they did not have to seek his approval for every ribbon or pair of gloves that they bought; it would surely have been possible for her to do the same for Ralph. Aunt Susan was parsimonious, she had seen her family lose a fortune and it affected her profoundly - but an allowance of two or three pounds a quarter, the same sort of sum she paid her cook, would have done a great deal for Ralph's self-respect. He might even have learnt to manage his money. But as it was he had to ask her for everything - no wonder he was profligate: *As I cannot imagine what you have done with all your large sums of money I will oblige you to write down how you have spent it as I cannot have my money wasted in this way & not know what becomes of it...* she ranted at him in a letter dated November 14th,1888.

But she continued to fund him. He knew if he sought her permission before buying items for his collection - spinning wheels in Shetland or stuffed birds in Manchester - she would have refused. So he bought them anyway and arranged for them to be sent by rail to Cheddleton station. Faced with a station porter and a bill Aunt Susan always paid up.

In August 1884, just a couple of months after he had been received into the Catholic church, Ralph visited Ireland. His cousin, Henry Bamford, soon to be ordained a minister in the Church of England, went too - perhaps Aunt Susan hoped that he would persuade his stubborn young cousin of the folly of his ways. If so she was much mistaken - and from her point of view the Catholic south of Ireland was an unfortunate destination for her impressionable and newly-converted nephew. Ralph revelled in his visits to churches and abbeys and monasteries. Years later he penned a lilting poem about *Erin's*

Isle. His main impression seems to have been of the monks.

> *True monks abide*
> *Near the foaming tide*
> *In Erin's Isle they roam...*

It went on for ten, rather repetitive verses. Catholicism would always impress him. Fifty years later his main impression of Nazi Germany, just before the outbreak of the Second World War, was its religion! *Hitler is a Roman Catholic & his name is held in great respect. He has made a concordat with Rome, & in this city on all sides are the Cross & the Swastika* he wrote from Trier to his housekeeper, Sarah Riley.

In 1888 Ralph went to Norway. It started as a trip to see his relatives in Edinburgh and Lethen, to be followed by an excursion to the Orkneys and the Shetland Isles - then much more remote and primitive than they are today. No doubt Ralph was looking forward to learning about the islands' folklore and seeing seabirds. But in Lerwick he met the captain of a fishing smack who was about to sail to Norway. It was too good an opportunity to miss - so Ralph went too. At that date he had no need of a passport - Queen Victoria's subjects could travel wherever they pleased. His aunt had no idea he had gone - she was still sending letters and money to the post office in Lerwick. Not until a telegram arrived from Christiania (Oslo) *Send £10 directly* [£680] did she realise that Ralph had gone abroad. Dutifully she got out her copy of *Feats on the Fjord* to read about the sights he would be seeing!

Ralph was pragmatic, and unfazed when plans went awry.

Aurdal

My dear Aunty,

I returned to Lyngoe on Tuesday last from Christiania, but found that the fishing smack which I intended to go back in had started without me, so today, Thursday, I came here ... I went a journey by train to Skien and from there went in a small steamer to Hitterdal in Telemark....

Of course Ralph had unlimited time at his disposal and all the confidence of an Englishman in the age of the British Empire. Britain ruled the world - so Ralph Sneyd believed he would be safe wherever in that world he chose to travel. He thought the best of people, trusted them - and they seldom seem to have let him down. And though his aunt might grumble, she would always send him money if he really needed it - though in this case not without a good deal of difficulty. Ralph was asking for a very considerable sum - and though in theory it was possible to telegraph money overseas, the postmaster in Cheddleton was very unsure about the procedure and the whole transaction took several days and caused Susanna Ingleby a good deal of concern.

Ralph seems to have loved Norway's mountain scenery. *Nearly all the way between Christiania and Hitterdal the scenery is very beautiful ...the pine clad northern mountains ... rise from the mirror-like fiords and nestling amidst the pine and the birch are the wooden houses of the peasantry...* he told his aunt. He would return to Norway at least twice more, once in 1895 with his wife, and again in 1906 with her and his ten year old daughter, Stella. Perhaps Norway inspired Ralph to learn more about Norse culture - for three years later, just a few months before his aunt's death, he visited Iceland. We know more about this trip than many of the others because, in November 1891, Ralph gave a lecture about it at the Nicholson Institute and wrote a pamphlet which he distributed to his audience. The descriptions it contained are more poetic and finely honed than the accounts his aunt received in his letters home, or the bald lists of places visited, people met and modes of transport used that appear in his diaries.

Ralph was adventurous. He was quite happy travelling by himself or with a hired guide, and would ride for miles across unknown country or scale high mountains - clad in his tweed plus-fours, thick socks and the stout pair of shoes he used for walking his native moors. Waterproof clothing was heavy and stiff - and only professional mountaineers had special boots and equipment.

In Iceland in 1891 Ralph and his guide rode, ... *for many hours over a desolate country, which consisted of miles of sand and stones, followed by miles of wasteland covered with grey moss ... interspersed with beautiful tufts of small pink flowers, we at length arrived in sight of Thingvalla Vatn or the Lake of Thingvalla.*

The local pastor put him up for a few nights in a part of his house *devoted to the convenience of guests.* We are used to booking our holiday accommodation in advance over the internet or through a travel agent. 19th century travellers had to put much more faith in the kindness of local people or be prepared to rough it. Later on in his visit to Iceland Ralph and his guide rode for four days across *a sea of lava, black and terrible, whose wild waves seemed as if they had suddenly been changed to stone.* He does not tell us where they slept or how they ate. Eventually they arrived at Mount Hekla where Ralph put up at a local farm, hired a local man to lead him and climbed the mountain:

It was with great difficulty that I dragged myself up the steep incline. I had taken hardly any breakfast, and nothing in the middle of the day but a little milk and water. [He was also recovering from a bad attack of bronchitis.] *Still on we went until we came to the snow. A glorious panorama met the eye. On one side was a vast extent of country of lava, grass and sand, and on the other the great snow mountains, which stretched far away to the horizon. There, under the canopy of heaven, gleamed the mystic peaks of old Iceland, clad for ever in perpetual winter.*

He was a born romantic - but he was also a sensitive and inquisitive traveller. In the Isle of Man in 1881 he persuaded local people to tell him folk stories - *I get a great many people to tell me legends about fairies etc* he told his aunt in a letter. In Iceland he went to a wedding and described the bride's costume in great detail. He even brought home some silver Icelandic wedding rings, large, elaborately-wrought with little discs attached like bells.

'And do you remember the stone querns Colin showed us?' asked Marion. 'One is in their pond - and he held the other for us to photograph - it weighed a ton.'

'Imagine getting them home!'

Ralph was obsessed with Catholicism, but he was curious about other peoples' religious ceremonies as well, and we know he explored the Greek Orthodox and Armenian churches in Manchester and sat in on a Jewish wedding in Bristol. Amongst his books there was a form of *The Coptic Morning Service* carefully annotated in his own hand. Wherever he went he described the vestments in minute detail - robes obviously fascinated him. Over the years he acquired numerous sets that he wore at ceremonies of his own devising, and he seems to have spent a considerable amount of money on them.

By 1885 he was experimenting with ouija boards (table tapping) as a way of testing his belief in the afterlife. A few years later in 1888 it was Buddhism - *Ralph read us a Buddhist catechism* wrote Susanna Ingleby in her diary that June, completely straight-faced. *A Buddhist Catechism* was a book by Colonel Olcott, Madame Blavatsky's partner in founding the Theosophical Society, and it was first published in 1880. The prospect of the family sitting in the library at Basford is almost comic - John William too deaf to hear what was going on but fuming about his son's pretentious ways, straight-laced Mrs Ingleby trying hard to understand, Ralph, totally immersed in his reading with no sense of his audience.

About this time he also became fascinated by psychometry. In 1886 he read a book on it and was so impressed that he exhorted his aunt to read it too. For a time the practice had a considerable following. It was a method of divining the supposed qualities or properties of objects and people by physical proximity. The chief exponent was a lady called Mrs Denton who demonstrated her powers by identifying common objects concealed in paper wrappers and pressed against her forehead. For many, it degenerated into a sort of party game, but there were those who believed it capable of much more important applications. *The influence of psychometry will be highly valuable in selecting persons for high office* wrote J.R. Buchanan in 1854. Ralph was interested in the mind as well as the spirit. For a time he made quite a name for himself as a fortune teller at various church bazaars and he was fascinated by astrology. No doubt he dressed the part - Ralph loved wearing outlandish costumes. He went to lectures and demonstrations on phrenology and thought-reading and to a whole range of 'spirit entertainments'. Ralph had never learnt to be analytical of what he saw or of what he read. Tricks with smoke and mirrors seldom failed to convince him.

In 1886, Ralph began a rather peculiar venture and we see the first signs of his growing confidence in his own ability to impart knowledge. That summer he spent time in Norfolk with the Nelsons at Holme-next-the-Sea and they seem to have introduced him to Father Faught. Frederick Faught came from Amersham and he was involved with the Theosophical Society. As far as we know this was Ralph's first contact with Theosophy and no doubt he and Mr Faught talked about it at length. Ralph was fired with ideas about truth and beauty that were part of his understanding of the cult of chivalry, and, urged on by Frederick Faught, he decided to form a society to promote them - very much part of the theosophical tradition.

It was to be called the True Philosophic League - TPL for short. Ralph drew up a list of aims and invented some grand-sounding titles. He planned a prayerful initiation ceremony at which he could dress up as a priest. On Thursday September 2nd 1886 there is one of the very few entries in the diary Aunt Susan had given him the previous Christmas, but it is not in Ralph's handwriting. His friend, Mr Faught, wrote it up for him - Marion recognised the handwriting from his letters.

The Philosophic League was founded at Holme House, Holme-next-the-Sea. Ralph De Tunstall Sneyd was by acclamation elected King and Chief and the following five members admitted Frederick Le Clerc Faught - Prov Governor Bucks & Berks, James Nelson - Prov Governor Norfolk & Lincoln, Thomas Nelson, Frances Nelson, Kate Hammond.

Next day four more members were admitted and the entry continues *the photographing of all the above took place at Holme House on the lawn.* The photograph shows all the participants wearing improvised white capes - one of the men looks very much as if he is draped in a tablecloth! Ralph himself is wearing proper vestments; he must have brought them from home in anticipation.

'How on earth did he persuade ordinary, sane people to dress up like that?' said Marion. 'I mean, this was a serious ceremony, with prayers - not a pageant or a play!'

'Charm? Charisma? I really don't know.'

On the 10th two more members joined and - *A unanimous vote of thanks was accorded to Mr Sneyd for his lecture on Buddhism and Oriental rites and customs and on the great Aryan migration. At the same meeting Richard Lane Freer Cheese was admitted as Departmental Ruler.*

Back in Leek Ralph set about enrolling other members. William and Eleanor Faulkner were the first on September 29th, then Frederick and Bernard Wardle, a Manchester man called Perkin, and William Goodacre. Mr Goodacre was vicar of Ipstones and Mr Faulkner was his curate, so the organisation had a degree of respectability. Meetings were held at friends' houses. Then Ralph went to a 'Thought reading party' and found himself another Provincial Governor (this time for Middlesex), Mr Stuart Cumberland. John Howerd became Provincial Governor of the Isle of Man and Ralph's good friend Jeremiah Beardmore of Bucknall became Provincial Governor for Staffordshire. Needless to say, Ralph's father refused to have anything to do with his son's tomfoolery, but, desperate to please her eccentric nephew, Susanna was enrolled as a dame. Ralph borrowed a set of vestments, acquired a cassock and a set of blue robes and bought candles to make his initiation ceremonies more impressive. *John William and Ralph had a quarrel about the League robes,* wrote Aunt Susan in August 1887, no doubt concealing, in her inimitable way, a spectacularly blazing row between father and son. But Ralph was not to be deflected. By the end of 1887 his True Philosophic League had at least thirty-four members (the men were Companions, the women, Dames), plus two Departmental Rulers and six Provincial Governors, not forgetting the King himself. Then Ralph decided it was time to do something more public.

He penned a series of rules and had them printed. Members of the league promised -

1. To oppose false principles of Philosophy and Religion.
2. To uphold true principles of Philosophy and Religion.
3. To create an interest in Science, Art, Poetry and Literature.
4. To perpetuate all beautiful Institutions and Usages.
5. To benefit mankind by constructing beautiful and Interesting Objects
6. To benefit mankind by preserving beautiful and Interesting Objects.
7. To prevent the extermination of Species of Animals and Plants.
8. To prevent the destruction of Ancient and valuable Monuments and Articles.

The aims, printed with a singularly inconsistent usage of capital letters, were perfectly laudable if extremely vague. Ralph was fascinated by the Arthurian legends and now the TPL was his very own Round Table. However it seems unlikely that his heroes, Arthur, Lancelot, Gawain and their companions, had much interest in preserving plant species or saving ancient monuments. Ralph's concept of the duties of knighthood had distinctly modern overtones.

In late October he hired a room in Leek for an inaugural ceremony and had tickets printed. He borrowed some banners from young Tom Wardle, Thomas's son. Tom had a collection of silk banners that he loaned out - they made regular appearances at functions in and around Leek. Ralph brought geraniums from the Basford greenhouse and made posters using religious symbols -crosses, stars, crescents and so on. His aunt provided white linen cloths and from somewhere he found a vase of peacock's feathers. Ralph was a good organiser when he set his mind to it.

The ceremony on November 5th was well-attended - Ralph had a lot of friends and it made a change from a firework party! Prayers and a reading of the *Aims of the True Philosophic League*, coupled with a lengthy explanation of them, were followed by a lecture by Ralph about wildlife conservation, specifically about the practice of decorating ladies' hats with plumes and dead birds. The proceedings closed with refreshments and a party at which the guests sang songs and played games. Ralph himself apparently sang *Dine Do* a negro spiritual, possibly while still wearing his blue vestments! No doubt his guests enjoyed this eclectic and very Victorian mix of the sacred, the educational and the entertaining, though to us it seems incongruous.

A reporter from the *Leek Post* was present and did his best to describe the proceedings as coherently as possible, though clearly he was out of his depth. Susanna recorded *June 5th. Fine until evening & then very wet. Ralph's Philosophic League Tea in the Coffee Tavern, there were 31 people there, about 45 tickets were paid for* - so there was a charge for the evening's entertainment. As far as we know, Ralph was too other-worldly to think of charging a membership fee for his League, but Aunt Susan was not prepared to subsidise his bunfight in Leek!

'I suppose his friends were happy to indulge him,' I said. 'After all, there wasn't a lot to do in Leek in the long winter evenings...'

'I don't see it like that at all,' Marion answered sternly. 'I can't imagine that people like the Wardles, or the local vicar for that matter, would have lent their name to something they didn't believe in. I'm sure they were behind him every step of the way. After all, they are very laudable aims...'

'I'm not entirely convinced. Thomas Wardle is quoted as having said at the inaugural meeting in Leek that the League was 'as good a way as any for a young man who had nothing better to do to occupy himself!' Scarcely the most resounding of endorsements!'

Of course, not all Ralph's activities were so eccentric. Leek supported flourishing dramatic and operatic societies in the 1880s, and according to his aunt's diaries, he went to numerous productions at people's homes. Fancy dress parties, tableaux vivants and theatrical productions acted and produced by family and friends, whiled away the evenings in many middle class homes.

In 1887 Ralph began to appear in productions; in *Snowdrop* and as *a paramour in Rumpelstiltskin.* The maids from Basford went to watch him perform. In February 1889 he acted the part of Nathaniel Winkle in a production of *Bardell and Pickwick* at Leek Town Hall. He had a fine voice and sang at a variety of concerts and events in the area though he does not seem ever to have joined the Operatic Society.

Staffordshire had an active natural history society, the North Staffordshire Field Club, founded in 1865. Members met monthly, and travelled by train or on foot to some place of interest, collected plant specimens or watched birds, had a picnic or a pub meal and went home. There were evening meetings with speakers and visits to private properties. Ralph joined and was in his element.

He also became a member of the Royal Antediluvian Order of Buffaloes on December 28th, 1888, as a member of Moorlands Lodge No 698. His tattered, dog-eared certificate survives. Together with his aunt he joined the Primrose League, a Conservative organisation founded in 1883 by Lord Randolph Churchill to promote his ideals of Tory democracy, notably reforms that would give the ordinary members more influence. The league took its name from the primrose which was Disraeli's favourite flower. Members were divided into 'habitations' and they became 'knights' and 'dames' of various degrees - Ralph was a 'knight harbinger', a title which no doubt pleased him greatly.

Leek had other, more low-brow entertainments. Travelling showmen and circuses set up in town from time to time and if he was at home Ralph usually went. In 1884, he went to see *the two-headed woman* while his aunt visited friends. The woman was more likely to have been a fake than a freak - but there was a gullible streak to Ralph's nature. Yet in other ways he was in the forefront of scientific theory, reading Darwin's *Origin of Species* in 1887, and foisting it on his aunt at a time when his church dismissed Darwin as sacrilegious and his erstwhile school friends were sending him postcards suggesting Darwin invented his theory to explain his own ugliness!

The Victorians were keen on self-improvement, and lectures were arranged - usually at the Nicholson Institute - on all sorts of subjects from travel to anatomy. Because of Mr Wardle's London connections, Leek often attracted major names as speakers. In 1884, Oscar Wilde came to speak and stayed with the Wardles. Ralph was there too, and Wilde held him spellbound. Over the next few weeks Ralph followed him around North Staffordshire, listening to his lectures; Wilde's wit and fluency and cynicism were unlike anything he had heard before. In all, Ralph heard him speak six times.

Ralph also gave lectures himself. On October 2nd 1885, aged 23, he organised his first presentation. Aunt Susan described it:

Fine until evening. Ralph went to the Belmont and Ashcombe woods for fungi. I went to Basford Hurst and Cheddleton in the morning, in the afternoon Ralph gave his lecture on fungi and sang in the school at Cheddleton, about 12s [£39] *were received at the door, tickets were 6d and 2d* [this would have differentiated between the gentry and the villagers - so Ralph probably had an audience of about 40] *there were 13 dishes of cooked fungi & 3 kinds of - wholesome, doubtful and poisonous.*

In many ways young Ralph De Tunstall Sneyd was busy and happy, but life at home was difficult. His religious views were always a source of conflict and rows with his father were an occupational hazard. Ralph's financial dependence on Aunt Susan was an embarrassment, and while she was, in fact, quite generous to him, her constant nagging about money must have grated. And it emasculated him. There is no suggestion that he did meet anyone he wished to marry during his aunt's lifetime, but marriage would have been impossible for him, both psychologically and financially. Aunt Susan was ever willing to help, arranging things in his museum, lining his cabinets, writing out his lectures for him, but her help bordered on the intrusive. He loved her but she stifled and infantilised him.

In the early 1880s Ralph began to worry about his health. Dr Somerville in Leek was his first port of call. After a while his aunt became worried and called on the good doctor to *ask him not to give Ralph any more medicine.* In November 1884 she saw him again, *I... spoke to Dr Somerville on the road about Ralph.* Undeterred Ralph took himself off to doctors in Manchester and bought all sorts of strange potions. His aunt wrote to them, too. She also called on his friend, Hartley, the chemist in Leek, who seems to have brewed some sort of concoction of his own and *told him not to give any more medicine to Ralph.* In the spring of 1887 both Ralph De Tunstall and his aunt began taking *Dr Wallace's medicine* at 10s-6d [£36] a bottle. She had already written to Dr Arledge at the North Staffordshire Infirmary about it - maybe she thought the only way to keep a check on what Ralph was taking was to try it herself! There was a good deal of correspondence with Mr Wallace and in total that year Ralph spent £2-15s-3d [£176] of his aunt's money on this particular patent cure.

People often bought these proprietary, over-the-counter (or out-of-the-newspaper-advertisement) remedies, many of which promised to cure an improbably wide range of complaints.

Taking medicine, prescribed or otherwise, was always a risk. Some remedies could contain heavy metals or poisons. Aunt Susan took something called Gelsemane, distilled from the deadly aconite root, to improve her sight. Other remedies contained mercury and strychnine. A key ingredient of many Victorian medicines was opium; it appeared in everything from remedies to quieten crying babies to powerful pain killers. 'Morbid craving' (addiction) was recognised in Victorian times, and deplored, in much the same way as drunkenness. But no-one talked of banning opium. *Nothing did me any good,* wrote Florence Nightingale, in her later years a martyr to all sorts of ailments, *but a curious little new fangled operation of putting opium under the skin which relieved one for twenty-four hours.*

Ralph had no need for opium but at about the same sort of period that she was approaching his doctors we find numerous letters to and from Aunt Susan complaining about her nephew's absent-mindedness.

Ralph has been so that he could not remember anything, such as posting a letter or knowing what day it is & always is surprised when it is Saturday evening & his lesson has to be prepared for School on Sunday - I wrote to tell Mr Faulkner his memory was going...

After every trip there would be a flurry of letters - usually written by Aunt Susan - tracking down lost belongings or purchases. Ralph may just have been forgetful - a story still circulates in Leek from much later in his life when he drove into town, hitched the pony and trap to a lamp post, did his shopping and bought a book - and walked home reading it!

Susanna Ingleby was over-protective but in this she may well have been right to be worried. Ralph's youthful absentmindedness might easily have been the result of taking too much opium-based medication.

At this period Ralph does seem to have been something of a hypochondriac. He experimented with homeopathy. He was interested in Mesmerism - a system of curing the body by the use of magnets which sometimes resulted in patients lapsing into a trance-like state - developed by Franz Anton Mesmer in the late 18th century. Ralph certainly believed in something similar and would not use a tool after another person had handled it for fear of 'acquiring their magnetism' and he hated shaking hands for the same reason. It was one of the many superstitions that he lived by.

Ralph also discovered what he saw as a magic potion, a brew called 'Number 1' produced at home by the Reverend Neville of Stoke Golding in Devon. Delighted with his discovery, Ralph despatched bottles of Number 1 to all and sundry. Mr Neville was interested in Theosophy and it is probable that Ralph met him through Mr Faught. Ralph visited them both in the summer of 1887 - and in a sort of spiritual quid pro quo he enrolled Mr Neville as Provincial Governor for Devon in the True Philosophic League!

They gave him an introduction to a third theosophist, Father Ouseley, in Brighton. The three reverend gentlemen lent Ralph theosophical literature, in particular to a book by Anna Kingsford called *The Perfect Way*. It was an introduction to the doctrine of the one-ness of all things and it instantly appealed to Ralph. He set out to learn more.

Chapter 12
Ralph the Theosopher

'She was a liar, a crook and a blatant charlatan!' said Pam vehemently.

'Countess Constance Wachtmeister adored her, Colonel Henry Steel Olcott and William Q. Judge almost worshipped her,' I responded.

'All duped. The first was an overly-romantic widowed Austrian countess with more money than sense - ripe for deception by the likes of H.P.B. The second was an American former soldier and would be 'do-gooder' who was blind to the real world, and the last an Irish lawyer used to being surrounded by fairies!'

'Oh, come, come, that's bit harsh,' I said laughing. 'I gather you don't like her?'

'I don't know why you're so fascinated by her and her wretched movement!'

'Because Ralph was. It reveals a lot about the way he thought doesn't it? And we can only get to know him as a person by trying to understand his beliefs. Immersing ourselves in....'

'Well I suppose so. But I think our readers are going to struggle with theosophy - after all, we do...'

We were discussing Madame Helena Petrovna Blavatsky, founder of the Theosophical Society, who Ralph met as a young man in London. So you have been warned - you might want to skip this chapter!

As early as 1886, friends had been sending Ralph books about theosophy. Susanna recorded their arrival in her diary and even listened as Ralph read some of them to her. But for him 1889 was the 'red letter' theosophy year - he met Madame Blavatsky. Away from home from the beginning of June until well into September, he stayed with numerous friends and relatives. Susanna recorded in her diary where Ralph was - or where she thought he was - but she didn't know everyone he was seeing. Ralph was quite capable of organising his life without her help - though she financed every day of it.

In his diary of 1889 Ralph wrote:

June 6: I went to London. I called on Madame Blavatsky & had some tea &

stopped for a meeting.
June 7:   I had tea with Madame Blavatsky & afterwards went with the
Countess [Wachtmeister] *to an evening meeting of Theosophists.*
June 12: I had dinner at 12 Lansdowne Road where I met Mrs Wolfe who
comes from America

He also recorded his frequent visits to the Oratory in Brompton Road, attendance at a new Catholic sect - the Army of God - and attending Mass at a Greek Orthodox Church. He went to Brighton to stay with the Reverend Ouseley and attended the Catholic Church there with him.

I discovered on the internet that 12, Landsowne Road had been rented by the Countess Wachtmeister who seems to have taken Madame Blavatsky under her wing after she fell ill in Germany. She recorded:

All that was possible was done to ameliorate her physical sufferings. After a few months' stay at Maycot, Upper Norwood, London, in 1887, a pleasant though small house was taken at 17 Lansdowne Road, Notting Hill, and a large group of earnest men and women of literary ability and recognized public standing, such as Dr. Archibald Keightley, Bertram Keightley, E.D. Fawcett, G.R.S. Mead, and others, who had not been affected by the Coulomb slanders, gathered around her.

I found out about the 'Coulomb slanders'. Madame Blavatsky and her close associates had had to leave India rapidly and in a most humiliating way after she was exposed cheating at a séance by an extremely angry man called Coulomb. He wasted no time in broadcasting her fraudulent practices. She was disgraced and they ran - pursued across India by extremely irate Indian disciples who felt cheated and let down by someone they had venerated and supported. Westerners who had become part of her circle rapidly withdrew, not willing to be tainted by the scandal surrounding her. It was the beginning of her end.

But Ralph probably did not know of that episode; all he would have seen was an open, companionable house with men and women on an equal footing, smoking, sitting up all hours of the night talking, debating spiritual matters, with Madame Blavatsky herself the exotic centre-piece. Ralph had discovered Bohemian London. His aunt would have been appalled at what she would have regarded as gross ill-manners and lack of decency. Madame Blavatsky ran to no timetable. She ate when she felt like it, slept when she was ready, and her followers fitted in round her. She drank and smoked heavily, dressed sometimes in old, comfortable, loose robes, at other times *decked herself in finery, a perky hat, fake diamonds, a dozen or fifteen rings on her fingers.* She made no provision for her house-guests. Ladies who had been accustomed to having their every want speedily administered to by a servant found themselves having to learn how to make their own tea in the kitchen. *There is tea and hot water,* Countess Wachtmeister wrote on a note she pinned on the door, *and hopefully milk and sugar.* Letters reported with incredulity that *men and women slept in the same room* and that once Madame Blavatsky had appeared in a doorway to the sitting room *completely naked!*

Coming from the rigidity and cold formality of Basford, where family prayers started and ended the day and meals appeared like clockwork at the appointed hour, Lansdowne Road must have seemed a magical place. Ralph blossomed in the informality and friendliness he found there. Susanna had no idea that he was about to get himself involved with some pretty dubious company. But Ralph was an idealist; he saw only the good. These were heady, spiritual and exciting days for the young Ralph Sneyd and like many people before him he fell completely under Madame Blavatsky's spell.

When Spiritualism and Mesmerism were all the rage, when Darwin's scientific discoveries had undermined the authority of the church, and a magical-occult revival was underway in France, theosophy caught the mood of the time. The movement flourished, disseminating occult and Eastern teachings to anyone who was interested and providing a powerful alternative to the restrictive dogmas of the conservative churches, the arid vision of materialistic science and the wishful thinking of Spiritualism. Within a few short years other movements and organisations had sprung up alongside it - like Mary Baker Eddy's Christian Science, the Society for Psychical Research and the Hermetic Order of the Golden Dawn. The occult renaissance was flourishing. Ralph was not to know that it would last only a few decades before conservatism once again took over, and he would not live long enough to see its next revival in the 'flower power' of the 1960s.

Helena Petrovna (nee Hahn?) was born in Russia in July 1831. She ran away from home and married the elderly Count Blavatsky when she was just seventeen. That much is more or less certain. But there are many stories about her family and childhood. One of the most macabre is of her baptism into the Russian Orthodox Church. The service was held in a room in her parents' country mansion. It was crammed with people, pairs of godmothers and godfathers, dozens of relatives, friends and spectators, all the servants. Candle-smoke and incense hung heavily in the air. A little girl was there as proxy for an absent relative. The child got bored by the tedious proceedings in the stuffy room and, unobserved, crawled amongst the legs of the adults. She had a lighted taper, as had all the guests. The ceremony was drawing to its close. The officiating priest, flanked by his three assistants in flowing golden robes with long beards and hair, was just in the act of renouncing the Evil One for baby Helena when, inadvertently, the crawling toddler set fire to his robes. There was pandemonium. The ageing priest and several guests were severely burnt. The catastrophe was seen as a message from the gods. Helena Petrovna was a sorceress. Servants were afraid of her. Even as a small child she claimed to see goblins and spirits and said she would cast spells on the staff if they did not obey her. She became unmanageable, always got her own way and was finally shipped off to be brought up, away from the rest of the family, by her grandmother.

Like other equally colourful stories about her it may or may not be true. What is certain is that in 1875 Madame Blavatsky founded the Theosophical Society in New York.

'The difficulty is knowing how much to put in and how much to leave out. I've got an absolute mountain of information!'

'Well burn it!' said my testy companion. 'Have you read any of her stuff? I have - well, tried to. I spent a deeply boring day at the British Library ploughing through her book *Isis Unveiled*. Absolute rubbish! Indian and Tibetan Buddhism, Egyptology and mysticism rehashed. It makes no sense at all. Deliberately obscure if you ask me. The ultimate con-artist...'

'Well, you may well be right but I'd still like to put a bit in our book about what theosophy was and how it came about.'

You cannot be serious!' Pam groaned. Just look at this account written by the Countess Wachtmeister! If you believe that you'll believe anything!'

In 1851 Madame H.P. Blavatsky went to London with her father. One day, while walking in the street, she saw coming towards her some Indian Princes, and, amongst these, a very fine looking Indian... a man of seven feet high... and to her great surprise, [she] *recognized in this man one whom she had always looked upon as her guardian angel. Ever since childhood she had seen him, and in moments of trial he had helped her, and when she saw him in the physical form in London... he made a sign to her to move on. The next day, she went to Hyde Park, and while there this man came again to her, and said it was true that he had watched her from childhood, because he saw in her a good instrument for the formation of this Society. Then he told her he had this work given to him to do by those above him, and that therefore he was most anxious that she should accept this position he offered her, which was to form this Society. ....After three days' cogitation, she decided to accept this position offered her. He then said she must go to Egypt, and that there she would have to stop for some time to be taught, so that she might be enabled to teach others. Then she went to India, and was taken, hidden in a hay cart, through a country where no European is ever permitted to pass... At last she reached the place where the Masters live.*

'I know the Countess was completely besotted with H.P.B.' I said thoughtfully, 'but I am not sure we should dismiss her out of hand. It is true that she dabbled in the occult, producing all sorts of weird and wonderful 'happenings' at séances, seeing mystic princes and spirits who were her guides, making things and people appear and disappear. That was her undoing. She was branded a fraud, but I still have sympathy with the ideals of the Theosophical movement. Whatever her motives, a movement that promotes unity between nations is surely a very good thing?'

'It's not that I disagree with the ideals,' said Pam wearily, 'far from it. But I think Madame B. came to them by accident. Her main objective, it seems to me, was to establish herself as someone with special powers. I don't think she cared how. She started out as a medium, then met Olcott, who talked to her about Buddhism and eastern religions. She latched on to the old ideas about the 'chosen ones' up in Tibet, the guardians of the secret wisdom of the ancients - and claimed to have been taught by them. I think the whole 'brotherhood-of-the-enlightened-working-for-the-benefit-of-mankind' bit was just a way of ensnaring the gullible. It didn't matter what they believed - as long as they saw her as their guru! She was much more bothered about the good of Helena Petrovna Blavatsky than the good of mankind!'

'A basic tenet was 'do no evil to any living being or creature, do only good'. No wonder Ralph was drawn to it. But you think he was just being gullible?'

'Oh, I'm sure his motives were sound. And I expect most present-day Theosophists are perfectly honourable people. It's the pseudo-science that worries me. Remember that book Sebastian showed us?'

The cousin of a friend of ours had been interested in theosophy. He'd shown us a book - a detailed work on astrology, published by the Theosophical Society in 1911, which seemed to have moved away from the ideals of the founders into pure fantasy. The characteristics ascribed to the various star signs were detailed and sometimes quite ridiculous: I, a Taurean, would do well as *the favourite slave of a Turkish harem.* Pam loved that idea. I was less than enthusiastic!

Sebastian even introduced us to his cousin. She was a pleasant old lady, living in a local nursing home, but clearly she could no longer understand who we were or what we wanted. We sighed. It was a theme that ran all the way through our searches - we had lost count of the number of people who had told us their old mother, father, aunt, uncle or neighbour could have told us 'all about Ralph De Tunstall Sneyd' - if only we had met them a year or two ago!

We had first learnt that Ralph had become interested in theosophy through reading Susanna's diaries. She wrote in August 1887 that Ralph was reading her *The Perfect Way.* Susanna never made any comment in her diaries about the books she read, but on this occasion she was moved to describe Anna Kingsford's work as *a queer book.*

No doubt Ralph had thought it would be a gentle introduction to theosophy for his aunt. Ms Kingsford's thesis was that Christianity was *the symbolical synthesis of the fundamental truths contained in all religions.* In other words, Christians were Theosophists but didn't know it!

'Are you sitting comfortably, esteemed colleague?' I emailed Pam one night. 'Get this - I've just carefully read all the letters in the last batch we had from Colin and Joyce. Amongst them is one to Ralph from the Countess Wachtmeister and, wait for it, there's a note on the end of the letter from Blavatsky herself! How many Smarties do I get for that!'

'Send me the text of the letter in full - and I'll see!'

From Countess Wachtmeister. 1st October
17, Lansdown Road, Nottinghill, London
Dear Mr Sneyd,

H.P.B begs me to write and tell you that a probationary chela's life is anything but a pleasant one and she advises you to wait before taking the final step and to ponder on the subject a little more seriously.

Colonel Olcott is now in England for the purpose of lecturing and if you would ensure him good audience and pay his expenses he would go to Leek and give a lecture on Theosophy. You, of course, would have to take the Hall, do the advertising and business arrangements - should there be any profit after all the expenses have been paid then you would hand the money over to the lecturing fund.

> *yours fraternally,*
> *Wachtmeister*

This is a very good suggestion. Don't say you cannot. There is nothing a man is unable to do if only he sets to work for it with real energy. By what you will do I will judge whether you are fit for chelaship; and if you succeed you may consider yourself as accepted by those whom I serve, as chela.

> *Yours fraternally,*
> *H.P.B.*

I emailed Pam again. 'What's a chela, most learned one?'

'The definition is that a chela is simply a disciple - in theosophical terms it seems to have meant someone who was following their own path and no longer needed constant support from their guru.'

'Ralphy doing his own thing again then?'

'Madame Blavatsky giving him a meaningless title in return for him giving her yet more publicity, I'd say!'

So Ralph invited Colonel Olcott to Leek and must have paid for the Nicholson Institute and for any advertising that was done. Or to be more precise Susanna must have paid. She recorded that she helped Ralph to write the introduction he gave when Colonel Olcott visited Leek in November 1889 to give his address about theosophy at the Nicholson Institute. She even attended the meeting herself, taking with her one of the maids, Annie. Facing them from the rostrum was an American...

...of fully fifty years of age, of medium height, robust, broad but not fat... His face was handsome and pleasant, and suited his bald head, and was framed in a full and perfect beard. He wore spectacles somewhat concealing the one defect of his appearance which was, none the less, 'a real spoonful of tar in a barrel of honey'- ...that one of his eyes was extremely disobedient and from time to time used to turn in all directions, sometimes with startling and disagreeable rapidity...'

Madame Blavatsky may have been a charlatan but she was largely responsible for the growth of interest in the occult and the paranormal in late 19th century Europe and America. Though many question her intelligence, of her energy there can be no doubt. The facts and ideas she managed to collect, from a huge range of sources, and disseminate in her books, is staggering, though the organisation is chaotic. The thing that we both found completely mystifying was that Ralph was not only interested in the movement but obviously absorbed a great deal of the arcane and abstruse information. Given his rudimentary education it is nothing short of miraculous that he could read and interpret these extraordinary writings. The following short extracts from the writings of Helena Petrovna - which run to thousands of pages - will give some idea of the sort of thing he ploughed through.

The Secret Doctrine

THE PRIMORDIAL SEVEN, THE FIRST SEVEN BREATHS OF THE DRAGON OF WISDOM, PRODUCE IN THEIR TURN FROM THEIR HOLY CIRCUMGYRATING BREATHS THE FIERY WHIRLWIND......

FOHAT TRACES SPIRAL LINES TO UNITE THE SIX TO THE SEVENTH - THE CROWN (a) AN ARMY OF THE SONS OF LIGHT STANDS AT EACH ANGLE (and) THE LIPIKA - IN THE MIDDLE WHEEL. THEY (the Lipika) SAY, 'THIS IS GOOD' (b) THE FIRST DIVINE WORLD IS READY, THE FIRST (is now), THE SECOND (world), THEN THE 'DIVINE ARUPA' (the formless Universe Thought) REFLECTS ITSELF IN CHHAYALOKA (the shadowy world of primal form, or the intellectual) THE FIRST GARMENT OF (the) ANUPADAKA (c)

It made no sense to us at all, but Ralph wasn't alone in accepting it.

'Remember Ralph's friend Ouseley?' said Pam.

'What do we know about him?'

'Not a lot - but he was that thoroughly disreputable cleric in Brighton. I'll send you the copies we made of his letters - they all got muddled up with the Holy Grail stuff I've got here.'

Whilst waiting for the letters I looked Ouseley up on the internet. Gideon Jasper Richard Ouseley was born in Lisbon in 1835, the son of Sir Ralph Ouseley KCB. He was educated in Ireland, ordained into the Church of England and got married. In 1870 he *voluntarily renounced all eating of flesh, strong drink and tobacco, as inconsistent with the humanity and the true religion of Christ, as taught by Him and His apostles* - an original take on Christian teaching at a time when vegetarianism was regarded as the province of cranks.

'Mind,' I said, 'he claimed the highest authority for his decision - a manuscript which he had somehow acquired from Tibet'.

'Where else?!' said Pam irreverently.

'He published this manuscript in 1892 as *The Gospel of the Holy Twelve*,' I went on. 'It contained most of the familiar gospel stories together with a number of others, many of which related to not eating meat and being kind to animals.'

'Such as?'

'Well, apparently God ordered the Virgin Mary not to eat meat while she was pregnant. And the Three Wise Men were so intent on following the star in the East that they forgot to feed and water their camels - so the star disappeared until they did so! Then there was the man who was tormenting a cat and Jesus made his arm wither...'

'I approve of that!'

'Thought you might. Ouseley apparently had two cats who he regarded as almost human - bit like you with your three spoilt moggies.'

'So he wasn't all bad!'

Inspired by his friend, Ralph De Tunstall also became a vegetarian. Susanna Ingleby had always fussed about Ralph's diet - now she really had something to worry about. *Ralph had plum pudding made with tapioca instead of suet* she wrote in May 1888. Plum pudding was a birthday treat in the Sneyd household. She set about collecting vegetarian recipes - lentil cutlets, scalloped eggs, corn oysters, macaroni cheese, fried vegetable marrow. *He should eat lots of beans* his Aunt Chrystobel wrote authoritatively. Susanna was not so sure - she thought he should drink quantities of milk.

Gideon Ouseley was a strange character. I awaited the letters with interest. They came. Ouseley's hand-writing was a nightmare and none of the letters was dated - just *September 25th, July 1st,* no year - but it soon became obvious that he and Ralph were in touch fairly frequently. Ouseley addressed him as *My dear friend and brother* and ended *Yours fraternally* or *affectionately.*

Trying to unravel Ralph's religious beliefs was getting more complex by the minute - and trying to understand the content of Ouseley's letters was little better than reading Madame Blavatsky's books. We found copies Ralph had made of his letters to his friend.

I wrote to Brother Ouseley. If every one of the 7 principals of man is 2 fold consisting of a corporial and also a sychic principal [then] *why in your terminoligy are the King Sovereign and Monarch not used always for the same person?*

Is there a separate Hierarchy intended for the underground cities, villages etc. Are not the churches divided in the present way with the present rituals to be alowed as well as the others in the renewed earth?

Would it not be just as well if the statues in your churches were covered with luminous paint?

With them were many pages of diagrams that looked like Egyptian hieroglyphics in carefully ruled squares and what seemed to be mathematical charts. They were incomprehensible to us but obviously made sense to Ralph and the Reverend Ouseley in their arcane and magical kingdom.

But if Ralph was enamoured of the theosophical Mr Ouseley, his wife was not! Amongst the correspondence was one page in her handwriting. Unfortunately it is only part of a longer letter - the rest seems to be missing - but her feelings are crystal clear. Ralph was away from home and seems to have gone to see the Ouseleys in Brighton.

...My husband is too much of a gentleman to see the crafty ways of people, but I am a little more far seeing. Tell my husband not to buy any of your silly books or I shall burn them when they arrive here... [signed] *Not an Ouseleyite.*

Presumably Harriett kept the copy of her letter to show Ralph on his return. It is hard to guess what Ralph thought about it. We know that Ouseley was thrown out of the Catholic Church without a pension. Was he scrounging off Ralph? He was certainly playing on his sympathy.

Ralph's cronies seemed to be as odd as the creed they followed. But not all theosophers were so strange.

'I found a nice quote you might want to put in while I was fishing around on the net the other night' said Pam, putting down my printed pages and taking a sip of the gruesome 'catering brown stuff' that masqueraded as coffee in our favourite pub in Market Harborough. The town is halfway between our two homes and a useful meeting place to swap ideas and discuss what we have written. The staff happily allow us to spend whole afternoons sitting in the bar after lunch - but their coffee is truly awful!

'I wrote it down for you - it's attributed to Katherine Tingley. She became big in theosophy in America after Blavatsky died. She travelled worldwide, establishing schools in several countries, emphasising practical humanitarianism, education, prison reform - and world peace! In 1900 she moved the international headquarters to Point Loma, California, where she established the Raja-Yoga School and College, the Theosophical University and the School for the Revival of the Lost Mysteries of Antiquity. She built the first open-air Greek Theatre in America and formed youth and adult symphony orchestras. A very practical and useful person in other words.'

'What did she say?'

'Just this - *We are not brought into existence by chance nor thrown up into earth-life like wreckage cast along the shore, but are here for infinitely noble purposes.'*

'That's good. Ralph would have approved of that. Let's leave theosophy there.'

Ralphy as a toddler

Ralph De Tunstall Sneyd

Alton Castle

Oakamoor station - for Cotton College

Cotton College

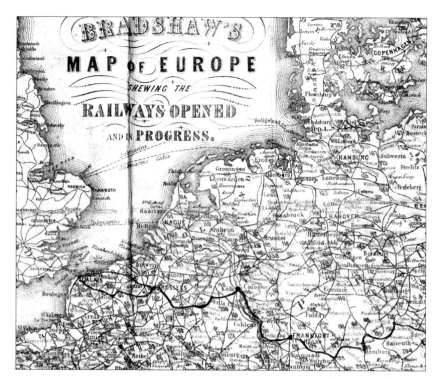

Lightoaks, Oakamoor, the home of Maj-General Thomas William Sneyd from 1884-1913

Madame Blavatsky and Henry Steel Olcott,
founders of the Theosophical Society

We believe this is Father
Anderson, parish priest in Leek
1860-1884, who instructed Ralph.

Members of Ralph's
True Philosophic
League on the lawn at
Holme House, Holme
in Norfolk in
September 1886.

Ralph (grey-haired) seen in a procession of the Royal Antediluvian Order of Buffaloes.

The W.H. Smith's stand at Leek railway station c.1900.
But then, Ralph travelled around the country a lot; the sight of young Mr Sneyd and his luggage on Leek station... would not have caused much comment. Chapter 13

The Brookes' cottage in Belle Vue in Leek. Harriett lived here with her parents and siblings until she married Ralph in 1894.

One of Harriett's sisters

Postcards from Ralph and Harriett's South African honeymoon.
Table Mountain and the fynbos.

Postcard of St George's Street and the Cathedral, Cape Town.

Rose Cottage, home to Ralph's Aunt Emily Jane Sneyd, where Ralph and Harriett lived after they married.

Harriett and Ralph, taken about 1894.

Fair View, which was left to Ralph by his aunt Susanna, and where they lived for the rest of their married life.

Chapter 13
Ralph and Harriett

While we were writing *Finding Susanna* I'd slowly grown to dislike Susanna Ingleby. We'd been sorry for her when we first read her diaries - she'd been so unlucky in her marriage and then Ralphy seemed to be such a disappointment to her, and John William was difficult. But once we'd met Colin and Joyce, and they'd shown us her letters to Ralph, she'd begun to lose my sympathy. She nagged him, belittled him and treated him like a naughty little boy. I dreaded to imagine what she'd said to him face to face.

'Yes, yes,' Marion interrupted, 'you've said it all before.'

'I know, but I think its worth stressing. I mean - look at this! He's going to stay with Uncle John at Barton Bendish - it's July 1884, so he's twenty-two. And remember, he's already travelled round Australia and Ceylon by himself: *.... as soon as you get to Lynn ask a porter to take your luggage to be put into Mr Read's carriage at Wright's Livery Stables, you will have to ask what you have to pay for a man taking it perhaps one shilling* [£3]*, Mr Read will be ready to start at 4 o'clock, take care you do not get wrong yourself, or your luggage, it will be a long drive from Lynn to Barton & a box would cost a great deal if it had to be sent after you....* And that's not all,' I went on. 'Aunt Susan nagged Ralph endlessly. When he went to Devon she ordered him not to swim if he went in the sea because he might drown - and then listed all the people she had ever heard of who drowned! She didn't like his friends either - remember Mr Menzies?'

In May 1884 Ralph received a letter from his aunt complaining at length about <u>*That stupid old Mr Menzies...*</u> who had been writing to Ralph and fishing for an invitation to Basford. We do not know who he was or how long they had known each other, but Susanna Ingleby was thoroughly rude about him. She could not *fancy him a nice person, if he had any sense he would see we do not care to know him ... do not fix to do anything with him he has more money than sense.* Ralph was a gentle, attractive, young man - maybe his aunt feared there was something improper in Mr Menzies advances. But whatever she felt, the sentence that appears partway through her diatribe is unforgivable *...I do not like any of the friends you have made yourself, they are a vulgar set & the* *sooner you cast them off the better.*

I had got the bit between my teeth now. 'When he went off to see people,' I went on 'his wretched aunt sent letter after letter implying that they found him a nuisance!   Oh yes - and there's that long rant about vegetarianism!'

In 1888 Ralph seems to have told his aunt that he was planning to visit *a nerve doctor.*   Aunt Susan let rip:

....it will be no use your going to him without you act by what he says, which of course will be to eat animal food & plenty of it, you have tried vegetables quite long enough & found they are no good, so go quickly back to meat, you have made yourself so delicate. I am sure it would make an 8th wonder of the world to see an old vegetarian, they never live long & look such poor, soft, half-baked people, at any rate you have tried foolish eating long enough & it has failed in your case....

We laughed. We both had vegetarian children who were anything but soft and half-baked!   We'd asked Ralph's grandsons whether he remained a vegetarian but they couldn't remember.

It seemed to me that Susanna Ingleby's treatment of Ralph verged on emotional abuse - she seemed to go out of her way to destroy every vestige of his self esteem.

'Right,' said Marion, 'you've made your point!   Now, what happened after Aunt Susan died in 1891?'

'Well, that's the problem...'

'OK, let's start with what we do know.'

Sometime between 1892 and 1894 Ralph moved out of Basford Hall and for a while he lived at Belmont. We were not surprised. John William Sneyd had often threatened to throw his son out of the house. Perhaps this time, without Aunt Susan to mediate, he'd made good his threat. Or perhaps Ralph had simply got tired of his difficult and uncommunicative father. For Ralph, the good thing that came out of Aunt Susan's death was that he was financially independent at last: apart from a £50 [£3,300] a year annuity to her sister Emily, Susanna Ingleby left him her entire estate - valued at £9,917 [£662,000].

No doubt Ralph missed her.   He wrote poems in her memory, re-inventing her as the loving aunty of his childhood.

> *Thou didst mend my small garments,*
> *And wisdom instil;*

> *That wisdom that flows*
> *Like a beautiful rill.*
> (*The Guardian of Childhood - Susanna*)

But in reality, his sense of loss was probably tinged with relief. There would be no more nagging, no more ill-informed criticism of his church. He was free to be himself.

He continued to collect and it was his love of curiosities that would bring about the next, and happiest, stage of his life. Sometime in 1894 Ralph heard that a soldier, recently returned from India, had some Indian artefacts he wished to sell. Ralph visited him at his parents' home in Leek. Sergeant Major Brookes was out, but his sister Harriett was at home and she invited Ralph in to wait for him. It was, it seems, love at first sight. Eventually Samuel Brookes must have come home and maybe Ralph did buy some articles from him to add to his collection. But that was not the end of the affair. Ralph was smitten! He poured out poem after romantic poem.

> *As, 'mid the pine woods, I would wander far,*
> *I thought - 'Shall this strange lonely state endure?*
> *Shall I be, ever more, condemned to roam,*
> *A weary wanderer through this world alone?'*
> (*My Wife*)

Through Ralph's rose-tinted spectacles the Brookes' modest house in industrial Belle Vue Road became a lilac-framed cottage!

> *There is a cottage, near some lilac trees,*
> *Whose hanging blossoms scent the laden breeze;*
> *But, in this home, a radiant girl was born*
> *Fair as Aurora, goddess of the morn....*
> (*My Wife*)

And so it went on. How long Ralph courted Harriett we didn't know, but it was probably not long or the affair would have become public knowledge. Leek was a small place.

'When does lilac bloom?'

'April-May.'

'Then I guess that's when they met ....'

Once again, Ralph was set on following the dictates of his heart instead of convention, regardless, or perhaps oblivious, of the cost.

> *Better my own true love,*
> *Than all the world!*
> *Better than fame or fortune,*
> *Lands or gold!*
>
> (*My Own True Love*)

And as we shall see, that was exactly what his wedding was to cost him.

Even Ralph seems to have recognised that marrying Harriett was an extraordinary thing to do. Harriett's parents, or maybe Harriett herself, planned carefully to keep the wedding secret. They were more worldly-wise than Ralph. Harriett went off to stay with her married sister, Sarah Annie Pitt, at Cheadle, and Ralph put up at a nearby pub, the Packhorse Inn on Millgate. The banns were read at St Mary's, Stockport, while they both sat out the three weeks necessary to qualify as residents, and Ralph visited the Pitts' house daily.

People in Leek were told that Harriett had gone to stay with her sister to further her education - it was a plausible story; the Pitts were childless and were already giving a home to the youngest Brookes sister, Alice. Sarah Annie had married well; her husband, Charles, was a paper merchant in Manchester and the couple lived in a pleasant villa in Charlotte Street, Cheadle, and kept a servant. Harriett's secret may have leaked out; there are press reports of *anxious enquiries* being made for Ralph in the days prior to the wedding and that a *watch was kept on Lea Side* [the Pitts' house] *by strangers to the town -* though it is unclear who they were, if indeed they existed. The reporter, however, was sure that:

....at the eleventh hour suspicion had been aroused on the part of Mr Sneyd's friends, and that means were employed to, if possible, prevent him from carrying out his intention....

There is no indication who these 'friends' might have been; the only person who had any interest in stopping Ralph's wedding would have been his father and he is not mentioned.

On October 24th they were married.

> *Pursuit and opposition did we brave;*
> *In distant church our secret vows we gave,* wrote Ralph.

He went to London immediately after the ceremony and a day or two later Harriett joined him there. They then set sail for a long sea voyage and an exotic winter honeymoon in sunny Cape Town, well out of reach of John William Sneyd and the mythical friends. Ralph no doubt wrote to his father and told him he was married - and then left the country and hoped John William would have calmed down by the time they next met! It was very much the same technique he had used when he converted to Rome.

'Think about that for a moment,' said Marion. 'It must have been an incredible experience for Harriett. She'd probably never been to London before, let alone abroad. When did they decide on South Africa? How did she know what clothes to take...?'

She was right. I did think about it. Harriett probably took all the clothes she owned with her when she left Leek. Women's clothing in the 1890s was voluminous - even a working-class girl like Harriett would have had a trunk-load of dresses and gloves and boots and petticoats and camisoles and drawers. There would have been at least one hat-box containing her best hat - large, cartwheel, flower-and-feather trimmed hats were then in vogue. It was October, so she would probably have worn her thickest winter jacket and her heaviest, stoutest boots to lighten the load in her luggage. For a few pence her trunk would have been transported to her sister's house by barrow or horse and cart - all stations had porters in those days. She was after all thought to be moving to Cheadle.

For Ralph it was more difficult. He had to have enough clothes with him for a three week stay in Stockport, for the voyage and for the time in Cape Town. How did he explain that away? But then, Ralph travelled around the country a lot; the sight of young Mr Sneyd and his luggage on Leek station, waiting for the Manchester train, would not have caused much comment.

Harriett probably wore her existing best dress to be married in - there were no guests or photographers to admire her outfit and it was quite common not to have a special dress for your wedding. Poor families considered it a needless expense. Ralph was so besotted that he would not have cared what she wore - though no doubt Sarah Annie and Alice made sure she looked her best.

'They probably stocked up in London,' I decided.

Cape Town in November would have been sunny and warm - the climate is almost Mediterranean. English summer dresses would have been perfectly appropriate, though Ralph probably bought his bride a parasol to prevent her getting a tan.

It was one of the most surprising of all Ralph's journeys. Harriett had been born and bred in Leek and had worked in a silk mill since she left school. It is unlikely that she had ever travelled further afield than her elder sister's home near Manchester. Quite why Ralph decided to take her on such a long sea voyage it is impossible to say. Maybe he regretted not seeing more of the Cape when he passed it on the way to Australia. Maybe he had read that it was a naturalist's paradise and wanted to see it for himself. Maybe Harriett's soldier brother had told her tales of Africa and she had always nurtured a secret desire to go there. Whatever the reason, sometime in November 1894 Ralph and Harriett Sneyd set sail for Cape Town. The voyage - to judge by Cook's 1894 brochure - would have taken nearly three weeks and would have cost both of them £31-10s [£2,200] each way, or £21 [£1,500] if Ralph economised and they travelled second-class.

No-one kept their letters at home - if indeed they wrote any - so we don't know where they stayed or what they did. They bought a souvenir pack of postcards and a book of silver leaf made of silver mined on Table Mountain. We found them safely stowed away amongst Ralph's papers. The postcards showed Table Mountain, respectable Europeans strolling among the huge trees that formed Government Avenue and along St George's Street towards the cathedral, and a series of grand colonial buildings. No doubt they saw them all. They almost certainly climbed Table Mountain - on foot, as the cable car was not built until 1929 - and explored the 'fynbos', the vast range of reeds, heathers and beautiful proteas, where orange-breasted sunbirds, the cape sugar bird and the cape rock jumper abound. On the beaches they would have seen penguins, and in the wetlands flamingoes and pied avocets. It must have seemed like a journey to paradise for Harriett.

Ralph's marriage to Harriett Brookes shocked Leek and shocked his family. One rumour that circulated was that Ralph believed that in spending time alone with Harriett while waiting for her brother to return, he had compromised her. Ralph, some suggested, felt that he had put Harriett in a position which might damage her reputation - so he had no choice but to do the honourable thing and marry her - bizarre as such reasoning appears in the 21st century. But it seems much more likely that Ralph spent an improperly long time alone with Harriett because they were getting on so well.

The local press made a great feature of the *Leek Matrimonial Romance between Peer and Peasant*, claiming that the marriage had seen Ralph disinherited of a fortune and pointing to an immense social gulf between the couple. It made a good story. But we knew their estimate of the fortune Ralph had lost was exaggerated and it seems likely that their assessment of the Brookes family was inaccurate too. Ralph wasn't a peer - and the Brookes were not peasants. In his obituary notice - which we found amongst Ralph's papers -

Arthur Brookes, Harriett's father, is down as a timber merchant, which is also how Harriett had him entered in the marriage register, and how he described himself to the census enumerator in 1871. But by 1894 Arthur was not a timber dealer or a wood turner (as one newspaper report of the wedding claimed) but a sawyer. His family came from Horton. Harriett's mother was born Eliza Fallon and her father was a small landowner in Ireland. They married in 1858. Certainly the Brookes were not Ralph's social equals, and that mattered a lot in 1894, but nor were they paupers.

Nonetheless we knew frustratingly little about the family. Even the spelling of their name was uncertain - some accounts gave their name with an 'e', some without.

'It would have been so much easier to trace them if they'd had an unusual surname,' I grumbled. 'Why couldn't he have fallen for a Featherstonhaugh or an Abramovitch?!'

Actually the Brookes proved surprisingly easy to trace - for a relatively cheap registration fee, I had access on line to the 1871, 1881, 1891 and 1901 censuses, the benefit of name indexes and access to the national registration data for births, marriages and deaths post-1837 - and a whole heap of other databases.

'Be impressed. Be very impressed!' I emailed Marion in Thailand, before giving her a detailed account of Harriett's siblings and their parents.

The Brookes family lived at 96 Belle Vue Road and in 1891 Arthur was 58 and Eliza was 53, Harriett was 18, her sisters Mary Ellen and Emily were 26 and 15, and her brother Harry was 10. The rest of the family had left home, but by looking them up in the 1881 and 1871 censuses I discovered that the other siblings were Sarah Annie (born 1859), Samuel (born c.1861), William (born c.1867) and Alice (born 1878).

Sarah Annie married Charles Pitt in 1887, and by the time of the 1891 census they were living in Charlotte Street, Cheadle. I also discovered that, though Harriett's brother William had started out as a *bobbin turner,* by 1901 he was a clerk at Smallthorne Colliery and had married a Leek girl, Mary Ann Hall, in 1889. Harry, the youngest of Harriett's brothers, was working in the silk mills as a *measurer* in 1901. Colin vaguely remembered his Aunt Emily - she married and had a daughter. Young Alice Brookes eventually married a Mr Slack.

Mr and Mrs Brookes allowed Ralph Sneyd to court their daughter, but they were not at the wedding and nor were any of Harriett's other five siblings. Maybe they thought that their absence from home would call attention to the event, maybe they did not want people to know they condoned the marriage, maybe they couldn't get time off work.

The Brookes sound an eminently decent family, ordinary hard-working people, several of whose children did quite well for themselves through a combination of intelligence, luck, and in the case of at least two of the daughters, good looks. Samuel rose through the ranks to become a non-commissioned officer in the army. William moved away from the family trade of wood-working to take an office job. Sarah Annie and Harriett married outside their social class and young Alice took advantage of her eldest sister's good fortune.

According to his obituary Arthur Brookes was well-known for his knowledge of local history, which probably endeared him to his son-in-law, and also suggests he was a man of intelligence even if not highly-educated. However the big social disgrace for Ralph's family would have been that Arthur's wife and daughters worked. Harriett's mother was a silk winder and her daughters Mary Ellen and Emily both worked in the silk mills - as had Sarah Annie before her marriage. Harriett had the most respectable job of them all; she was employed at Sheldon and Fenton's silk mill in Leek to give out work and do book-keeping. But it was a job, nonetheless. There was snobbery about women working - the first step up the social ladder for many small tradesmen was to earn enough to allow their wives to be ladies of leisure. *My opinion,* explained a correspondent to the *Englishwoman's Domestic Magazine* in 1866, *is that if a woman is obliged to work, at once (although she may be a Christian and well-bred) she loses that particular position which the word 'lady' conventionally designates.*

Many working class Victorian parents would have worried about their daughters 'getting above themselves' and have been as shocked by Harriett's marriage as the gentry were. She would have been denounced as a scheming hussy, 'no better than she ought to be' - a meaningless phrase if ever there was one. But the Brookes family had no illusions about the value of their daughters 'knowing their place' - if there was a better life on offer they were refreshingly willing to allow their girls to take it up.

Inevitably there were jealous rumours. 'Ralph De Tunstall Sneyd's wife? She was a prostitute from Mill Street!' we heard from one elderly lady. Belle Vue Road runs downhill into Mill Street.

'Her parents were coming home from the pub one night, drunk as usual,' said someone else 'and the old lady fell over in the gutter. 'Hey up,' said Arthur, 'pick yersen up, we're related to royalty, now!'

Neither of our informants had known the Brookes family personally - they were repeating gossip they had heard from their parents or grandparents, and like all gossip it had probably grown with the telling. However, that these stories are still remembered at all is a measure of just how extraordinary the union was seen to be and of the passions that it aroused.

While the Brookes may have accepted Ralph and Harriett's marriage, John William Sneyd never would. Ralph had angered him when he became a Catholic; the marriage was the last straw.

Aunt Bertha Palliser (nee Cotton) wrote to Ralph in 1905 - with a glorious disregard for punctuation - and spelled out the situation:

....your change of religion and then your marriage beneath you of course gave your Father cause to feel very angry with you as were all your best friends, but as your Wife has shewn from all we hear she is fond of you & makes you a good Wife, my sister & I hoped that some day your Father might forgive you & at any rate if he heard your children were brought up well & in a refined way not mixing with those beneath your position, he would leave them well provided for ...but I do think he has acted in a most vindictive & cruel manner...

She went on to hope that the will disinheriting Ralph was an old one. Sadly, it wasn't. John William's final will is dated 1903. By that time he and Ralph were on apparently cordial terms again - there are letters between 1896 and 1902 arranging visits, though it has to be said that none of them mention either Harriett or the grandchildren. But stubbornness was a Sneyd trait; Aunt Bertha was probably right. Once John William had made up his mind to disinherit Ralph - whether it was in 1884 or 1894 - there was no going back.

'I suppose we'd better explain about John William's life at Basford'.
'What do we know?'
'Well, not all that much, but there are anecdotes - and the letter to Emily.'
'Oh yes - and the one from Aunt Bertha ...'

A curious letter to Ralph from his Aunt Bertha survives, undated, but from before 1891 as she tells him his Aunt Susan had just given her his address. For seven-and-a-half closely written pages, Aunt Bertha urged Ralph to renounce the Roman Catholic faith, assuring him that God forgave people who made mistakes if they were not *too blind* to admit them. But before she got to that she wanted to ask him about a rumour that was circulating in the county - a rumour which she clearly believed had some substance. First she urged her nephew to go and see Mr Challinor:

...I think you should know what is settled on you & must come to you at your Father's death & what is in his power to leave away from you, should the report which we hear is believed in Staffordshire be really true viz that he has married his cook. I cannot think that he can have so degraded himself as he was always so proud of his family & unless he was quite in his dotage (which he cannot be yet) or under the influence of a most designing woman he surely would not do so discreditable a thing. We do hope there may be no grounds for this report beyond indiscretion in playing as we hear indoor games in the kitchen which certainly is not good taste & I think your Father ought to be informed as soon as possible of the rumour that is going about to his great discredit...

There was a great deal more in similar vein. She went on to suggest that Ralph ask either his Uncle Dryden or Aunt Emily to talk to his father, and offered to write to him herself if they would allow her to.

'Indoor games!' I spluttered, 'what on earth do you suppose they were? You don't think she means...?'

'No I don't!' answered Marion tartly, 'he was in his sixties and he doesn't seem to have looked at another woman after Agnes died - sounds like nasty gossip to me. But I wonder why she didn't ask Aunt Susan?'

'I don't know. But this can only be a few years before Ralph married his Harriett - it gives some idea of the dreadful sort of things that must have been said about that marriage, doesn't it?'

'True. I do find it interesting that she's writing to Ralph about it though - treating him as a responsible adult. The Sneyds never did!'

The fact that the rumour about the cook was widely believed is an indication of just how isolated John William Sneyd was by the late 1880s - but the real fault lay not with him but with his servants. Over a decade later Aunt Fanny Stewart would write to Ralph about *that wretched woman & her family who lived upon your father.* In his will, John William left £200 [£13,000] to his cook, Mrs Elizabeth Annie Robinson, and gave permission for her and her husband to live on at the Hall for four months after his death.

Elizabeth Annie Lomas, Susanna's former housemaid, married Arthur Robinson at Cheadle in 1894. Not only had John William promoted her to cook, he was also employing Arthur as his gardener-cum-secretary-cum-odd-job-man. And there were two more women servants at the Hall by 1901, Ann Dale and her fourteen year old daughter, Mary Anne - more than there had ever been in Aunt Susan's day.

'So why was the place so neglected?'

'They were robbing him blind! Poor old man.'

Annie had certainly got her feet under the Basford Hall kitchen table. Not only did she and her husband live in the Hall, they had four young children there as well - little Annie who was five in 1901, four year old William, two year old Charles and baby Albert! The three youngest were actually born in Basford Hall. No wonder she didn't have time to keep the place clean! And, also living out of John William Sneyd's pocket, down at the Round House (part of the Bath House complex) were Annie's parents, old Mr and Mrs Lomas!

'You don't think little Annie could have actually been John William's child, do you?' said Pam.

'Who knows!'

There were certainly some odd goings-on at Basford. There's another letter, dated June 13th 1894, this time to Aunt Emily from someone called Hannah Carr.

Mam,

I am writing a very strange letter but I think it is in my place to tell you Annie at Basford Hall is carrying on most Abominable. She as got one of the street walkers out of Leek staying their & I believe that Mr Sneyd knows nothing about it & she is regular filthy woman & Annie goes to visit them at Leek & there is about 14 of them regular bad women & they get their living with men going seeing them, the Post Man at Cheddleton as told me he as seen her their & knows her well she is regular filthy & that bad woman Annie wount let eny one see Poor Mr Sneyd & I believe he is getting very childish but I do think Annie ought to be very much punnished....

We had no way of knowing what Hannah Carr's motives were. She might simply have had a grudge against Annie - who does seem to have been a singularly manipulative and dishonest young woman. If Emily did try to intervene, she was unsuccessful - Annie and her family were still in place ten years later, still taking advantage of their increasingly frail employer.

'And remember what Humphrey said!'

I giggled, remembering a summer picnic on the lawn at Basford Hall. We were all drinking wine and talking and Humphrey Scott-Moncrieff had gone indoors to look for something - suddenly his head appeared out of an upstairs window, calling 'I think this was where old John William had his toothbrush on a string!' We didn't know what he meant but he came down and explained. As an old man John William Sneyd was reputed to have taken to his bed; he never came out of his room, the maids took him food and water to wash with and emptied his chamber pot - and he kept his toothbrush on a string hanging by the bed!

We felt there was every likelihood that Ralph's father had become rather strange after Susanna Ingleby's death, if not before. They had been close since childhood and she had been his companion for nearly thirty years. Victorian men were not expected to understand domestic matters or deal with servants and old Mr Sneyd was no exception. With Mrs Ingleby dead and Mr Ralph gone, the servants seem to have run rings round him. In the end, both he and they probably found it easier if he stayed in his room all day.

Ralph described the decay at Basford in a poem. His descriptions ring true. It hadn't been the happiest of homes in Aunt Susan's day, but at least it was clean and the gardens were tidy.

> *...A noble hall is standing*
> *Neglected on a hill;*
> *No sounds of mirthful pleasure*
> *Its lonesome chambers fill.*   .
>
> *The passages and staircase*
> *Are dark and lone at night:*
> *Within the old man's chamber*
> *There burns a single light....*
> (*Basford Hall in the Past*)

We knew that when Ralph's first child, Stella, was born in 1896 he took her to see his father. John William was in bed - which fitted in with the toothbrush-on-a-string story - and pulled the sheet over his face so he wouldn't have to look at his granddaughter. Ralph pulled it back and shouted 'You will look at this child!' It was probably true. Colin had heard the story from his mother who was the baby in question - and no doubt she had heard it many times.

John William died in 1904. He wasn't senile - a perfectly sane letter survives from December 31st 1903, written in his own hand.

'We're running ahead of ourselves, you know,' said Pam.

'Sorry.'

'Let's get back to Ralph - and Harriett.'

Chapter 14
Married life

After the excitement of their secret wedding and their honeymoon in South Africa, sometime in 1895 Ralph and Harriett returned to North Staffordshire. No doubt they were rather nervous about their reception - but at least they had somewhere to live. Aunt Emily Jane Sneyd had offered them a home. Emily was seventy-two in 1895. She had never married and had spent much of her life shuttling between relations, helping out in various family crises and living in whichever of the family properties happened to be vacant. In 1895 she lived at Rose Cottage, Bradnop.

If Charles and Susanna Ingleby had made a go of their marriage, it would have been Emily who John William Sneyd would have called upon to live with him and care for his motherless baby boy. Maybe she was jealous. She seems to have been fond of her nephew, but there are letters that indicate that she did not approve of the way her brother and sister were bringing the child up.

In 1895 with her sister Susanna dead, and her eldest brother, John William, all-but-disowning his son, Emily could at last make her contribution to Ralph's life. It is unlikely that she approved of her nephew's marriage any more than his father did, but she could dress up her offer of accommodation as Christian charity - and score posthumous points off her sister Susanna at the same time. She had played the same game when Ralph converted to Rome. She was a staunch Anglican and had been brought up to fear and loathe Roman Catholicism with the same intensity that Susanna Ingleby did - but on the matter of Ralph's conversion she was, as far as we can see, diplomatically and uncharacteristically silent. Somehow, however late in the day it was, she was determined that her nephew should come to love her as much as he had once loved his Aunty Susan.

So Ralph and Harriett moved to Bradnop. It must have been quite nerve-racking for Harriett at first for old Miss Sneyd was a dragon, a lady of the old school. But Harriett was intelligent; she made herself pleasant, she watched and she learnt. She must have had to remember not to talk much about her family or her past life. Harriett would have worked in the mills for nine or ten years before she married, but it must never intrude into her conversation. She would have had to drop her old friends and neighbours - which would not have made her popular and fuelled unkind rumours - and she would have had to meet Ralph's friends, Thomas Wardle, his wife, his sons, Gilbert and Tom, Tom's French wife, Gabrielle, the Berminghams, Mrs Cruso, the Challinors. In a small town like Leek, these would be people who Harriett recognised, but to whom, before her marriage, she would never dare to have spoken.

As a factory girl they would not have noticed her - but they all now knew who she was and where she came from. They would have been scrutinising her closely, watching for her to make a mistake that betrayed her origins. Nor dare she risk spending too much time with her own family - at least not until she was confident of her new persona. The contrast between who she had been and who she was trying to become was too great. But Harriett was a strong, clever woman and she kept her nerve. Their first few years were idyllic.

Two years after the marriage, in the autumn of 1896, Harriett gave birth to their first child, Stella - or Elsie Dorothea Stella as she was christened. Ralph was overwhelmed and enchanted by his baby daughter. Aunt Emily was probably overwhelmed too - the mess and noise a small baby makes would have been a lot for an elderly spinster to cope with. Fortunately, like John William, she was deaf! Baby Stella's birth consolidated Harriett's position; she was now the mother of a Sneyd.

Even her father-in-law recognised that this made a difference. On December 30th, 1896 John William made an agreement with Ralph about the £8000 [£566,000] that had been his mother's marriage settlement. Ralph was only to have the money on his father's death, and in the interim the fund was to be administered by two trustees, Robert Henry Goodacre, vicar of Ipstones, and John William's cousin, Henry Sneyd of Lenthill. Ralph would get the interest.

Added to the money and stock he had inherited from his Aunt Susan this would enable Ralph to live the life of a gentleman. He would never be a rich man - but he would not have to work for his living. The settlement also marked the beginning of a grudging rapprochement between father and son.

We decided that we needed to see Rose Cottage for ourselves to help us envisage what those first few years with Harriett had been like - so we drove out to Bradnop to find it. It proved remarkably difficult and we made numerous attempts. 'Finding Rose Cottage' came to be a theme on our Staffordshire visits - whenever we had an hour or two to spare we would drive to Bradnop. Each time we would be armed with a new piece of apparently conclusive information - it was up Cook's Lane, it was the house now called 'Rosemount,' it was a farm cottage. Everyone had heard of it but no-one knew where it was! It was most frustrating.

'Well, I don't know where it can be,' said Marion, exasperated as yet another lead came to nothing. 'That's Jasmine Cottage all right - but the woman who came to the door said it had never been two cottages - and when you look at it you can see that it wasn't...'

'Turn right at the Moss Rose,' we'd been told, 'and you'll come to Jasmine Cottage, opposite Stile House Farm. It's been knocked into one now, but half of it used to be Rose Cottage at one time. The cottages were named after two sisters, Rose and Jasmine.'

We had heard that story several times and it sounded convincing - except that, when I thought about it, Jasmine seemed a very modern name - I had never come across any Victorian Jasmines.

Rose Cottage was elusive, but eventually, with the help of an old map and transcripts of the 1891 and 1901 censuses for Bradnop, we did find what we believe to have been Aunt Emily's house. Both censuses placed it on the Ashbourne Road between Throstle Fields and the Blacksmith's Arms. Throstle Fields is still there but the pub burnt down in the 1940s. However, we discovered that it stood at the cross roads where you turn off the main road up School Lane into Bradnop village proper. There are only two properties on that stretch of road - one a substantial Victorian house, now much modernised with new windows and a porch and set back from the road behind a pretty, tree-screened garden - and a modern house right next door to it. The Victorian house must, we feel sure, once have been called Rose Cottage - though it no longer bears that name. If we are right then it would seem that Aunt Emily Jane Sneyd lived in some style.

In 1898 Harriett had another baby - Arthur Lionel Llewellyn, called Lionel - and when he was one Aunt Emily decided to move yet again, this time to a house in Leek. Maybe it was the only way she could see to dislodge Ralph and his growing family. Maybe she felt it would be more convenient for her to be in town, near the shops, her friends and her doctor - after all, she was seventy-five. Whatever the reason, Ralph and Harriett had to find somewhere else to live.

Aunt Susan had owned some property in Onecote parish - a dilapidated house with a bit of land and an adjacent farm. Old William Moss, the tenant, had died in 1895 aged seventy-four, he was a widower and lived alone so Fair View was vacant. This, Ralph decided, was to be their family home. They moved in 1900. Harriett was pregnant again and later that year she gave birth to baby Ralph Clement Cotton in their new house. Ralph gave all his sons 'family' names - but when his grandson, Lionel's son John, was born he was adamant that the boy should not have 'Ralph' as his second name - to have three Ralphs in the family, would, he firmly believed, bring bad luck! It was another of his many superstitions. The 1901 census shows Ralph and Harriett in residence at Fair View (Ralph would later call it Fair View Hall) together with a 17 year old cook, Annie Blakeman, and a 26 year old nurse, Lucy Cartledge - and Harriett's parents, Arthur and Eliza Brookes. They seem to have been living there permanently - the census enumerator recorded that the head of the household back at 96, Belle Vue Road was their eldest unmarried daughter, Mary Ellen. Emily and Harry were still at home with her.

'Do you really think Harriett's parents were living there permanently?' asked Marion.

'I don't see why not. They were in their sixties, it would be quite natural to go and live with a married daughter - especially one whose husband could afford to keep you.'

'They could just have been on a visit when the enumerator called.'

'True.'

'I really can't imagine them living there,' Marion was adamant. 'I suppose it could be just another example of Ralph misunderstanding the rules about who it was 'proper' to share your house with if you were a gentleman.'

'But Ralph never cared about that sort of thing!'

It seemed to me she was being just as snobbish as Ralph's relatives! Seven years married and living in isolation up on the moors, Harriett might have been glad to have her parents for company and to help with the children. Ralph was busy with his collections and his studies and his ceremonies, and there were many things he needed her to do to help. She had taken on Aunt Susan's role as his secretary, checking and copying his notes and writing letters for him - a time-consuming business. Socially things had changed too. Old Aunt Emily had moved to Leek - she died there in 1901. There were no longer any members of Ralph's family that Harriett had to impress on a daily basis and she was probably more relaxed about having her own family around. As I tried to tell Marion,

Ralph himself was lacking in any sense of class consciousness - back at Basford Hall he had always been happiest in the kitchen with Mrs Bloor - and his friends came from all walks of life.

At the bottom of the garden at Fair View stood a big, old, two-storeyed barn. Ralph probably spent more time in the barn than he did in the house - it housed his collections, and fairly soon he converted part of it into a chapel - not just any chapel but 'the Chapel of the Holy Grail at Fair View.' It was the site of family services and of all sorts of rituals of Ralph's own invention. On April 26th, 1902, barely eighteen months after the Sneyds moved there, The *Leek Times* reported one of them, under the heading *St George's Day at Fair View.*

It began, *The blessing and elevation of the sword took place at the Chapel of the Holy Grail on Wednesday April 22nd... The Grandmaster informs us: 'We wish to symbolise the everlasting wisdom, which is the sword of spiritual power. We also wish to show that the guardians of truth should ever be ready to defend the same, if needs be with their earthly life, and that it is the glorious duty of all true knights and heroes to uphold all just causes and to protect the weak from the attacks of the oppressor.'*

It was an odd life that Harriett had found for herself, but she seems to have been happy in it - and compared to Messrs Sheldon and Fenton's mill it must have been paradise. In 1901 everything was going well; her husband adored her, her children were healthy, she was encouraged to read books, write poems and go for long walks across the moors with Ralph. She had servants to help in the house and more money to spend on herself than she had ever had before - she liked nice clothes and now she could dress fashionably in silks and furs. Harriett had good reason to sing as she went about the house. It charmed her husband.

> *...All our hearts with grief are sore,*
> *Now we hear thy songs no more;...*
> (*On the Death of My Wife*)

wrote Ralph after her death, and he recorded some of the words she sang in the voluminous notes he made for his future biographer. A love of music was something they had in common.

For Ralph, Harriett was his 'sweet lady-love', his 'fairy princess', his 'fair lady' and the 'light of his soul'. He was a hopeless romantic.

'How could she live up to that?' said Marion.

'I don't think she had to. She was an ideal that existed only in his imagination - I'm not sure he ever saw the real woman underneath, the one who got ratty with the children and burnt the toast...'

Harriett's view of her new life was much more pragmatic. She had done well for herself, and having spent the first two decades of her life working extremely hard, she was going to make the most of her good fortune. She herself had come from a large family and her mother worked. She knew about small children and babies - but she chose to employ a nursemaid for her own little ones. She also decided that they should be sent away to school as early as possible. Harriett, her grandsons believe, was the one who made the decisions at Fair View. Maybe she was aware of the limitations of her own education and believed that her children would have a better chance of fitting into their father's social class if they were schooled away from home. Maybe she just wanted them out of the way so she and Ralph could enjoy each other's company and do things together. Harriett had seen very little of the world before she married but Ralph had always enjoyed travel. Now he had a companion. Postcards arrived at the children's schools from all over the country and beyond - London, Oban, Como, Boulogne, Norway.

In 1906 Ralph and Harriett's youngest child was born, christened Alfred William Augustine but known as Willie to his family and as Billy to everyone else. Harriett seems to have been a rather distant mother to her three elder children but she doted on her 'dearest Babs.' Now thirty-four Harriett was beginning to enjoy being a mother. As a little boy Billy went everywhere with his parents and was spoilt to death. In October 1909, for example, Harriett reported to Stella that three year old *Babs has got such a big teddy bear, we bought it this week, it was 10/6, so you see it is a good sized one.*

'How insensitive!' Marion exclaimed. 'Look it up - see, that bear cost £33 in our money! And there was poor Stella, stuck at Oulton with Ralph and Harriett hardly ever visiting. If they wanted to make the other children jealous of Billy they were certainly going the right way about it!'

Billy was sent away to school with his brothers for a year or two, but then he had an accident and hurt his head. Harriett believed it had caused permanent damage; thereafter he was labelled delicate and kept at home. That must have made his siblings very jealous too.

Ralph had their home renovated. The drains were checked, repaired and new pipes laid, the walls were re-pointed and propped up as necessary, the chimneys were rebuilt and given new chimney pots, new windows were cut in the kitchen and the bedroom above it, others were altered and a new porch was built. All the woodwork throughout the house was replaced and the hall was panelled in best yellow pine. The roof was re-slated and the guttering replaced. The kitchen range was improved to provide hot water for a new bathroom and an indoor lavatory was installed. For Harriett, this was to be a short-lived amenity - within the year, Ralph decided it was unhygienic and it was removed! The family went back to using the old two-seater, a long windy walk away in a brick outhouse at the end of the garden.

The rooms would have had to be redecorated after all this work and no doubt Harriett was proud of her new home. It was certainly a far cry from Belle Vue Road. Needless to say, Ralph had some strange ideas about what their home needed. An 'arms panel,' ten feet by five feet was created following a drawing Ralph had provided and it was mounted on the wall outside. He also had a local builder, 'old Guy', put up crenellated walls around his property to 'keep out the invaders!' They are still there - blackened, ugly and not high enough to deter a determined sheep!

The family must have moved out while the work was going on and it maybe that this was when they went to Sharpcliffe. Certainly, according to Billy, the family rented Sharpcliffe from Mr Sleigh for a time - no doubt returning to a former Sneyd house appealed to the romantic in Ralph. Sharpcliffe is a grand 16th century house, high up on a wooded hillside, which Ralph's grandfather acquired in 1846. Various of Ralph's uncles lived in it and his Aunt Susan spent the summer before her ill-fated marriage there. Dryden Sneyd sold Sharpcliffe in 1876 for £22,655 [£1,300,000] to Hugh Sleigh.

We do not know how long Ralph and his family lived there but he left a permanent memorial behind him. Deep in the woods he built - or had someone build for him - a circle of standing stones. According to local dowser, John Gilman, it is purely decorative; there is no significance in the alignment of the stones with the sun or the stars or with ley lines. Perhaps Ralph was just interested in the mechanics of building a stone circle.

Ralph and Harriett seem to have spent quite a lot of time away from Fair View, living at Bank House in Leek while their children stayed up on the moors with the servants. Bank House, on Clerk Bank, belonged to Tom and Gabrielle Wardle. Tom was the sixth of Sir Thomas Wardle's nine sons and he was ten years younger than Ralph. He was the most artistic of the Wardle boys and he became designer-in-chief at the family's Hencroft Works. Perhaps it was their shared interest in art that brought him and Ralph together. It looks very much as if he invited Ralph and Harriett to use his house in Leek as a base whenever they chose to spend time in town.

They were certainly very isolated up on the moors. Today Leek is a bare twenty minutes away by car, but the journey on foot or by horse and trap then took a great deal longer. A round trip to Leek for shopping would probably have taken a day, given that there were no supermarkets and you had to queue, and chat, in each shop you visited. Charles Bould, the carrier who lived at Pethills, ran a daily service between the Duke of York public house in Leek and Bottomhouse in the early 1900s, and other carriers going to Ford, Winkhill, Onecote and Grindon passed by Fair View. Goods bought in Leek could be delivered within the day - Harriett did not have to carry her own shopping. The carrier was an important figure. I can't better the description that appears in Nithsdale's *The Highlands of Staffordshire.*

He accepts all manner of commissions: selling eggs and butter and poultry, and purchasing all sorts of articles required by people of the moorlands who cannot attend the market. He will have a lawn mower for the parson; notices for the parish council; a repaired cornet for a village bandsman; cycle parts for a bicycling lass up country; a pair of spectacles for some old lady; a box from the station for a servant girl home for the holidays; ... and bread, groceries, and other necessaries of life for many families; and, by the time he starts for home, a fair cargo of liquor in himself!

This, of course, was because all the carriers started from one or other of the local pubs!

Nonetheless, for a town-bred girl, Onecote cannot have been an easy place in which to keep house. No doubt the family had produce from their own and neighbouring farms, but basics like flour and tea and sugar had to be fetched from Leek. A note scribbled in Harriett's handwriting survives giving instructions to one of her sons who was running errands for her in Leek.

29lbs meat Bayleys already ordered
2 brown loaves (Tattons)
2 tins Ovaltine (Boots) ....
Call for Daddy's boots from Salters
Be quick home like a good boy
1d for yourself

'Twenty-nine pounds of meat!' exclaimed Marion. 'That's over two stones! How could he have carried all that?'

'Maybe he had a bicycle? Maybe he just had to see it on to the carrier's cart?' I didn't really know.

There are also a series of little notes to Ralph on torn scraps of paper - perhaps Harriett attached them to the shopping lists she gave him. *Be quick home my precious as I am lonely without you,* and, more detailed *Be quick home my darling, as I do not like to be without you for any length of time. Don't mess reading papers. Bring me Sunday Stories for this week.* This was a family that kept everything!

Harriett and her cook would have had to plan carefully. Staffordshire weather can be extreme and Edwardian winters were harsh. Each year there was a very real possibility of Fair View being cut off by snow for days or weeks at a time. Perched on the edge of an escarpment Fair View would also have caught the worst of the wind and the rain - the family must often have cursed Ralph's fastidiousness in having that indoor lavatory removed! The house must have been difficult to keep warm - but people of Ralph and Harriett's generation were used to cold bedrooms and passageways. Even Marion and I can remember wearing gloves in bed and scraping ice off the inside of our bedroom windows.

Much as she seems to have loved her eccentric husband, there were incidents that tried Harriett's patience. In one letter to Stella she explains that *Daddy has gone to Leek to fetch a new cheque book* and then goes on to tell her daughter that this is his third trip to Leek for that purpose - on each of the previous visits he'd been sidetracked and come home without having been to the bank! She also seems to have had to take charge of Ralph's financial affairs - he was not very good with money. A letter from their solicitors dated October 25th 1905, is addressed to *Mrs Sneyd*, and reassures her that all Ralph's stocks and moneys were in order and that the interest was being paid. The £8000 [£525,000] that should have come to him the previous year when his father died was now to be in the form of a mortgage on the Basford and Consall estates, but there was some hold-up about the payment, which, the solicitor hastened to assure her, was a good thing because it meant they would be getting an extra £20 [£1,300] a year in interest. Ralph's total income for 1905 had been just over £670 [£44,000]. The letter was addressed to Bank House in Leek, and refers to their income improving *when you have let the house at Fair View* - which probably means the farm bungalow, not their own home. But it is the penultimate paragraph of the letter which is most telling:-

I believe that you have an account for cabs and one or two others still to be paid, and I should strongly advise you to get these cleared off and then you will know exactly how much you have to spend. I think the suggestion made when I was at your house the other day that Mr Sneyd should have a £100 [£6,600] of the yearly income or say £2 a week to do what he likes with would be a good arrangement.

Clearly they had got into financial difficulties. Ralph's father had died the previous year. It is likely that Ralph knew, back in 1894, that he had been disinherited of Basford and that it was to go to his Uncle Gustavus. Gustavus was only eighteen years older than Ralph and they had always got on well. As his uncle had no intention of giving up his lucrative living at Chastleton, perhaps Ralph had hoped he would let him live at Basford Hall. But after his father's death, Ralph was to see another side to his uncle. Not only did Gustavus rent Basford to his great niece, Phoebe Dugdale and her family, he defrauded Ralph of all sorts of items that had been left there. Ralph wrote to him on May 4th, 1904.

I should be much obliged if you would send me the knife, fork and spoon as they are my own & I will take full responsibility for them! There are numbers of things which belonged to my dear Aunt Susan which I have not yet received: poor dear soul she little knew in what a shameful way I should be treated... she and our blessed Lady will intercede with God that the rightful line of Sneyds may return to their rightful home ... if I may not have the house I think I am at least entitled to hang in my hall something which may remind me of the estates of which I have been dispossessed ...

'He meant a replica of the key to the front door of Basford Hall.'

'Interesting that he sees his right to Basford as God-given,' I observed.

Marion nodded thoughtfully. 'He was the only male Sneyd in his generation,' she said, 'and he had sons. Mind, it would have been a poisoned chalice. He couldn't have afforded the upkeep.'

A list survives of the items Ralph believed his uncle had stolen from him. It is on a yellowing sheet in old-style purple duplicating ink, and the sheet is number four of a larger, missing, document.

Debts and Claims for Jewellery and other objects missing from Basford Hall
Lent to my Uncle Gustavus   *£25 [£1,650]*

Lent to my Uncle Gustavus for farmer's cow which had died	*£17 [£1,180]*
Lent to my Uncle Gustavus	*£19 [£1,320]*
Hammerless gun (Sold by Gustavus' Butler) never used	*£13 [£856]*
Gold Watch (missing) value about	*£5 [£348]*
Ring (of Diamonds and Sapphires) worth at least	*£6 [£418]*
Necklace and bracelets of Amethyst set in Gold (very beautiful)	*£12 [£790]*
Valuable models of Animals etc. worth at least	*£8 [£560]*
Collection of Pebbles and Shells about	*£3 [£209]*

I also lay claim to the pictures which belonged to my poor Mother and the Furniture which belonged to her....

He never saw any of it. In some ways Ralph was a true Sneyd; he never gave up on his missing possessions or on the sense of grievance that accompanied their loss. And he was losing more than possessions.

As the 19th century gave way to the 20th, Ralph was becoming more and more estranged from his Sneyd relations. His immediate family were dying one by one - Aunt Emily in 1901, his father in 1904, Aunt Ada Hunt in 1911, Uncle Dryden in 1913. Most of his cousins were scattered or dead, and though Dora and Harriet Bamford still wrote to him at Christmas and on his birthday it is clear from the letters that they did not meet. They were spinsters in their fifties in the early 1900s. Ralph sent them photographs of his children and they commented politely - Lionel had such pretty hair and how was dear Stella getting on with her music - and what was his youngest son's name again? They sent news of their brothers, married clergymen, both living in America, and of their wives and children, but they pointedly refrained from asking after Harriett.

His Cotton aunts, Bertha and Fanny also wrote. There were invitations *...we would be pleased to see you both...* but Ralph seldom followed them up. One glowing letter from Aunt Fanny Stewart does talk about *the dear little boy you brought with you* (probably Willie) and they both remembered Stella's pretty singing voice, but they were old ladies in 1900, set in their ways, snobbish and forgetful. *I do hope your Wife is better, for the moment I have forgotten her name...* wrote Aunt Bertha. They chose to ignore Ralph's religion and were completely out of touch with his lifestyle - and he probably realised that it would be wisest not to meet them too often!

Those relatives who remained in the area were the ones who had inherited Basford Hall and Ashcombe over his head. Ralph paid courtesy calls on them once or twice a year, alone, but all the parties must have been uncomfortable. Dryden Sneyd seems to have ceased all contact with his nephew after 1894, and Gustavus Sneyd had hurt Ralph too deeply for them to have much contact for many years after John William's death in 1904. So Ralph De Tunstall Sneyd, the last of the Sneyds of Ashcombe Park to bear the family name, had lost his place in the family history. Another branch of the family had taken over the once-grand Sneyd estate. Ralph's Catholicism, his marriage and his own eccentricity all separated him from the relations he had left. Like Aunt Susan, they were conventional people who feared and distrusted oddity.

But whatever his relations thought, Harriett was a good wife to Ralph and he worshipped her. It is quite difficult to get a picture of what she was really like. We have only seen two photographs of her and she left very few documents. Billy kept all her clothes - but by the time we started our research they had been dispersed. Mrs Boulton up at Biddulph, who had contacted us after an article of ours appeared in the *Leek Post and Times* and who had been friendly with Ralph Clement and his landlady, had a fan that Ralph said had belonged to his mother. It was pretty, painted chiffon trimmed with lace. Other people remembered a fashionable fox fur jacket and muff hanging in the wardrobe. Harriett, we deduced, liked nice clothes. But it is not much to go on - and Ralph's idealised view of their family life is certainly not the one that his children remembered. Ralph wrote nostalgically after Harriett's death:

> *From mirthful tales to children,*
> *A deep affection springs;*
> *The wife endears her husband*
> *By the lullaby she sings;*
> *The simple meal at evening,*
> *With the smiling mother there,*
> *The flowers that she tended,*
> *With refined and gentle care....*
> (*In Memory Serene*)

But for his second son at least, there were no such memories. Ralph Clement was sent away to a school he hated when he was little more than a toddler, and he left school to go straight into the army and the blood bath that was the First World War. His mother was dead by the time he returned. Fair View held bad memories and he could not bear to live there ever again. Ralph Clement spent much of his working life lodging in the Unicorn public house in Leek, and when eventually he shared a retirement bungalow with his ex-landlady he often described it as the 'only real home' he had ever known.

It was different for Billy. He spent most of his childhood with his parents and lived on at Fair View after his father died, sleeping and living in two rooms and allowing the rest of the house to fall into disrepair - but keeping everything where it was when his parents were alive. He refused offers from picture dealers to buy two valuable, but damp-damaged, oil paintings that hung on the wall in what had been his father's bedroom on the grounds that his father's room must never be touched. His parents' clothes hung in their wardrobes until his death, unworn and moth-eaten. Perhaps by keeping the place unchanged he was hanging on to the memories of his childhood before his mother died, when he was her spoilt baby and the house was full of life and laughter and people.

Lionel and Stella married and had their own families. Memories of their childhood faded; they, too, had spent comparatively little time with their parents. They seem to have been fond of their strange, gentle father - but they remembered their mother as a strong woman who did not stand for any nonsense. We have already noted that Harriett was intelligent and capable. She also had a sharp pen which suggests she may have had a sharp tongue.

Your behaviour when meeting us in the public streets of Leek has been for some years both insulting and annoying, you have actually turned suddenly round as if you had seen a snake ... such behaviour one might expect from an uneducated person... but not from a lady. We have never intruded ourselves on your society and have no wish to do so ...

'Whoever was that to?' I asked.

'Don't know - the first page is missing,' answered Marion, scrabbling through the pile of letters, 'but she goes on to talk about inviting this woman's husband to John William's funeral and letting her have a photograph of the portrait of old Mrs Cotton...'

We couldn't work it out and try as we might we never did find the first page of that letter. But whoever it was, they had certainly got on the wrong side of Harriett Sneyd! She didn't think much of Ralph's friend, the theosophical Reverend Ouseley, either - we have already seen part of the diatribe she sent him. And in 1907, with Ralph away on yet another jaunt, she scolded him in a letter about one of his pet obsessions. *I think it is all a myth about the Holy Grail, my idea is that it is to get a fabulous sum for it, now don't you let yourself in for anything or I shall be distressed....* As she became more secure in her marriage Harriett could let her irritation show. But nonetheless, she continued to support Ralph in his various schemes. *Far have I wandered, When the moon shone bright, Over the distant dales, Arm in arm with the one I love, Listening to fairy tales,* she wrote happily. Harriett and Ralph were country lovers and in fine weather the moors around Fair View are wonderful, a powerful, inspiring, ever-changing landscape full of hidden secrets. *Where purple heather stretches wide,* wrote Ralph,

> *The grouse, both red and black, abide;*
> *And luscious bilberries do grow,*
> *And golden bright tormentils show.*
>
> (*The Moorlands Wide*)

He certainly took a countryman's interest in the moorland birds and plants. According to his son, Billy, he was especially protective of a colony of curlews and lapwings that nested across the road from the house. Then one day they stopped coming. Twenty years after Ralph's death they returned, just as suddenly. Billy lived almost all his life at Fair View and was delighted to see his father's much-loved birds return.

The Moorlands are a naturalists' paradise, but the area around Fair View is spectacularly wild and desolate. Even the grass looks short and stunted as if it is having a struggle to grow and there is little wildlife other than the occasional rabbit. But plovers and kestrels, ousels, larks, hen harriers and long-eared owls nest on the moors around, and blackcock, twite and dippers can be seen nearby.

The Sneyds' nearest neighbours were at Bottomhouse, a few hundred yards away across the fields, but it was only a tiny, windswept hamlet on a crossroads. There were two pubs - the Green Man, run, in 1901 by young George Burnett and his wife Sarah, and the Travellers' Rest run by Joseph Chadwick with help from his sister's children, George and Annie Bloor. Young John Chadwick farmed Bottomhouse Farm with his wife Mary, when she could spare the time from looking after their two tiny sons and baby daughter. Another family of Chadwicks had Newbarn farm, John Bradbury and his two teenage sons farmed at Spring Fields and two families of Mycocks ran the Upper and Lower Berkhamsytch farms. The Goulds with their two little girls, Lizzie and Gertie, were at Bott's (later Butcher's) Tenements. Other farms within a short radius of Fair View were Fellows Close, farmed by the Greens,

Backlane where the Barks lived with their four young children and Pethillshead run by an elderly couple, William and Ann Meakin and their son, Edward. To the west, just as close but across the boundary in Bradnop, were the Hampsons at Green Gutter, old William and Mary Anne Phillips at Goatfields (or Goat Fell - the farm names change from map to map), widowed Mary Berrisford at Standing Stone and Archie Cantrell and his wife and children at Lark Park. Decades later, Archie was one of the bearers at Ralph De Tunstall Sneyd's funeral - his family still have the letter of thanks Lionel wrote them. To the north of Fair View the land grows bleaker and James Wain, living at Pewit Hall with his wife and daughter, eked out his scanty living from the land by working as a mason's labourer. In an emergency, these were the people on whom Ralph and Harriett would have had to call.

Onecote village was about a mile away, the hamlets of Ford, Ford Wetley and New Street were slightly nearer. Ford is a picturesque little place, a cluster of fine old stone houses deep in the valley with the Hamps flowing between them, a little pastoral oasis amid the high moors. Most of the Sneyds' neighbours were farmers, working small, unproductive hill farms with strange sounding names: Dirty Gutter, Gooseneck, Hopping Head, Hobmeadow, Longditch, Blowo'rem. They would have known them all, of course, but it is unlikely that hard-headed, horny-handed moorland farmers would have been very much in tune with Ralph De Tunstall Sneyd's world.

Harriett seems to have been anxious to abide by Aunt Bertha Palliser's stricture that her children *should not mix with the class beneath them.* But in any event, the local farmers' children had little time for play. In Joyce Holliday's *Memories of the Moorland Child,* interviewee after interviewee detailed the work they had to do - letting the poultry out and feeding them, milking, butter-making, gathering wood - before clattering along the rough roads to school in their steel-tipped clogs and heavy boots, muffled in stout coats and jackets, braving the wind and the rain and the hidden terrors of the empty hills. When they returned at night there would be another batch of chores - collecting eggs, shutting the fowls in for the night - and at weekends and in the holidays there were stones to be cleared from the thin moorland soil before ploughing, potatoes to dig, hay to make, grain to tread. By comparison, the four young Sneyds led privileged lives. As adults, they would socialise with their neighbours - and Stella married one of them - but as children they were expected to know their place.

Ralph had a lot of friends and he and Harriett often entertained; visitors from Leek would stay overnight rather than face the dark, lonely journey home. There was a huge oak refectory table in the dining room at Fair View that was reputed to have come from Sharpcliffe, and seated thirty-two, and a blue and white transfer-printed earthenware dinner service with thirty-two place settings. Billy remembered his parents giving dinners that used all of it.

Ralph remained a devout, if somewhat eccentric, Catholic all his life and the family often seem to have had priests and monks to stay. *Father Dominic is coming to stay a few days with us* wrote Harriett to twelve year old Stella in May 1908. Father Dominic was a Franciscan friar. She went on *We had a party last Tuesday & Father Sperling was one of the guests.* Father Sperling was the priest at St Mary's. Ralph involved these guests in his various pseudo-religious ceremonies if he possibly could: *When Father Ignatius of Llantony came to Fair View we had a service in the chapel & went in procession from the house to the chapel, Brother David first in his habit & carrying my great cross of mountain ash....* The three men, with Ralph in the middle *wearing the habit etc of the Franciscan order* processed to the chapel, and Ralph recorded the event on a single sheet of notepaper, adding *we had my form of matins with incense!* Poor Father Ignatius had simply come to give a lecture in Leek. Many of Ralph's ceremonies were more elaborate.

On the Thursday previous to Whit Sunday I robed myself in two blankets in preparation for the blessing of the Sword, the Belt and the Scabbard; which were to be worn afterwards by myself during part of the ceremonial of initiation into the Order of Knighthood ... So begins eight-and-a-half pages of description, drafted by Ralph and copied out by Harriett in her neatest writing in an exercise book. Ralph had decided he wanted to be a knight, but as his version of knighthood was somewhat out of fashion in the early 20th century he had devised his own ceremony. His friends, Father Dominic and 'Brother Ouseley', the theosopher from Brighton who Harriett so disliked, helped him. Father Dominic blessed the various accoutrements *using a Latin formula.* Ralph made a *...solemn profession of Knightly faith and devoted myself to the cause of God and the ladies; faithfully promising to protect the oppressed.* He also gave a *short address to the people present, telling them how long I had wished for the knightly initiations and describing my aspirations to rightly fulfil my duties in chivalry.* Ralph was never happier than when he was expounding his views to a captive audience.

He then bathed, *put on the brown hose and the black shoes and afterwards arrayed myself in a white alb and a white girdle* and kept an overnight vigil in his chapel. There was also a lengthy description of how he kept himself awake, standing, walking, praying and consulting *a book on the ancient chivalry from which I gained many ideas for the future ceremonial.* The following morning, all by himself in the chapel, he lit candles, sang a psalm and put on a *gorgeous cope of blood red colour.* He was fond of this cope - it makes several appearances in the ceremony and twenty years later he would wear it in his self-appointed role as Chief Druid of Staffordshire! He then went to Leek, confessed and took communion, and returned to Fair View for a late breakfast.

'Wearing what?' I wondered. 'He must have got changed for church - I can't imagine the priests would have been too pleased if he'd turned up in his blood red cope ....'

'Then he went and lay in his bed...' Marion went on, ignoring me.

'I'm not surprised, he must have been worn out.'

'No listen - *which I intended to symbolise the rest of the holy ones!*' The family, together with their guests, then processed back to the chapel. Ralph put on armour with a white surcoat and belt and Harriett and Stella helped him on with his spurs. *The rowels of these spurs were composed of gold and the parts which were adjusted to the feet were beautifully gilded...*

'Where on earth did he get those from?' wondered Marion, 'And is that what he is wearing in those photos we found in the trunks? What on earth must his neighbours have made of it all?'

There was a lot more ceremonial - questions and answers, blows with swords, slaps on the cheek. Ralph was enjoying himself hugely. Stella was very much involved, asking the questions to which he gave the responses, helping her father on with his sword and finally intoning, 'Take this sword with the blessing of God....!'

'How old do you suppose she was?' I asked Marion. 'The boys don't seem to have been there...'

'Well, they might have been in the audience. I would guess Stella was about twelve - old enough to remember her lines - she had quite a lot to say. That would mean it was 1908 or thereabouts.'

There was a lot of dressing up. Ralph wore various combinations of robes, but he seems to have lent his 'habit and cord of the Franciscan order' to his friend Ouseley - *this habit and cord are amongst my treasured possessions and have frequently been used by myself* he wrote.

'Do you remember Arnold Corden's story?' asked Marion.

I laughed. We had visited Mr Corden when we were working on *Finding Susanna*. If my memory served me right we had been on one of our periodic searches for Rose Cottage and someone had suggested we go and see him - in those days he was the chairman of the Cheddleton Historical Society. He remembered how, as a boy at scout camp, he and a friend had been left behind on cookhouse duty while the rest of the troop went off for a hike. Suddenly, a tall, thin figure in a brown habit appeared, followed by two others, and they glided through the camp, heads bowed, looking neither right nor left. Arnold and his friend were terrified - they thought they had seen ghosts! Only later did they learn that the apparitions were Ralph De Tunstall Sneyd and two friends!

'He really would have liked to have been a priest or a monk,' I said. 'I'm quite surprised he didn't join an order after Harriett died - they'd have accepted him, even if he didn't have enough education to be a priest ...'

'I'm sure he liked the idea,' Marion replied, 'but I'm not sure he could really have coped with the discipline - he was too much of an individualist.'

But we still hadn't finished with the ceremony. Before Ralph could finally wear the red cope for the last time that day, see *the life of an errant knight before* [him] and drink *rich liqueur from a two-handled goblet...* [his] *long trials of initiation behind* [him] ... there was something else he had to do.

'Trials!' Marion exploded. 'Nonsense! He loved every minute of it!'

'Shhh! This is one of the best bits!' *Clad in my suit of armour I mounted my steed and was handed my lance and shield, and galloped off towards the quintain,*

'The what?'

'A target. In this case a cast-off tin tray from the kitchen on a pile of straw!'

'You're making it up!'

'Read it yourself then!'

And there it was - Ralph had written the account himself. It was worthy of Monty Python. We collapsed into uncontrollable giggles.

Chapter 15
Pam and Marion

'We really need to go back to Staffordshire,' I said to Marion one evening on the phone.

'Why? Look at the mounds of stuff we've got already — there's enough for a dozen books, not just one!'

'I know, but I'd like to have another look at those trunks of Colin's.

'He'll be delighted if he has to drag all that lot out of the loft again!'

Marion was working on the chapters about Ralph's schooldays and had more material than she could use. I was working on his later life and had far less to go on. When we'd first gone through Colin's archive we had been writing Susanna's story. I was sure that there were lots of things we'd ignored then because they were too recent. There was so much we didn't know about Ralph's later years - I hoped some of the answers were still in Colin's loft!

'And I'd really like to have a look at the area around Fair View...' I went on. Ralph lived up on the moors above Leek for nearly fifty years, but both times we'd visited his house it had been dark and wintry. I felt we needed to have a proper look around in daylight.

'And of course, we've never actually found Rose Cottage, or been to Thor's Cave - or Arbor Low, come to that,' said Marion, obviously warming to the idea. 'And we've never seen the pictures in Ford House that John told us about.'

Over the next few days we planned our visit and negotiated times that suited us both - and our respective husbands. We no longer had a place to stay - on our previous visits we had stayed at my little terrace house in Stoke, but I had given up my job at the university and the house was let, so I volunteered to find us a B&B in Leek. Not until I had actually made the booking and was emailing the details to Marion did I take note of the name 'The Green Man'. Marion has a passion for green men - heads with leaves growing in their hair, mouths and eyes, based on pagan deities - she finds them carved in stone and cast in iron all over the country. It seemed a good omen.

'Just look at that!' said Marion in delight as we pulled into the car park of the Green Man a few weeks later. 'Bang slap next door to St Mary's Roman

Catholic Church. Clever you - real Ralphy territory!'

'Sheer luck!' I admitted. 'The place looked OK on the website and wasn't too expensive - I didn't know exactly where it was, to be honest.'

The forbidding tower of the church Ralph had known so well loomed over us as we fitted our key into the lock of room number one. The Green Man is an old inn and our room was in the coach house. It was surprisingly spacious and there was a sofa, armchair, wardrobe, chest of drawers, an en-suite bathroom and two very comfortable single beds, as well as a TV and a kettle. Perfect, we decided as we settled down to our supper of cheese and biscuits, fruit and nuts, and the obligatory bottle of white wine.

I had also brought a present for Marion - a giant tube of orange Smarties! We shared them as we made our plans for the following day. In Staffordshire we led a strange sort of parallel existence; we now had a large circle of friends and acquaintances in the area who knew us but not our husbands and children. To them we were 'Pam'n Marion', two slightly odd middle-aged ladies who turned up once or twice a year and seemed obsessed with the Sneyd family. We had often been described as 'the Sneyd ladies'...

'Right, most respected colleague - what's on the agenda now?' said Marion the following morning, finishing off the last piece of bacon on her plate and downing her coffee.

'Ford House. They asked us to be there around nine so we'd better hurry.

We parked the car and were nearly there when suddenly Marion stopped. The gates to Greystones cafe were closed - they were beautiful wrought iron with an elaborate design of a tree - and over it was a green man! Marion photographed it - this, she was sure, was a good sign for the day ahead. 'It's going to be a good trip,' she said, confidently.

Ford House belonged to Ralph's grandson John Sneyd, and he had lived there as a child. He now rented it to a local firm of accountants, but there were still family portraits hanging in the stairwell, including, he had said, some of his grandfather. We had passed the house numerous times - it was opposite the Nicholson Institute - but not until we crossed the threshold did we realise just how grand a place it was. The downstairs ceilings were decorated with lavish art nouveau plasterwork and the fireplace surrounds were elaborately carved. The shallow, creaky stairs were illuminated by rich stained glass panels and hung with family pictures. Some we recognised, most were strangers to us, but that didn't matter, it was Ralph we were interested in. A series of framed press cuttings, tucked away under the stairs, showed him in the great hall of Winchester Castle, sword in hand, gazing up at the huge painted disc that hangs on the wall and purports to be the top of the table around which King Arthur sat with his knights.

'Isn't this a wonderful building!' we said to one of the young men who bustled past us on the stairs.

'Have you seen the bathroom?' he asked. 'No? Come with me!' and he led us back up to the landing and into a perfect Edwardian bathroom complete with a huge wood-and-brass shower!

John's father had done well for himself. Ford House is considerably grander than Fair View.

'Now,' said Marion as we retraced our steps to the car park and climbed into the car, 'where to next?'

'Fair View, I think. If we head out along the Ashbourne road that will take us past Rose Cottage - and we need to take a photo. Then on to Bottomhouse. And we need to time ourselves - work out just how far it is from Leek and how long it would have taken by horse and trap...'

We drove along the familiar road, noting the site of the old railway track on our right. Rose Cottage, we realised had been very conveniently situated for the Waterhouses line. A scatter of small houses make up Bottomhouse - and it was no more prepossessing than we remembered it to be.

'But don't you remember that letter from Chris and Frank?' said Marion. 'After we'd been to visit them they decided to come out and see Fair View again to see if it jogged their memories -in case there was something they hadn't told us.' The two men had been good friends of Ralph's son, Billy, but they had not been back to Fair View for years and they were amazed how much more prosperous and gentrified Bottomhouse had become. The pub, they said, had changed out of all recognition! We dreaded to imagine what it had been like in Ralph's day. We spotted what must have been the farmhouse belonging to his friends the Blores, and traced the track down which Ralph walked with books tucked under his arm for Sarah Blore to read, an apple in his pocket for her children. Then we drove up towards Onecote and right - there was Fair View. The house next door was new. In Chris and Frank's day 'Alan's bungalow', where Sam Riley had lived before him, and a clutter of farm buildings had stood in its place. And, they said, the road used to be nearer to the house.

'Whatever is that hideous scar on the horizon?' said Marion looking towards Waterhouses. 'It must ruin the view from that side of the house.'

On we drove, through the hamlet of New Street to the main road and an ugly 'Happy Eater'. Brambles covered the hedges and the ditches were full of nettles.

'There was a butcher's at New Street in Ralph's day,' I told Marion, 'run by the Murfins. I found it in a trade directory. I expect Harriett got some of her meat there.'

We retraced our steps and drove down into Ford, just half a mile from Fair View. The landscape changed dramatically as we dipped down into the valley. The Hamps flows through the village and a wide range of plants grow along the dry river bed attracting lots of butterflies. Like the Manifold further on in Waterhouses, the Hamps flows through limestone, and each summer the beds dry out as the water flows in underground channels. The most dramatic flower there today is the butterbur. It was brought to Staffordshire by Canon Hawksford in the 1880s and from his garden at the head of Cotton Dell it spread downstream and then further afield - Ralph would have seen butterbur as an invasive new species whereas now visitors admire it!

Then it was back to Onecote to meet Graham Riley. As part of our attempt to find people who had known Ralph we had contacted various local vicars. We had discovered that country clergymen often had a fund of knowledge that we could tap into - besides, as I said to Marion, at least they see it as their Christian duty to answer letters! Chris Scargill, vicar of Onecote, had put me on to Graham. He was the son - or was it the grandson - of the Sam Riley who used to farm Ralph's land. Graham was renovating a cottage he had just inherited. 'Seen yer in the paper this morning' he greeted us as he waved us into a living room filled with paint pots, newspaper, packets of plaster, lengths of wood and tools of every description. While I asked questions and scribbled down his replies, Marion read the article. The *Leek Post and Times* had done us proud - a full page spread with a lovely picture of Ralph and his buddhas, asking for information about Ralph and his collections.

'OK,' said Marion, when we had finished, 'What now? We're due at Colin and Joyce's at two.'

'Back into Leek for a drink? I don't think I could eat anything after that huge breakfast - and Joyce is certain to lay on a wonderful meal.' Neither of us were used to a full English breakfast - but when it was on offer we were happy to enjoy it! However, once ensconced in Greystones we decided that we could probably still manage a toasted tea-cake apiece with our coffee!

Colin and Joyce greeted us effusively. Tea flowed as we swapped family news and caught up on the events of the past year. It was nearly ten years since we had first met up at Ipstones village hall and they had invited us to see their archive. In that time we had become good friends. But we had to tear ourselves away - there was work to be done.

The three tin cabin trunks sat innocently on the floor in the garage. Colin had set up a trestle table for us and plugged in an electric fire. I opened one of them - and the enormity of the task we had set ourselves, and the limited amount of time we had to do it in, struck us both. We hesitated.

'What do you suggest we do?'

'We-ell' I paused. 'Look, I think all we can do is sift through it all and put on one side anything that looks interesting or the right date. We can't waste time reading everything carefully. Then if we take it back to the Green Man we can sort through it tomorrow morning. Joyce and Colin are out all day tomorrow but they said we could bring back anything that we didn't need and leave it in the shed...'

Soon there were piles of paper on the table - and of course, we couldn't resist reading some of them.

'What on earth is this? *I yearn for you and burn for you - hurry home...* it's a note with a shopping list! Wasn't Harriett romantic!'

'Heavens - here's a list of John William's cases. I've never seen one like this. Have you?'

John William was a magistrate and somehow notes of his cases for June 2nd 1875 had got mixed in with Ralph's papers. He heard eight cases that day, and scrawled brief details and the sentence he gave each on a folded sheet of foolscap. George Harrison, Edward Crumpton, J.H. Lane, James Wardle and Mr Shaw were all had up for drunkenness and fined 5s or 10s [£30] - a week's wages - according to whether they were just *drunk* or *beastly drunk; threatening and using foul language.* Joshua Leggatt had stolen a pigeon from Arthur Scarratt and was fined 2s-6d [£8] and ordered to pay 1s 6d [£5] for the bird. Thomas Hand seems to have got off a charge of criminal damage to some roof tiles and Elias Mellor was fined 6d [£2] for threatening behaviour!

We found a copy of the short address, in Susanna's handwriting, that Ralph had given when Colonel Olcott came to Leek to lecture on theosophy.

Ladies and Gentleman, it began *as I know several of Colonel Olcott's friends in London, although this afternoon is the first time I have had the pleasure of meeting him, I have been asked to introduce him to you...*

There were incomprehensible letters from Ralph's theosophical friends:

What do you think of my device? The triangles? From Egypt think Pythagorous to X2 ling? If [it] *is beautiful I would like to see it sculptured in marble.*

I thought I would send you the enclosed, it is an attempt to [put] *this portion of Genesis into greater symmetry than the English traditions allow to be done. The result is that the amazing correspondence between divisions of year, months, days to the narration is made quite clear and any supposed unprobabilily shows that the reader <u>must go behind the literal</u> account for the allegorical meaning...*

There were mountains of correspondence about the living of Dalbury of which Ralph was patron - including a letter from the Bishop of Derby telling him he couldn't officiate at the ordination of a new vicar and a press cutting describing the same ordination and the important role Ralph had played! Piles of share documents and insurance policies. Copy after copy of pamphlets, poems and newspaper cuttings. Numerous tedious letters from elderly relations. But just occasionally we found an item that showed Ralph in a new light.

There was an invoice, dated May 1935, from Finneys of Longton for *8¹/₃ dozen* ('Or a hundred!' put in Marion) china mugs *Jubilee & Gilt, Badged.* 'Those must be the coronation mugs he gave to the children at Berkhamsytch School,' said Joyce, disappearing into the kitchen. 'We've got one somewhere.' She returned carrying it. Marion reached for her camera.

I am writing to you on behalf of the Girl Betty Jones, ran one letter. *...it appears to me that her mind has in many respects not grown out of an infantile condition.* Betty Jones was clearly in serious trouble and Ralph was pleading her case. *I have slept little & have been obsessed with the horror of the whole thing. Trusting you to have mercy...* he concluded. Sadly, we were never able to discover who Betty Jones was or what she had done.

'Oh!' exclaimed Marion, as she picked up a torn sheet of paper 'that's what we saw on the hillside. No wonder Ralph was upset.' She passed me the copy he had made of a letter. *With regard to the proposed Cement Works at Waterhouses,* Ralph had written, *I am writing to express my dissatisfaction...*

That morning we had seen just how ineffectual his protest had been. The cement works had grown and grown.

Joyce provided a delicious meal for us - pork braised in apple and sage sauce, creamy cheese potatoes baked in the oven to a golden brown, beans, carrots... followed by a totally sinful trifle. Colin remarked that custard was his favourite - anything with custard. It was lovely, but we dared not linger at the table too long - we had to finish our trawl through the trunks that evening. We were still finding photos and letters - it was so difficult to discard anything. At last, several hours later, and after more tea and sandwiches and home-made cake, we carried four bulging carrier bags of documents to the car and set off for the Green Man.

'I've had an idea,' said Marion the following afternoon. Did you hear what Colin said at dinner? About liking custard?'

'Yes?'

'Well, we didn't take them anything this time, like we usually do...'

By then the piles of documents had been sorted and divided. We had made notes and two large bags of papers could now go back to Colin. But first we had to call at the Co-op and put Marion's plan into operation. Into our shopping basket went a tin of Ambrosia custard, a tin of Bird's custard powder, custard yoghurts, custard creams, custard tarts, rhubarb-and-custard sweets - and a large, shiny yellow gift bag to be labelled, by me, in wobbly felt tip 'Colin's Custard Doggy Bag'.

'They'll think we're crazy,' I demurred, well aware that not everyone shares our sense of humour. We did rather seem to regress to our childhoods on these trips!

'So?'

Colin may have seen the joke on this occasion - but when, a few months later we asked to look in the trunks 'just one more time' we got the impression he was less than amused! But he was far too polite to refuse...

It had been a packed couple of days. Thor's Cave and Arbor Low were still to come.

Chapter 16
Fatherhood

'Look at this,' said Pam handing me a photograph that she had retrieved from one of the tin trunks the day before, 'What do you make of it?'

She fiddled with her long rope of turquoise beads and watched me as I looked at the picture. Ralph De Tunstall was seated in front of a carefully draped curtain staring into the distance. Obviously a studio portrait. On his knee, perched awkwardly, was a small child, about three or four years old, with fair curls to his shoulder, dressed in a knickerbocker suit made of what looked like velvet with a large lace collar. Ralph's long, elegant fingers hovered near the child without seeming to hold him. There was a distance between them it seemed to me - even allowing for the fact that people in studio portraits always looked strained. I cast my mind back to a portrait we had of Ralph at that age, dressed in a kilt, with his father in the uniform of a Captain of the Yeomanry - his dear Aunt Susan sitting comfortably between them in a pretty dress. That too was stilted - but somehow there was warmth, a 'togetherness,' between them. I was probably being too fanciful.

'Oh look', said Joyce delightedly. 'It's Uncle Billy!'

This was the Billy we had heard so much about from Colin and Joyce and from Frank Roden and Chris Tatton - friends of Billy's for some years before his death in 1976. Back in the late sixties they were looking for somewhere to park a caravan in which to spend their weekends and someone put them in touch with Billy Sneyd. Ever anxious to make an extra bob or two, Billy agreed to let them park in his garden. 'Mind, if anyone from the planning department objects you'll have to move it, quick sharp,' he said.

Within a matter of months, any mention of planning permission for the caravan at the bottom of his garden had him reaching for one of the swords hanging on his walls.

'If they want you to move, they'll have to deal with this first!' he would threaten. Fortunately for them all, the caravan at Fair View never reached the top of any planning department agenda.

Frank and Chris repaid Billy by doing things for him - like taking him to pay bills which he had not got round to dealing with. Credit was no problem for him - he was respected as an honest man, a gentleman. Nonetheless, one local newsagent was delighted when they went over one day and took Billy to settle his four year old paper bill! They collected things for him that he had ordered, they took him to outlying villages for pub meals and they shared evenings with him up at Fair View, sitting by the fire in the kitchen and drinking whisky - his favourite tipple.

Billy had never married and had inherited Fair View and most of his father's huge collection. He was the Billy people still remember as 'good company', 'a terrific story-teller', 'a gentleman'. He stared out of the portrait at us - his podgy young face unsmiling.

'And, here are some more obviously all taken in the same sitting,' said Pam - handing me several others. Billy was perched every bit as uncomfortably in each one.

'Are there any of Ralph with the other children?'

Pam rifled through the bags of papers and photos spread around the room. We had one photo of Stella aged about fourteen. We had no photographs of Lionel or Ralph as children though there were quite a few of them as young men, and strangely, there were none of the three older children with either of their parents, and there was only one of Harriett.

'There are huge gaps,' I said - thinking that this was not going to make writing a chapter about the children's childhood much easier at all. 'How many letters have we got?'

Pam counted and sorted them.

'Four from Stella, five from Ralph and seven from Lionel, one from Billy, one from Ralph De Tunstall to Stella and a postcard of his to Lionel, quite a lot of letters and postcards from Harriett to the children - and one from Father Christmas!'

I looked at her sharply and wondered if I had filled her glass once too often! We read the letters. Most of them seemed to date from 1909 and 1910. All the postcards were undated and the postmarks were smudged and unreadable.

'It's not much to go on is it?' said Pam as we finished reading and sorting.

'I think I'll give John Sneyd a ring when we get back and see if he can help.' I said, 'We haven't seen him for quite a long time, have we?'

Dr John Sneyd is Lionel's son, Ralph's grandson, and a retired chemistry teacher. We had met him and his wife, Sue, several times when we were working on *Finding Susanna* and Sue had helped us by trying out recipes for us for *Susanna's Cookery Book* - she is an excellent cook. We knew that when Billy died they had gone up to Fair View and rescued papers and other small items that were being thrown away. It was possible that John had some more photographs and letters.

A couple of weeks later we made our way over to Nottingham and were warmly welcomed by John and Sue. John had been busy since my call and had ready a number of things that he thought we might find useful. 'Useful' was the understatement of the week. There were five more letters from Lionel, some dated much later than the ones we had from Colin and Joyce and much longer. There were many other photographs - including a delightful one of Stella, Lionel and Ralph as small children. And there was, amazingly, a complete draft copy of the ritual that Ralph had devised for the Gorsedd he organised at Thor's cave in 1928, with notes in his handwriting amending it. On the front was a note *Stenographer's Copy. Passed by Mr Sneyd.*

In the early evening we made our farewells and set off for our respective homes. John promised to send photocopies of the letters and the ritual - not only had it been a pleasant trip, it had been a most fruitful one.

'Well, information's still a bit thin on the ground,' said Pam as we parted, 'But I dare say you'll cope!'

Ralph De Tunstall Sneyd, we were discovering at every turn, was a complicated man. Nothing seemed as straightforward when we actually came to investigate it as it appeared on the surface.

Fact. Ralph married Harriett Brookes in 1894 and they had four children - Stella, born two years after their marriage in 1896, Lionel born in 1898, Ralph born in 1900 and Billy born in 1906.

Fact. The three older children were sent away to boarding school at an early age - Colin said his Uncle Ralph was only four years old. And he hated it.

Fact. Billy attended school for a time but then sustained an injury. He was then educated - after a fashion - at home by a governess. Later he was sent to Leek High School. Notebooks of his that we have seen suggest that he was not a natural scholar - though he was obviously able, intelligent and socially adroit.

All that seemed to suggest a perfectly normal family. But was it? How could you have a normal family life when your father was a Welsh Druid, had been since the early 1900s and presumably took off to Wales frequently? What would school friends make of a father who had a Buddhist temple, Druids' altar and Catholic shrine in his back garden? And, later, what would friends think of the Druid ceremonies that he initiated, organised and made you attend? In later life Billy would tell friends that his father 'lived and died a Catholic but tried every other religion as well, including black magic!' Trying to reconcile Ralph the Druid and Welsh Bard, Ralph the Knight of the Round Table and the strange ceremonies that he and Harriett performed in their barn/chapel with letters to him from his sons which start *Dear Dad*, was difficult. Even more was accepting that the Ralph who signed himself *Taliesin Peredur Amadis* on his compilation for the 1928 Bardic Gorsedd was the same Ralph who signed himself *your dear old Dad* on a postcard to Lionel!

Edwardian men did not have much to do with babies - that was a job for mothers and nursemaids. But many men in Victorian England came from large families and had some knowledge of small children - their own siblings or cousins or young nephews and nieces. But Ralph knew nothing of babies until he had his own. But like most men of his generation he read to his children and taught his sons to be gentleman - though it is difficult to know just how much time he really spent with them.

As a child Stella seems to have been Ralph's favourite. She was his only daughter and very pretty, with striking eyes and a delicate face. But Stella had another side that Ralph was to see rather more of later on. Though she participated in her father's ceremonies, though she wrote affectionate letters to her *Darling Mother and Father* and signed them, *your loving little daughter,* she was not averse to playing tricks on Ralph.

Ralph was convinced that Fair View was haunted, that angels walked about in the house. Late in his life Billy told Frank and Chris about the things that he and his brothers and sister did when they were children. More than once, he told them, Stella tied a tin-can to a long piece of string and then, at night, dragged it up the stairs, bump, bump, bump, past her father's study - whilst her younger brothers watched and doubtless giggled. Her father was convinced that he had heard ghostly footsteps! She would blow through the ventilation holes in the air bricks; Ralph was sure that the whistling sound that produced was the sound of angels' wings!

Ralph told his children to draw any angels that they saw - and it was amazing just how many they did see, though perhaps not so amazing when you learn that they were given a shilling [£3] for every one that they drew! We have seen some of these drawings. Billy remembered his father looking at their sketches and saying, 'Ah, yes, I saw an angel like that just the other night!' It was a home where fact and fiction, reality and fantasy were inseparably mixed.

It is easy to dismiss the tales of ghosts and angels as yet another aspect of Ralph's vivid imagination. But was that all that they were? Stella and her brothers may have played practical jokes and drawn pictures of what their father wanted them to see - but who is to say that Ralph did not see and communicate with spirits that were unseen by people less sensitive and open to magic and spiritual ideas than himself? The moors above Leek are a strange place, and folk tales and stories about acts of magic abound. Stone circles dot the whole area, and ley-lines and natural energy lines criss-cross it. Practically anyone walking up on the moors and seeing those strange rock formations, the Roches, stone fingers grasping at the sky, can feel the ancient belief which still lingers in the stones and in the soil.

It is not surprising that Ralph should have been influenced by such a place - even Frank Roden and Chris Tatton, two eminently sane, sensible 20th century men, believe that strange things sometimes happened at Fair View. They have seen the evidence with their own eyes. One evening they were with Billy in the kitchen together with some other guests. One of the women in the company borrowed a torch in order to use the two-seater privy at the bottom of the garden - Billy had seen no reason to reinstall the indoor lavatory when his father died. On her return she clutched at her throat and said, 'Oh, I have lost my necklace - it's a gold one with a gold heart on it.'

She was distressed as it was of great sentimental value to her, so Frank at once went to look for it. He couldn't see it but promised to look again in daylight. True to his word he did - Chris helping him. They raked over leaves and searched diligently for a long time but no necklace was to be seen. A few weeks later Frank had occasion to use the privy himself. To his amazement there, on the seat, was the gold necklace with its gold heart - laid out in a perfect circle. No one could explain how or when it had got there, and thirty years later Frank still shakes his head in puzzlement as he recounts the event. Billy denied any involvement and they believed him.

Chris and Frank also remember a strange feeling in the house, not frightening but odd, 'as if there was something there that shouldn't have been' is how they describe it, though neither of them ever saw any ghostly manifestations. They said Billy's dogs always refused to go upstairs - they seemed to sense something strange and would sit at the foot of the stairs and howl. But that was many years later and we have no way of knowing whether there was any ghostly presence at Fair View when it was a family home, full of pets and children and guests. Certainly the family who live there now do not think the house is haunted.

Harriett, unlike her husband, was well used to children and she was diligent in the way she brought up her own - even Aunt Bertha Palliser complimented Ralph on what a good job she was doing. She and Aunt Fanny had firm views on how Ralph should educate his children. *I fear Leek will not be a suitable place for education,* Aunt Fanny fretted. She suggested they get a governess who would -

....be with your children all day and attend to their manners and deportment, it would be far better than sending them to second rate schools.... Such a governess as I have described to you would know the rudiments of French also music quite sufficient for young children and I think it would be a help and comfort to your wife to have some one to look after the children when she was looking after the household duties & your comforts to have someone to help her & I feel sure there are many ladies who for a small salary would be glad to take such a situation ....

Some months later she wrote again:

....I often wonder you do not go to some bright place where there would be good upper class schools for your children or where you could get a good daily governess ....

She and her sisters had been educated by governesses -

.... then we were all sent to a school in Cheltenham ... It was considered a very good school & there were first rate masters for Music, Drawing, French, Italian & German, Dancing, etc., etc. but in those days they were very particular about their being Ladies and not rich Tradesmen's daughters, if they were ever so rich they were not admitted but that is all changed now....

Cheltenham Ladies' College, she thought, might still be a good place for Stella. Ralph had other ideas. The children were sent to school at St John's Convent, Alton, which was run by the Sisters of Mercy. It was where he had gone to see the priests as a young man of 17. When Ralph's children went there, there were, of course, two schools - one for boys and one for girls. We do not know how long Stella stayed - certainly she was still there when Billy started school because she mentions going over to the boy's school to see him - but at some point she moved on to Oulton Abbey whilst her brothers went to St Wilfrid's College at Cotton.

Educating a large family was expensive - though much less so than it would be today. It cost Ralph £30 [£1,500] a year for each of his sons and in 1916 that rose to £35 [£1,450 - money was fast losing its value in the early 20th century], with extras for games, repairs to clothes, pocket money and so on. Oulton seems to have been more expensive - £12 [£720] a term in 1913. But Ralph was determined that his children should grow up to be good Catholics. When they were at home he and Harriett took them to church each Sunday - years later his daughter-in-law would recall how they were always late. As a child she remembered seeing her future husband and his brothers and sister straggling into church behind their parents, laces untied, buttons undone, part-way through the morning service each week! Once they were at school Ralph handed responsibility for their religious training over to the priests and nuns.

St John's Convent, Alton
May 22nd 1909
....Lionel sent Stella a medal for her first Holy Communion and I sent her a Holy Picture. Please will you come and see us soon. Some of the boys' fathers came on Thursday....

A month later,

St John's Convent, Alton
June 19th 1909
My dear Mother and Father,
....Thank you for the post card you sent us. There are 21 boys here. Please will you come to see us soon....

This was Ralph Clement, Ralph De Tunstall's nine year old son, writing to his parents. *Please come and see us* was a constant refrain in the letters that have survived. The schools the children had been sent to, unlike the one their father attended in Debenham, were only a short train ride away from Leek. Getting to any of them would have been quick and easy, but Harriett and Ralph De Tunstall were otherwise occupied - they seldom visited their children.

Other parents did. Possibly the children felt rather hurt, and their letters reflect what they were not getting by citing what other children had: visits, letters, presents and outings.

Charlie Walker's mother and father came on Wednesday... [Ralph]

Aloysus Lenordt's mother went back on Tuesday. Louis Adams's mother is going back on Monday, Eddie Tomkin's Mother has come today... p.s. Shall you come to see us on Corpus Christi for my First Holy Communion? [Lionel]

Will you please both come to my first Communion and bring Baby and the puppy? [Lionel]

Mrs Dobson came to see Ruth and Joan on Thursday and they all went a motor drive... I hope you will write to me soon, I would love a letter... It was Joan Dobson's birthday on Tuesday and she received heaps of presents ... [Stella]

But the letters seem to have had little effect and, disappointingly for Lionel, his parents did not attend his first communion - with or without Willie and the puppy! Oddly, Ralph and Harriett do not seem to have attended any of their children's first communions - though they obviously set great store by them. A postcard of Joan of Arc, posted in Leek to *Master Willie Sneyd* at St John's Convent, Alton, is inscribed *To my darling on the happiest day of his life, With heaps of love & all good wishes from his devoted Mother. March 14th 1915.* He was nine and it commemorated his first communion.

Like the letters Ralph De Tunstall used to send home to his 'Dear Aunty' when he was at school, his sons' letters do not say very much about their lessons. An early one from Ralph (the lines for big and small letters have been carefully pencilled in for him) gives some indication of his day. Perhaps his parents had asked him to tell them. Poor Ralph was writing under duress though. Although he starts the letter *My Dear Mother and Father*, the last sentence shows a little boy not fully engaged with what he was writing!

The little ones go down to play at six o'clock at night. We had French on Wednesday. We do our tables at night. Thank you very much for the letters you sent me. We had poetry on Thursday. Please will you send my prayer book. How are Mother and Father?

with love and kisses to all from Ralph.

Even as young as nine all the three elder children wrote in a well-formed hand, and their letters are both grammatically correct and correctly spelt.

None of Ralph's children seem to have inherited his difficulty with spelling. Presumably then, reading and writing were well taught at Alton, together with French, poetry and arithmetic.

Some letters suggest that the children were sometimes despatched to school in something of a hurry and without all the clothes and other things that they needed. Perhaps Ralph and Harriett had been away and they had been packed up for school by the housekeeper - we don't know. But we do know that they had to write home for things:

Sister wants you to send the rest of our clothes.

Thank you for the post card you sent us. Will you please send me my toothbrush?

We are holding the College Annual Sports tomorrow. Please ask Mama to send me the 5/- for the two of us.

Please will you send my cricket outfit also sports money?

I got 2/- [£5] worth of eggs from Reg last Wednesday as we had run out. I suppose it is alright.

And so on. During the war the schools seem to have charged extra for supplying the children with eggs and milk. Stella's school bill in January 1915 included ten shillings [£25] for *extra eggs, milk, etc.* Many parents seem to have provided them themselves - it was probably cheaper.

Other letters from Ralph and Lionel report how many boys there were at the school and the games they played - football, rounders, cricket and hockey. In one detailed letter Lionel described a game of 'Fox and Hounds' - a vigorous cross country chase with two of the boys as foxes pursued by all the rest as hounds. He had been chosen to be a fox with his friend and together they had outwitted and outrun the hounds - to his great satisfaction.

January 1910 - It is very cold, we have had a good deal of snow here. We have played football this week. We made a very good slide. I am quite well and working hard at my lessons. We shall have twenty boys here when the others come back. Thirteen in the big class and seven in the little class... How are Grandma and Aunt Emily? Lionel wrote.

He was keen on sport and obviously followed what was going on nationally as well as at school.

....both sides did good bowling but neither of the sides made many runs. We

got their side out first innings for 20 runs. I caught two for our side. They got us all out first innings for 11, and we made 22 for 2 wickets in the second innings. The Australians won England by 9 wickets in the second Test match... Please will you come and see us soon....

In another letter Lionel wrote, *Alton beat Oakamoor on Wednesday by 10 goals to 0 at Alton. Manchester United have won the English Cup this season.* Some things don't change!

Though we have hundreds of letters between Ralph and Susanna from when he was at school, there are comparatively few that have been kept from his children - Harriett lacked Susanna's sense of history and she had a larger family to look after.

Far more of Lionel's and Ralph's letters seem to have survived than of Stella's. We have six of young Ralph's - all written in 1909. There are twelve of Lionel's which range from 1908 to 1915. There are only four of Stella's, none of which is dated though it is clear from the handwriting and content that she could not have been more than about ten or eleven years old when she wrote them. There are none that she wrote as an adult or during her later years at school, even though we have heard that she stayed at school until she was nearly twenty. Only one of Billy's survives, written in huge letters in a curly, loopy script, in pencil on ruled lines on a ridiculously tiny sheet of paper. He could only fit one or two words on each line.

> *My darling*
> *Mammie*
> *and Daddy*
> *I like school*
> *very much.*
> *I am very*
> *well.*
> *Love & kisses*
> *from*
> *Willy.*

A 'PS' in violet ink in a more adult hand explains, *This is a little letter Willy wrote while I guided his hand. He had not time to write a longer letter to you.* It is headed *Alton Castle, November 1st* and probably dates from his first term at school. He was about seven.

The letters that the three older children wrote are very loving in tone.

Love and kisses from Ralph, aged ten. Aged seventeen Lionel ended a letter to his mother, *I remain your loving and affectionate son Lionel* followed by a row of kisses. The ones Harriett wrote to them are also overwhelmingly affectionate. Where Susanna had always started her letters to Ralph *My dear Ralphy* - or when he was older - *My dear Ralph,* Harriett was much more effusive. *My darling Boy,* starts one to Lionel when he was seventeen, ending *Heaps of love to my darling from your devoted mother HS. Darling Girlie,* starts one to Stella, ending rather more formally, *believe me, your devoted mother H.S.. Heaps of love* Harriett would write on postcards.

Ralph himself seldom seems to have put pen to paper, but when he did it was with straightforward affection and advice - so very different in tone from what one might expect from a Bard, Druid, Knight of the Round Table and eccentric collector that one is brought up short. In one letter Stella seems to have thought that she had done something to displease him. He replied:

My Darling Stella,
We were very much pleased to hear from you. I hope you are not upsetting your poor little self in any way; I am sure I have nothing to forgive my pet. If everyone was as good as you, we should all be marching to glory.
Your Affectionate old Dad, Ralph De T Sneyd.

Apart from the information they contain about what the children were doing at school, the letters also display, especially the ones from Stella, evidence that they were written to satisfy what Ralph and Harriett wanted to hear. As a little girl she craved their approval. In a letter written shortly before she made her first communion - about 1904 - she wrote to Harriett *I am trying to be a very sensible little girl and give you and Daddy pleasure.* In later letters the theme continued:

Oulton Abbey
Near Stone
My darling Mother and Father,
I hope you are both quite well. It was the Lady Abbesses feast on Saturday and the big ones went a picnic and the little ones played tennis and in the morning we went to see Lady Abbesses presents. It will be Willy's birthday soon and I will try to write to him. We have instruction every day with Dame Magdalen and we are learning a lovely hymn called Jesus the only thought of thee. It is Dame Magdalen's Feast on June 3rd and I am looking forward to it because

we have a whole day's holiday. It was Dame Bernard's feast the other day and she came round to thank the girls for their holy pictures. It is Ascension on Thursday.
I must now say goodbye.
I remain your loving little daughter, Stella E de J

Oulton Abbey
Thanks so much for the lovely letter you sent me the other day. It was Ascension on Thursday and in the morning we wrote a composition for Dame Magdalen, and after Vespers we had study and then recreation. I hope you are keeping the baby puppy for me for when I come home. I am learning a piece of music called Chassenett and I think I am going to play it in the workroom at Midsummer. We all go in for the examination in music in July. Miss Bladen has made my summer coat for me. How is baby? Give him my best love and a big kiss.
I remain your loving little daughter, Stella E de J

What 'E de J' meant we have no real idea - but we supposed it might be some sort of title connected with the Grail ceremonies. It was obviously of significance to Stella and Ralph.

Oulton Abbey (undated but obviously July)
My darling Mother,
I enjoyed Daddy's visit very much. Thank you so much for sending the eggs and the lovely book.... On Wednesday Father Patrick Nolan came to stay here and he asked me if I remembered having tea with him at Father Sperling's house. On Thursday we all went up to the guest room to see him and he told us ghost stories. We all go in for the music exam on Friday next so please say a little prayer for me that I may pass....
I remain your loving little girl

Though undated, the hand-writing in this next one indicates that it was probably written a year or so after the others we have quoted. But the content is the same. Little seems to be happening in Stella's life or education.

The children seemed to write each week. From the boys' letters we learn about the animals that lived at Fair View - pets were obviously a large part of their childhood and are frequently mentioned in their letters. They must have missed them when they were away - just as their father had missed his. On May 15th 1909 Ralph wrote, *How are Floss and the canary?* He must have received a reply for a week later Lionel wrote, *I am pleased to hear that Floss has had her pups. What have you called the pup you kept?* Others letters show that apart from the dog Floss, her puppy and the canary, the Fair View menagerie included goats, bantams, rabbits and a parrot!

As we have said, most of the letters date from 1909 and 1910. But the ones that John Sneyd had, written by his father Lionel, are later. They date from the period when he and his younger brother Ralph were at school at St Wilfrid's, Cotton. How long they had been there or when they left Alton we do not know. All that is certain is that by 1913 they had been moved to Cotton. From the letters it is clear that Lionel was developing into a young man with clear ideas of his own and an interest in many things. In a letter written when he was only twelve, he comments on an election. *...I was very glad to hear that Heath got in, but they say that the votes are to be counted again, but all the same, we are hoping that he will get in.*

In 1913 he wrote to his little brother Willie. It is a charming letter decorated with flowers, a bird on a watering can and scouts standing under a Union Jack by a tent. Perhaps he and Ralph were in a scout troop. We don't know. He says that he will be home in two-and-a-half weeks and will bring his brother *something nice,* congratulates him on his success in breeding rabbits and commiserates that his beautiful parrot has died, adding, *Ask Mama to read you this letter as I suppose you cannot read what I am putting down...* Willie was seven and doesn't seem to have started school yet - Harriett was loath to part with her youngest son. To his mother Lionel wrote,

Thank you very much for the cakes Daddy brought us. I hope you are keeping quite well at home. I suppose the governess is come now and then Willie is learning his ABC... There are about 90 boys at the college now, about 20 are new boys. Ralph is keeping quite well, he sends his love to all. The College has been fitted up with electric lights but the engine has not come yet... Please will you send us some more paper and stamps. We have plenty of envelopes....

Cotton College was strict and Ralph, in particular, was very unhappy there. In later years he would speak of the beatings they received and how they were always hungry. At night they would sneak into the kitchen and steal food and beer - though the punishments if they were caught were severe. Lionel seems to have coped with school better than his younger brother - maybe he was more able or better at looking after himself. He certainly comes over as a very confident young man.

There are no other letters until these last two - both written on the same day two years later. It is clear that by then Lionel was fully aware of the woeful shortcomings of his education and was not afraid to say so - though his letters are at all times polite and most affectionate. He wanted to leave Cotton. Aged seventeen he wrote with some style on the subject to his mother, whom he always refers to as 'Mama', and to his father - addressed more informally as 'Daddy'. These letters are interesting as they show his quite different approaches to his parents in trying to solve his dilemma - not at all unusual of course. To his mother - anxious that her sons, the sons of a gentleman, should be properly educated - he harped on about the teaching being inadequate and the syllabus restricted and not really suitable to a young man in the 20th century because of its bias towards religious studies. To his father, who would presumably have been pleased that he was studying religion, he chalked up the fact that the boys were not really suitable companions for him - a Sneyd and a gentleman. He was using a considerable amount of diplomatic skill to appeal to what he knew would impress each of them the most.

St Wilfrid's College, Cotton 12/5/15
....Paul Emery wrote the other day, he seems to like engineering all right. He says he gets paid (pocket money) to learn by his employer. Ralph seems to like the idea of being an engineer very much, in fact he is looking forward to it, and is always ready to talk about it. I for my part am perfectly satisfied to do my best whether success or failure. But here they do not seem exactly to take as much interest in a modern career (commercial) as they do with church students: for instance at my age I should really be doing chemistry, science, hygiene and other studies which they do not take here; but this is a church students college so they give the maximum of their attention to them.   How is Floss, she must be getting quite old now, poor old dogee. Please wish Daddy many happy returns of the day for us....
Your loving and affectionate son
Lionel xxxxxxxxxxxxxxxxxxxxxxxx
ps Please write soon as I have not heard from home since my birthday.'

12/5/15
My dear Daddy,
I wish you many happy returns of the day. I hope you are keeping well, also Mama... Stella came to see us today, I seem to have outgrown her. Have you

made up your mind to send me to Chesterfield, I hear from one of the boys
here that it is a rather decent place, so I am not sorry I am leaving Cotton in
a way, since the boys here are mostly of the shop-keeper class, and in general
are not well mannered. I am trying my best with my lessons and am looking
forward to the time when I shall reap the benefit of my not altogether pleasant
school days.... Please will you write and tell me whether I am leaving or not
as I should like to know.

I am looking forward to another theological discussion with you next
holiday, but mind not to make me a heretic.

Please will you come and see us as soon as possible as you have not
been this term....

Again wishing you a most happy birthday and many to come,
I remain
Ever your devoted son
Lionel
Love to all at home xxxx
P.S. Has Willy got his goats yet?

And that is it. We don't know what sort of things Ralph and Harriett did with their children, whether they went on train trips, went to the seaside, visited London, or Manchester or any of the other places that Ralph went to when he was young. We don't know what books they read, whether they grew things in the garden up at Fair View, whether they went birds'-nesting and fishing and so on. In fact we really know precious little about their childhood. All that we can say with certainty is that they all seem to have retained a deep affection for their father.

Stella stayed on at school until 1915. Lionel and Ralph left Cotton at about the same date, even though they were rather younger, and both lied about their age and joined the army. The Great War had started, Ralph and Lionel were soldiers - childhood was at an end and life would never, for them or anyone else, be the same again.

Some weeks later, I gave my completed pages to Pam over a leisurely lunch in our favourite restaurant in Market Harborough for her approval, correction, and input. It was the way we always worked. She read it carefully, then said, 'Well, yes, but what about the letter from Father Christmas. You can't leave that out!'

I had forgotten it. Amongst Colin and Joyce's papers was a short letter in Harriett's handwriting dated 1902. At this date this children were all aged under nine - and their mother had forgotten their Christmas stockings!

Dear Children,

I am sorry I did not come to you on Christmas Eve but I got fast in your chimney. I have borrowed a stocking from your Mama as yours were too small, and in it are one apple and one orange and one box of chocolates for each of you. I am sorry I have not got the Christmas stockings to bring, as I gave them all to some poor children and I knew you wouldn't mind. I hope you are all very good children to your Dada and Mama and behave yourselves when you go to bed. With love to you all until next Christmas when I hope to hear a very good account of you,

Believe me
Yours very affectionately
Santa Claus

Ralph is in the crowd at this Druid ceremony in Wales in the 1920s.
One wonders what his children thought!

Billy

Stella, Lionel and Ralph c. 1902

Stella

Vision in loft at Fairview, of B & M:
seen by Stella,
Iralph de Tunstall Snepp.
                                    The Daughter of

The eyes were blue.
Vision in Barn. The outer robe was
dark blue, and the inner robe white,
ornamented with gold, the hair was golden.

Stella's drawing of the Virgin Mary, as annotated by Ralph.

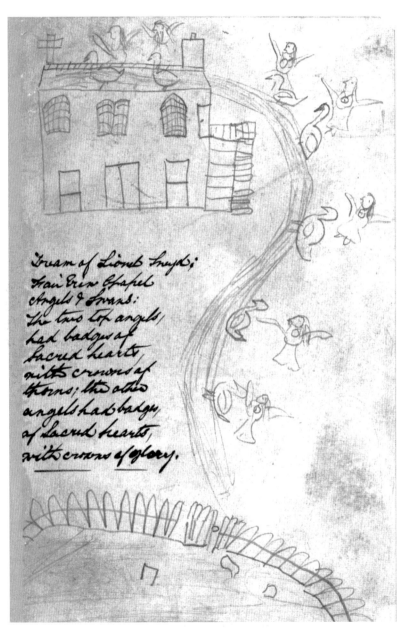

Dream of Lionel Smyth;
Fairview Chapel
Angels & Swans:
The two top angels,
had badges of
Sacred hearts,
with crowns of
thorns; the other
angels had badges,
of Sacred hearts,
with crowns of glory.

Lionel's drawing of angels and swans around Fair View.

Ralph and 'Willy', his youngest, in 1910.

Billy

Stella

Lionel and Ralph Clement
c. 1916-1918

Card sent to Ralph
by Lionel in 1917.

Chapter 17
Tracing Ralph's Collections.

'Oh goody!' said Marion. 'A treasure hunt! Lovely. Green Man again -will you book or shall I?'

It was her usual enthusiastic approach to research in Staffordshire. This time I had suggested that we try to see whether we could track down any surviving items from Ralph's collections.

We had already asked people who knew Fair View in Billy's day what they could remember. There were, apparently, stuffed animals and birds in all the bedrooms - people spoke of an orang-utan, an alligator, a golden eagle, a Tasmanian devil and lots of birds.

Everyone remembered the 700 buddhas. Ralph seems to have begun collecting statues of the Buddha some years after Harriett's death. In 1933 he converted his barn into a temple to house his growing collection, and the local and national press reported the story. Buddhism, in the 1930s, was still seen as unusual and exotic. There are a number of press photographs of Ralph and his buddhas at that date. However, given the size of Ralph's collection and the importance he attached to it, remarkably little documentation survives.

Many people also remembered the mummies. They used to stand, upright, on either side of the stairs. There was a little pump attached to each case that supposedly sucked the air out so that the bodies were kept in a vacuum. Until she put her foot down, one of the housekeeper, Sarah Riley's, jobs was to pump the cases out each week! Graham Riley, her great-nephew, remembered how, each year, his father was roped in to help Ralph with these mummies. They would be carried outside and 're-varnished.' I dreaded to imagine what Ralph had used and what damage it had done. Conservation work is highly skilled and scientific; I had worked in museums with Egyptian collections - no conservator of my acquaintance had ever felt the need to re-varnish a mummy! Furthermore, these two were said to be Ptolemy Philadelphus II and Arsinoe.

'Guess who they were?' I asked Marion after a session on the internet.

'I don't know.'

'Ptolemy Philadelphus II was the grandson of Anthony and Cleopatra.

Arsinoe was the daughter of Ptolemy I and married King Lysimachus and had the sort of life that reads like a Greek tragedy...'

'Go on.'

'She married three times - one husband was killed in battle, another murdered two of her children...'

Other accounts said that the second mummy was Antiochus II, King of Syria, Ptolemy Philadelphus' son-in-law who was poisoned. Either way, it seemed highly unlikely that the mummies of two such famous people had ended up in a barn on the Staffordshire Moorlands. We suspected that whoever had sold the mummies to Ralph had had a vivid imagination.

Fair View was certainly a treasure trove. Chris and Frank remembered Roman door knockers in a cabinet. Graham Riley remembered a huge red and yellow feathered Red Indian head-dress. We were told there were skulls and skeletons in the chapel. There were also heads of big game, we could see them in the photographs, gazing incongruously down on Ralph and his buddhas. Chris and Frank talked about trays and trays of birds' eggs and butterflies and our old friend Sebastian remembered a display case of brightly-coloured exotic butterflies hanging in the stairwell of the house along with frame after frame of samples of hair from generations of Sneyds. That made sense - we recalled Ralph's grandmother's diaries up at Keele with their snippets of her childrens' hair, folded into little paper packets and neatly labelled. Hair collecting was obviously a Sneyd thing!

All these items were left to Billy, along with the house and the lion's share of the contents. Lionel and Ralph were each left a number of named items - furniture, family pictures, silver bearing the Cotton crest, jewellery, a *King Lung* plate apiece (presumably one of the set of 18th century Chi-en Lung plates which bear the Sneyd coat of arms -most of them are still at Basford). They were each left some curiosities -Lionel had leaves of the 'Sacred Bow Tree' and a mother-of-pearl baptismal shell, Ralph's share contained an eastern helmet and cases of stuffed birds and snakes. Sarah Riley inherited a lot of furniture, some jewellery, ornaments, Sleigh's *History of Leek*, a metal chalice, the wireless set and half the cutlery, crockery and bed linen. Books, photographs and cases of stuffed creatures were to be shared between the sons. Curiously, none of the chattels were left to Stella. She also received a much smaller proportion of Ralph's money than her brothers did. Reading it now it seems a most capricious will - but no doubt Ralph had his reasons.

Over the years Billy sold his inheritance piecemeal. It was his main source of income. He sold to dealers and museums and to people who arrived on his doorstep and to others he met in pubs and to people recommended to him by people he met in pubs. Sometimes he got a fair price for Ralph's things, sometimes he didn't. Billy's chief adviser seems to have been someone called Tom, who wrote to him a number of times from Stretford in Manchester about textiles. We have no idea who he was. Tom wrote to the Victoria and Albert Museum in London about altar frontals and Indian textiles from Fair View, he advised Billy on their care, fumigated things and restored a silhouette for him. The two men seem to have been friends and Tom wrote to Billy thanking him for his hospitality, sending his regards to Billy's dogs - *your furred friends* - and telling him he was killing himself with overwork - *...work, work, work is not as noble as all that and, you will agree, it is too much for one man, yet you have in your house such amazing things that would keep you... Those silver crowns must be worth a deal. Keep some of them if you will but sell the others and invest the proceeds ...and live in a small but lovely place with the best of your stuff...*

But Billy could not bear to give Fair View up, even though, as time went on, he lived in greater and greater discomfort, sleeping on a camp bed in the kitchen which was the only warm room in the house.

We wished we knew more about how and where Billy sold his father's collections. He was quoted as saying the mummies had been sold to a museum in Vancouver. I contacted colleagues there and the Canadian Museums Association. Neither the university nor the town museum in Vancouver has any record of them - indeed, mummies are in very short supply in Canada. Only a handful of Canadian museums have examples - and none of them are the Fair View ones. Some of the larger buddhas were supposedly sold to America - to the 'Buddhist Society of New York.' No such society exists...

Billy, we suspected, was deliberately misinforming people about the fate of his father's collection - but whether out of embarrassment or mischief it is impossible to say. It may be that he did not want his brothers to know exactly how much he was getting for their inheritance, it may just be that he thought transatlantic museums sounded more impressive than Manchester dealers - Billy was known for never allowing facts to interfere with a good story. Certainly his activities caused neighbours to be concerned for his welfare. Indeed, one of the people who contacted us was the former Onecote policeman, now retired, one of whose duties was to go up to Fair View and check on old Billy Sneyd because he was known to be 'a trusting old boy who had a lot of dodgy dealers visiting him!'

We knew that what was left of Ralph's collection was sold after Billy's death. We advertised in the local press for people who had bought items at the sales - there had been several. The best stuff had been sold at Osmaston, near Ashbourne; less valuable items had been sold in Leek. Several people replied but none of them had bought very much. And then, a week or more after our appeal had appeared and we had given up hope of any further response, Marion took a call from Chris Tatton and Frank Roden. They'd known Billy well and would be delighted to show us what they had... We have mentioned Chris and Frank several times already and they have been enormously helpful to us - but in fact we did not meet them until we had almost finished this book.

As usual, we planned our Leek visit carefully. We both had many other commitments and it was always difficult to dovetail our free time - so we had to fit as much as possible into every trip. The first person we visited was a Mrs Boulton. She had donated some items from Ralph's collection to the Potteries Museum in Hanley. She lived in a large modern bungalow on the outskirts of Biddulph, in fact, she had only just moved in. We sat in her light, spacious drawing room sipping coffee while she explained how she knew Ralph's son, Ralph Clement and how he had given her some things from Fair View. She used to live in Longsdon and had been a neighbour of Ralph Clement and Ivy Brentnall. Ivy had been the landlady of the Unicorn pub in Leek where Ralph had lived for many years. He had always felt uncomfortable at Fair View and spent most of his working life living in lodgings. When Ivy retired they bought a bungalow together in Longsdon - they shared the costs, but, Mrs Boulton was anxious to point out, there was nothing remotely improper about the arrangement - Ivy, the ex-landlady, was a widow with grown-up sons. Ralph was a shy, quiet man, very well-spoken, a true gentleman, he kept himself to himself, liked his television and his glass of whisky.

Gradually the Boultons had got to know him. Occasionally he talked about his father and his childhood home. He brought oddments from his father's collection to the bungalow - a helmet used to hang in the hall there, she remembered. After Billy's death Ralph took Mr and Mrs Boulton up to Fair View to look around. Mrs Boulton was clearly shocked. 'It was so bare.

Not a scrap of comfort anywhere. Mustn't speak ill of the dead - but fancy living like that...!' Fair View was already being cleared and there was very little left - she remembered the chapel with the holes in the ceiling that had once accommodated the heads of the taller of Ralph's buddhas. There had been some fossils lying around - one fascinated her because it looked like a bird's nest full of eggs. Ralph Clement urged her to take it. In the end she took four fossils - they used to decorate her fireplace in Longsdon, but eventually she donated them to the Potteries Museum in Hanley. She had some photographs in little wooden frames that she had cleaned up, a fan that Ralph said had been his mother's and, perhaps as a memento of the trip to Fair View, some photographs of Ralph De Tunstall with his collections. There were pictures of him, tall, serious and slightly stooped standing in the chapel with the buddhas - we had seen similar pictures elsewhere.

'And here's one of one of the mummies,' she said, handing us a rather gruesome photograph. We gasped. That one photograph made the whole visit worthwhile. Ralph's mummies were not, as we had imagined, encased in painted sarcophagi like the mummies you see in museums. This figure was very definitely a dead human being, face and hair wizened and blackened but very visible, the rest of the figure swathed in loosening bandages. If they had peered into her glass cabinet this mummy's friends would still have recognised her. It was macabre. We understood now why Sarah Riley, Ralph's housekeeper, had hated them so much.

Our next trip that day did not appear to have anything to do with Ralph De Tunstall. Marion has long been interested in dowsing and we had been given an introduction to John and Annie Gilman in Leek by a friend who knew of her interest.

'*Anyone* can dowse for water,' Marion had assured me one day, showing me a pair of dowsing rods. 'You hold them like this, lightly -now, if I lean over that puddle they'll swing together - see.' She demonstrated. 'We traced the drains in our garden like this,' she went on. 'Now you try.'

I did as I was told, with absolutely no faith that it would work. I am notoriously insensitive to anything remotely paranormal. The rods whirled round and round, backwards, forwards - wherever I held them -over water, concrete, indoors, outdoors. As I had suspected, dowsing was not my thing! My youngest son tried - with similar results. Marion was incredulous but she had to accept the evidence of her own eyes. *Not* everyone can dowse!

John and Annie took dowsing much further than finding water - John describes himself as an 'historical and archaeological' dowser. They could find lost animals, objects, things in the ground - they could even dowse over a map without going to the actual site. We were assured that they were extremely successful at it. I liked them both enormously - but this was definitely Marion's afternoon, I decided, so I sat back and listened. We chatted, John gave us some notes he had carefully prepared for us and gave Marion an intensive lesson in the technique of dowsing. Then the conversation turned to what we were doing, where we had been, what information we were seeking. Anxious to explore the limits of the process, Marion asked John whether it was possible to work from a photograph. Mrs Boulton had lent us the one of the mummy - Marion fished it out of her briefcase.

'We'd really like to know where this is now, wouldn't we, Pam?' she said. I nodded uncertainly.

'You have to be very careful what you ask,' John said, 'and it's very important to ask permission of your subject before you proceed...' Annie was looking very worried.

'Billy said the mummies went to a museum in Vancouver,' I said cautiously, 'perhaps you could ask whether they are there?'

'I'll try,' he said, pausing for a moment to compose his thoughts, then he held his little dowsing pendulum over the photograph. Almost immediately he became distressed. 'Oh dear, oh dear...' he cried, rubbing his forehead, 'she's in a terrible state, so angry, hurt, confused...'

'Do be careful,' Annie warned gently.

John bent over the photograph again. We watched. I didn't want to be rude, these were such nice, kind, sincere people - but really, this couldn't possibly work! Thank goodness my museum colleagues couldn't see me now...

Then, out of nowhere, it hit me. A wave of heat, of airlessness, of uncontrollable emotion. I felt breathless, nauseous, tearful, appallingly guilty - for being here, for troubling this spirit, for being part of a culture that could treat a fellow human being with such contempt, for all sorts of things I knew but couldn't name. I was aware of Annie and of John, but I couldn't see or sense Marion. The room whirled round and round, I twisted in my seat, trying to escape and at the same time unable to believe what I was feeling.

'Don't be so silly, get a grip, this isn't happening...' said my rational mind. John stopped. Gradually the room returned to normal. He looked exhausted and strained. 'I didn't get very much, she needs help, she's been harried from pillar to post, she's 'over the sea' but whether that is Canada or not I don't know - Poor, poor soul. You felt her too, didn't you?'

I nodded foolishly. 'Is there anything we can do to help her?' I asked. At the time it seemed a perfectly sane query. And I didn't need an answer, I knew what was needed - she wanted a proper burial, respect, to stop being a curiosity, an exhibit. As a museum curator I was aware that attitudes to human remains in museum collections have changed radically over the years, but wherever our mummy was - and it turned out not to be Vancouver - those attitudes had yet to catch up with her. It was very distressing.

Marion was sympathetic - but untouched. 'You were as white as a sheet,' she said later, 'so was John. I didn't know what to do.'

'Were you in a fit state to do anything?' I asked. 'I mean, the atmosphere in that room ..'

'I didn't feel it,' she replied to my astonishment, 'but I could see the rest of you did. This one is your responsibility, it seems...'

It is. And, after some deliberation, I decided that we should not include the mummy's picture in this book. She has suffered enough indignities. But if anyone out there knows the whereabouts of a mummy (or a pair of mummies) impregnated with varnish and in glass cases made by a firm of joiners from Leek... well, you know what you have to do.

Our third visit of the day - as we have said, we worked hard on our trips to Leek - was to meet Chris and Frank. They lived in a caravan on a park south of Stoke-on-Trent. John Gilman advised us as to the best route to take through Newcastle-under-Lyme and Frank and Chris had given us detailed instructions about how to find their park - but I was full of foreboding as we set off. Marion was excited about her newly-won knowledge of dowsing - and we get lost when she's excited! Besides, it was a dark, wet, windy February evening and a caravan site by a railway line, behind a boarded-up pub, at the bottom of an unlit, twisty country lane sounded, at best, very easy to miss!

'How do you suppose George would feel if he knew you were going to meet two unknown men in a dark, empty caravan park by a derelict pub?' I asked her as we turned off the main road.

'Not sure,' she answered cheerfully, 'so I haven't told him! What would Paddy say?'

'I don't think he'd be too thrilled!'

We'd found the right turn but surely we'd come too far? 'Ring them,' said Marion authoritatively, 'tell them we're by a farm with a sign about breeding Aberdeen Anguses...!'

I picked up my mobile... Chris answered the phone at once. 'Keep straight on,' he advised, 'then there's a sharp turn, you should see a train going by just about now...' - there was a rattle and a streak of dim carriage lights somewhere over to our right - 'you're very close, see there's the park, turn right over the cattle grid, right to the end, I can see your lights, keep coming, keep coming...'

The park seemed deserted, no lights in any of the vans, no street lights - the perfect setting for a television murder mystery! And there, as they had said, right at the end of the row was a van with coloured fairy-lights looped round it. Chris was outside to greet us. He ushered us up the small flight of steps that led up to the caravan. Surrounding it was a tiny patio, not more than two-and-a-half feet wide but complete with barbecue equipment, chairs and potted plants. To the left there was a white painted shed - topped with illuminated glass ducks! Another shed to the right, more steps up to the entrance of the caravan. The door opened into a little entrance lobby with the heater full on. The kitchen next - tiny and dominated by a glass cabinet full of dinner services and other pieces of colourful porcelain. Past a computer, then through to the lounge with a huge television and an arrangement of oriental carvings, vases, and pictures over the gas fire. Patterned carpet fought for domination over a very modern standard lamp with piercing spot-lights mounted at the top, which glared down on the shiny maroon leather sofa and footstool. We were ushered down two steps into another tiny room which seemed to be suspended in thin air - we were outside the van again, at the back. A train roared by - shaking everything - and we realised we were right next to the railway line. It was the craziest dwelling we had ever seen! Seated at a small round table we had time to take stock of our hosts. They were men in their late fifties, casually dressed - Chris was sporting a wonderful pair of Inuit-style slipper-socks - quiet, pleasant and friendly. They brewed tea and chatted about Billy and the time they had spent in their caravan at Fair View.

We soon realised that Billy had struck lucky. He could not have wished for better part-time tenants, for Frank and Chris are the sort of people who make the world a better place. As they talked, it was clear that they had spent their lives helping - whether it was running the Regent Theatre in Hanley or visiting old ladies or organising quiz nights at their local pub. Billy had given up his car by the time Frank and Chris arrived and did not go out much. They spent a lot of time in the house with him, chatting and drinking, but they also took him out, drove him around and brought him dinners cooked by their respective mothers. Frank is good with his hands and he mended and restored chairs and household items that Billy had confined to the cellar. And in return Billy had given them things - the silver pen and inkwell which, he said, Ralph had used to write the poems in his book. Mind, most of the draft poems we had seen were typed - or in pencil on scraps of paper! A 'Saxon dagger' which actually turned out to be oriental. Locks of Ralph De Tunstall's hair. Billy had idolised his father so these were precious possessions. When he was dying he had invited them to help themselves to anything they wanted - but wisely and honestly they decided not to. 'The house was full of money,' said Chris, 'he always saved fifty pence pieces for some reason. And there were lots of valuable things - we didn't know what was what and we didn't want the family accusing us of stealing...'

In the end the only things they took, after Billy's death, were a collection of seedpods from some exotic plants Ralph had encountered on his travels that had been abandoned, unremarked, on the floor of the chapel. Frank and Chris would prove to be an amazing source of stories about Ralph De Tunstall Sneyd.

'Those are two of the nicest people I've met for a very long time' said Marion, as we headed back to Leek.

'Weren't they just!'

The next day we visited our friend, Jodi Peck. She had been at the Osmaston sale and had bought a sword which she believed to have been the one Ralph's father, John William Sneyd, had as an officer in the Yeomanry. After a while she grew to dislike having weapons about the house and sold it on. She had also bought some glass and china, a book, a pastel portrait and an 18th-century silver spoon - she showed them to us - but these were household goods rather than items from Ralph's museum. But most importantly, she still had a copy of the sale catalogue, carefully annotated with the prices everything had made - and what is more, she knew exactly where to find it! Jodi is incredibly well-organised. We thumbed through it eagerly as we sipped tea from china mugs and nibbled freshly-baked Canadian cookies in a kitchen fragrant with the smell of cooking. Many of the lots were household goods, or items like Jodi had bought, collectibles that would have doubled as household ornaments.

The catalogue listed ceramics, copper and brass wares, glass, pewter, silver and silver plate, books, pictures and furniture. An *ivory mounted elephant (damaged)*, a pair of miniature bronze statuettes, various oriental bells, vases and incense burners and the intriguing *Lot 155. Oriental Miscellany including Dragon shaped moulds, etc.* might have been curios Ralph acquired in Ceylon - or bought from Harriett's brother. Many of the other entries for brass jugs, trays, vases and bowls gave no clue as to their place of origin but might easily have been items Ralph picked up on his travels.

We thought we recognised some of the items - was the set of Brass Troy Weights the same set he had bought in his first term at Debenham? There were horn spoons, two ostrich eggs and a tortoise (we guessed they meant the shell) - was that from the tortoise Ralph had had from Mr Palmer when he was a little boy in Armitage? There was a pair of buffalo horns, a carved wooden tablet depicting a Buddhist monk and a couple of dozen oriental gods, goddesses and other figures in metal, ivory and wood. There were some of the weapons poor old Mrs Bloor had polished so carefully - *2 Spears, Pike head, Axe, Bayonet and Long Dagger, Small Sword with pierced hand grip and chaise* [sic] *decoration with leather sheath*, four more swords including the cavalry sword Jodi bought, an *Ivory handled Oriental Dagger*, a 19th-century pistol, a Yeomanry helmet and various shields and horns. Rather surprisingly, there was also an Edison phonograph and a series of cylinders - we guessed that those had been Harriett's or Stella's. There were two patchwork bedspreads, *a Priest's Cloth*, whatever that might have been, and Victorian underwear, capes and a dress. 'Were those Susanna's?' I wondered.

There were also books - presumably the oldest and the ones with the nicest bindings. No doubt the rest were sold in Leek or went to a book dealer. There was a family bible with brass fittings, two scrapbooks dated 1858 and 1867 and *Souvenirs of Belgium*, also dated 1858. We wished we'd seen those. 1858 was the year Ralph's Aunts Susan and Emily spent abroad with their father and step-mother. The 1867 scrapbook was probably one of Ralph's own, made when he was just five years old. There were also copies of

Edward Topsel's *The History of Four Footed Beasts* and *The History of Four Footed Serpents* dated 1658. We guessed they would have been the sources for some of Ralph's stranger childhood drawings. And Marion would really like to have had a look at Edward Jones' *Bardic Museum* of 1802 - she was sure it would have shown her where Ralph got his ideas for the ceremonies at Thor's Cave.

Over the next few days we made several more visits - but many of our contacts asked not to be identified for security reasons. We drove out to cottages hidden up twisty country lanes, grand houses, remote farms and little terraced properties in the back streets of Leek. We were shown beautiful, delicate pieces of 18th century English porcelain, Chinese plates and strange pieces of Oriental brassware. One gentleman showed us a watch that Ralph Clement had given him at Billy's funeral in 1976. 'Billy wants you to have this' Ralph had said, thrusting a green baize bag into his hand and hurrying away before he had time to unwrap it. When he looked inside he found a beautiful pocket watch in a shagreen case. It was almost spherical - a sure sign of age. 'It dates from 1702,' he told us, 'but I don't know the maker.' He must have been a very good friend to Billy to have been left such a beautiful piece.

But our star discovery, one sunny morning, was a little bodhisattva. He was sitting on the top deck of a what-not in a dusty living room full of fine antiques and pictures, and cluttered with books, piles of papers and empty wine bottles. The curtains were drawn to protect the pictures from the sun and a fire burned brightly in the grate. 'I bought this at the sale at Osmaston,' the owner told us 'fell in love with him and decided if I was going to have one thing this would be it. I had him valued at Spinks' in London - he's 17th century, a nice piece, they said.' The little figure was serenely beautiful, covered in worn gold lacquer and wearing an elaborately carved headdress. We photographed him carefully, on a stool in a shaft of sunlight, in front of an antique Chinese screen.

'Time to pick up Sebastian!' said Marion, as we climbed back into the car, delighted that we had at last found an item of real quality.

We had arranged to take our friend Sebastian out to lunch. He had helped us a lot on previous research projects and we owed him a meal -besides, he had known Billy and might have some anecdotes about Ralph. He had suggested we go to the Three Horseshoes at Blackshaw because he had heard they did a good carvery. Staying at the Green Man, Marion and I had already eaten a large cooked breakfast. Diana, who runs the B&B with her partner, does excellent breakfasts, good quality ingredients, not at all greasy - normally they lasted us until the evening. But Sebastian lived alone and we suspected he didn't feed himself very well - so if he wanted a cooked lunch, then that was what he should have. Besides, we had another reason for wanting to visit the Three Horseshoes. Christine - one of the many local people we had got to know in the course of our research - had told me that Ralph's two suits of armour had been bought by the landlord there and had been on display in one of the bars. Mind, she hadn't actually seen them for herself...

She was a keen local historian who had known Billy well and had visited Fair View. I had contacted her because I thought she might know the whereabouts of items from Ralph's collections. Her response had been disheartening. 'Billy told me he put the whole lot on a low-loader and tipped it down a mine shaft!' she said. 'He never would tell me which shaft though!' As time went on we began to think he had been teasing her. Christine is interested in mining and we suspected that Billy wanted to tantalise her into thinking that one of her beloved mines held his father's mummies and stuffed birds...

The carvery was a good one. We ploughed through plates of lamb and roast potatoes, gravy and vegetables - Sebastian had charmed the young woman behind the bar and she had given him double portions -washed down with glasses of white wine. We enjoyed his company but he had little to add to what we already knew about Ralph De Tunstall Sneyd. We enquired about the armour. The young bar staff were helpful and gave us the address of the former manager who had known the inn for over thirty years - if anyone knew anything about the armour he would. But he didn't - we'd drawn another blank. We seemed fated not to get to see the collections we had heard so much about.

Later that afternoon, after a quick visit to see Averil in the old people's home, we drove up to Basford Hall. I had some more documents for Humphrey and Judy - a dealer friend sends them to me, I copy what is useful and pass them on to the family. I always enjoy going to Basford. We are always welcomed with open arms and Humphrey has a generous hand with the wine bottle, which is lovely - for me, if not for Marion who has to drive - and, to me, Basford is at the heart of our research. A visit to Basford, where Susanna Ingleby was born and died, Ralph's boyhood home, the house he expected to inherit, is a tangible reminder of what our book is all about.

Ralph sat in this kitchen, he walked down this passage, he came in through this door, he would have known many of these pictures...

'How LOVELY to see you, do come in, we're in the kitchen,' Judy gushed, chasing the twins, Alexandra and William, and their homework out into the family sitting room, much to their annoyance.

'Now I've lost it!'

'It's your fault!'

'You've had two hours to finish that and you still haven't done it! Hurry up, do!' - the usual stuff of family life. The wine flowed, we were to stay to supper, Judy was roasting a chicken and there were potatoes and beans from the garden...

'Super!' we said, weakly, exchanging glances and anticipating our third cooked meal of the day - the last thing our waistlines really needed - but hey, this was Staffordshire!

Humphrey arrived and I handed over the documents. He put on his reading glasses. 'Now, what's this one about...?'

Soon the twins returned and Judy served up the chicken. We chatted about our research, asked Humphrey and Judy what they remembered of Ralph De Tunstall, of Billy, of the collections at Fair View... There was little that was new, we had had these conversations before but we never quite knew what would jog people's memories. We talked about what we had found and about the mummies and buddhas we had so dismally failed to locate.

'Of course, it was my father who put him in touch with the dealer in New York,' said Humphrey, 'he had all sorts of contacts. Yes, we did hear they went to the Buddhist Society - it doesn't exist, you say? Well, perhaps I've got it wrong. There was Billy, stuck up at Fair View with all this stuff - he didn't know how to get rid of half of it and dealers were ripping him off.'

That sounded believable.

'He brought a piece of a pirate ship for my father as a sort of thank you - he wasn't very gracious about it as I recall. 'I suppose I'd better give you something so I've brought this' he said, or words to that effect!'

'Pirate ship?'

'Yes, a Chinese pirate ship - it hung over my bedroom door when I was a boy... it's part of the poop deck. I'll get it, it's in the attic somewhere...' Humphrey laid down his knife and fork and went upstairs. William followed. In a couple of minutes they were back with a huge parcel. They unwrapped it. Bubble wrap and brown paper covered the entire kitchen floor. And there it was, beautifully carved and lacquered and gilt.

'I didn't know we had that!' Judy squealed delightedly, 'I want that on the wall, where can we put it?' She took a cloth and started to clean the carving, carefully, lovingly...

'That's what I like about this place!' I thought to myself happily. 'The unexpected always happens - and it happens at once. Most people would have said 'It's in the attic - I must look it out sometime.' Here it arrives immediately!'

The panel disappeared into the hall, followed by Judy with her duster and Marion with her camera. We'd just found another piece from Ralph's collection! Not that I thought it was part of a pirate ship - it looked much more like a ceremonial vessel to me...

'So, respected colleague,' said Marion on our final evening, pouring out yet more wine from a screw-topped bottle into our plastic picnic wine-glasses, 'as a museum curator - what's your verdict on Ralph the collector?'

I took a long swig of wine. And another. 'We-ell...'

'Yes?'

'We can't really say so in the book - but I think he was a bit of a nightmare!'

'Really? Why?'

'He collected all this stuff, but then he didn't look after it properly. All those early natural history specimens - I expect they just decayed. Those mummies - I'm sure we can't track them down because he made such a mess of them that any museum that acquired them had to throw them away. Mummies aren't meant to be impregnated with creosote or what-ever...'

'But he had some wonderful stuff - think of that little statue...'

'Yes, if you collect enough some of it's likely to be good! And the stuff that could stand neglect - stone, metal, ceramic, coins - was probably OK. But most of the organic material probably had to be scrapped and the textiles would have been in very poor condition. Tom, in Manchester, fumigated things for Billy if you remember, it says so in the letters, so there were insect pests in the house and they would have worked their way through all sorts of stuff - Harriett's furs - remember Chris and Frank described her fox fur jacket and muff? And they'd have attacked stuffed birds and animals too.'

'Oh!'

'And of course we don't know if he had any sort of system for labelling things - he'd collected it all so he probably knew what most of it was. But if you collect - say an Icelandic basket, he had one of those - it's not good enough to say that it's Icelandic, you need to know which village or district it came from in case there were regional variations, and when, in case techniques changed, and that information needs to be recorded. Ralph knew what he'd got, but no-one else could ever be sure.'

'But it was a private collection...'

'But that's the point about big collections - they're only private for a lifetime. There are all sorts of things that worry me. Conservation work that probably did more harm than good. And his lack of intellectual rigour...'

'What do you mean?'

'Well, for example, I don't know that I'd trust a man who was sure he'd seen a plesiosaur to identify a fossil! And - I suppose this is the big one - it was such an eclectic collection. No-one can know all about everything - yet, the thing that is really, really surprising is that he never seems to have asked for advice! I would expect someone collecting on that scale to be in touch with other collectors - writing to them, sharing information, swapping stories - but there aren't any letters like that. No-one other than friends and family ever came to look at his collections -no-one in any position of authority even knew they existed. He had this huge collection, a lifetime's work - and now there's hardly anything left.'

'OK -so what should he have done?'

'Well, the obvious thing would have been to leave it to a museum... or establish one of his own.'

'You mean he could have founded a Ralph Sneyd Museum in Leek!'

'Why not?'

All in all, of Ralph's vast collection, his life's work, we had managed to locate fewer than twenty specimens. It was such a *waste*!

Chapter 18
Ralph the Widower

On July 7th, 1916, Ralph and Harriett Sneyd set out for a holiday in Wales. They caught a train from Leek to Stoke-on-Trent and went into the refreshment room on the station to have a cup of tea while they waited for the train to Crewe.

Train travel was never particularly comfortable and that summer the carriages would have been packed with troops - men coming home on leave, others returning to the front, new recruits, and, saddest of all, the wounded, men with blood-soaked bandages, men with missing limbs, men on stretchers with attendants. It was a grim sight and one that must have been particularly distressing for Harriett and Ralph as their two eldest sons were at the front. Station refreshment rooms were seldom pleasant places so it is unlikely that the couple were much enjoying their cups of stewed tea - and Harriett was feeling distinctly unwell. Sitting waiting for the train she began to feel worse and worse. One hand was very cold and she was losing all sensation in it; she really did not feel fit to undertake a long journey. She turned to Ralph...

The couple returned to Leek by the next train. By the time they got there Harriett was almost paralysed and they had great difficulty getting her into a cab at Leek station, and when they did she was driven straight to the Cottage Hospital. By the time they arrived she was unconscious and had to be carried into the hospital on a stretcher. She never fully regained consciousness and died the following day. She was just forty-three.

Ralph must have been devastated; it was all so sudden. Within twenty-four hours, instead of finding himself in Llandudno as he had anticipated, he was back home arranging the funeral of his beloved wife. His two eldest boys were risking their lives overseas, his daughter Stella had just left school and was at the age when she most needed her mother's guidance, and his youngest son, Willie, was a child of ten.

It was a small funeral. After a ceremony in St Mary's, Harriett was interred in the Sneyd family vault at Cheddleton; they might not have accepted her in life but she would be with them in death. What must have hurt Ralph greatly is that none of his relations seem to have written letters of condolence - or if they did, none survive.

> *Oh my darling! Thou art dead!*
> *Darling, my darling!*
> *Like a bird, thy soul has fled,*
> *Darling, my own!*
> *Lest this life should fetter thee,*
> *Death has set thy spirit free,*
> *Near the pure translucent sea*
> *Where angels roam.*
>
> (*On the Death of My Wife*)

Ralph mourned, but doubtless his unwavering religious certainty helped him to cope, as did his ability to immerse himself in other things. For the rest of his life he carried Harriett's picture in his wallet - and in his memory he carried the picture of her as his soul mate, his fairy princess. Little Willie, his mother's favourite, heartbroken at her loss, had to cope as best he could. He had missed a good deal of his education but Ralph seems to have been less willing to mollycoddle him than Harriett had been. When Willie was eleven he was sent to Leek High School, staying in lodgings in the town during the week - boarding school in all but name. Running the home was left to Stella and the housekeeper. Ralph was not an uncaring man but he was spoilt, someone else had always taken responsibility for the more mundane aspects of his life - what else was a grown up daughter for?

Stella had other ideas. Within two years she was married. James Shenton was the local slaughterman, a successful businessman it would seem, even if his trade was generally held to be a particularly unpleasant one. It had been love at first sight for him. On Stoke station, in uniform, on the way to the front, he had glimpsed a beautiful young woman. 'When I get back I'm going to get to know her better,' he confided to a friend. The young woman was Stella Sneyd. Ralph may not have been entirely happy about his daughter's marriage but he was still willing to fight her corner. Stella's husband was not a Catholic and so she had married in a registry office. The church did not approve and she was publicly humiliated from the pulpit, Ralph wrote an irate letter to his friend, Father Sperling. *You will no doubt have noticed that I suddenly left the Church when you had ceased speaking on the subject of the three marriages in Registry Offices. I did this as a public protest, not against you, but against what I consider the foolish regulations which have lately been promulgated by the Vatican....*

Ralph went on to remind his priest how much he had given up to join the church and criticised the *tiresome restrictions to private liberty with regard to marriage, sex and other things which have been imposed on the laity by a dominant party.* Ralph was a devout Catholic, but where the Church's rules conflicted with what he thought right he was quite prepared to make a stand. Stella knew she had her father's support - for the copy of Ralph's letter to Father Sperling is in her hand. No doubt she was grateful.

Stella and James Shenton moved to Thorncliff and had nine children, six of whom lived to adulthood. Ralph and Stella saw little of each other; her children knew their grandfather mainly through meeting him in the streets of Leek. It was all perfectly civil and very formal. Visits to Fair View were a rarity, Ralph seldom visited Thorncliff and the Shenton children were never close to their uncles. True to their genetic heritage, another generation of Sneyds were almost cut off from their family. But in this case, the younger generation took matters into their own hands. When Stella's youngest son, Colin, was a young man, he met his uncles Ralph and Billy in a pub. They became friendly and he visited them regularly for the rest of their lives - and eventually, Billy Sneyd entrusted him with the precious family papers.

With his daughter married and his two elder boys away fighting for their country, Ralph became very dependent on his housekeeper, Sarah Riley, and her family. Sarah's parents lived at Ford and her brother Sam farmed at Onecote, but after he married he also farmed the land at Fair View and lived in the bungalow there. Sarah took over the organisation of the household where Harriett left off. She cooked, she cleaned, she looked after little Billy - and she seems to have taken charge of all the household finances. She even acted as Ralph's secretary, writing official letters on his behalf. Many domestic accounts survive, written in Sarah's clear hand, and she was obviously in charge of paying all the bills.

Looking at the accounts we had a sneaking suspicion that Miss Riley had done rather well for herself. Her wage was £1 [£38] a week - but in amongst the bills for bread and meat and groceries there were numerous entries *Sarah Riley - £10* [£387]. Joyce Shenton was with us as we skimmed through the household account books.

'That was a lot of money,' she observed.

It was indeed.

We talked to Lionel's son John. He remembered Sarah. She'd lived in Leek after she retired from Fair View - he was only a child and his chief memory was that she had a yapping dog. 'We looked after it for her one weekend,' he said, 'I don't know why. It barked solidly all the time and the neighbours complained....!'

Sarah Riley still seems to have seen the Sneyds as family. 'But,' John went on, 'I do remember my father saying he thought she did all right out of my grandfather...' Sarah would remain with Ralph for the rest of his life and she was an important part of the household - 'A wife in all but the bedroom,' said Joyce.

Sarah cared for Ralph faithfully. Family and friends always asked after Sarah and as time went on her role in the household became more and more established. She was tolerant of many of Ralph's oddities, but there were things she couldn't abide - his mummies were a case in point. She hated going near them, hated dusting their cases.

She could also be quite outspoken with Ralph. John Sneyd, his youngest grandson, remembers visiting his grandfather on Boxing Day one year. They had the tea Sarah always served to visitors - boiled eggs, bread and butter and a slice of fruit cake - and then Ralph and little John sat down with John's new painting set. But they omitted to clear the table first. A globule of scarlet paint landed on Sarah's pristine, starched tablecloth. She railed at Ralph - and her anger is something John still remembers fifty years later! Miss Riley was a force to be reckoned with.

In his will Ralph left Sarah £200 [£5,400] but in a letter dated November 10th, 1944 (four days earlier than the date of the will) he drafted a note in his own hand on two lined pages torn from an exercise book. We found it, in an envelope, amongst papers that had come from Challinor and Shaw, his solicitors. It is not addressed to anyone in particular and we have no way of knowing whether his solicitors acted on it or not - but in it he described Sarah as *a faithful and kind companion* and paid tribute to her prudence and economy and the way she had nursed him *through very many serious illnesses.* In recompense he wanted her to have *One Thousand pounds* [£27,000] *from me before the mony of my estates is divided...*

Ralph was not good with money as the solicitors' papers reveal - but it was not entirely his fault. When John William Sneyd made Agnes's marriage settlement over to Ralph in 1896, shortly after Stella's birth, the mony, came in the form of a trust - but the document implied that when John William died Ralph would have access to the capital. This never happened. Ralph's trust fund provided him with a comfortable income, but if for any reason he needed capital he had to go cap-in-hand to the trustees. Documents survive authorising, for example, £400 [£24,000] for the children's schooling in 1913 and £200 [£6,000] for Stella's marriage in 1918. The original trustees were John William's cousin Henry and the local vicar. Henry died in 1920 and his wife, Evelyn, took over the trusteeship. She was nearly forty years younger than her husband and outlived Ralph. For a while, Phoebe Dugdale, Averil's mother, was the second trustee - though latterly Evelyn administered the fund alone. It must have been galling for Ralph to have his intimate financial affairs overseen by two women who were both many years his junior. Furthermore, they lived in the properties Ralph knew he should have inherited. Phoebe Dugdale was Gustavus' tenant at Basford Hall - when she was not in London, or Cannes, or travelling on the Continent. Evelyn Sneyd bought Ashcombe in 1918 and lived there until 1925 when she sold it, moved south and married Mr Shove. Thereafter, Ralph only dealt with her through his solicitor.

Solicitors in the early 20th century seem to have fulfilled the sort of functions we expect of accountants; Challinor's dealt with Ralph's income tax, his insurances - they even paid his children's school fees. They do not seem to have been very efficient. Numerous letters survive complaining about the late payment of insurance premiums and taxes. Challinor and Shaw had been the Sneyd family solicitors since Ralph's grandfather was a young man. Mr Joseph Challinor was the soul of discretion, a diplomat who saw it as his role to make life run smoothly for his clients, a wise counsellor and a personal friend. Aunt Susan and John William Sneyd had trusted him implicitly. But times had changed. Mr Joseph Challinor died in 1910 and his successors saw their role rather differently. They did what Ralph asked but do not seem to have advised him in any way. And Ralph sorely needed advice when it came to giving his sons a start in life.

Lionel went to the Royal Veterinary College at South Mimms after he left the army, but he found it hard work - probably because he had learnt so little science at school - and he soon left. Ralph did an engineering apprenticeship at Rolls Royce in Derby. In 1922 they established a garage, 'Sneyd Brothers, Motor Engineers,' in Brook Street, Leek. It was the town's first

Ford dealership.   Ralph De Tunstall persuaded the trustees to give Lionel £1,500 [£50,000] and Ralph £800 [£27,000] of the trust capital to start the business, in return for the sons paying him an annuity of £186 p.a. [£6,000] between them out of the profits.

Lionel - by then Major Sneyd - was very much the driving force and for a while they were quite successful. In 1922 the trustees stumped up another £500 [£17,000] for the business in the form of a mortgage on Fair View. In 1927 Billy was 21 and joined the firm, bringing with him a further £800 [£29,000] agreed by the trustees. But the motor trade was badly hit by the Depression.   In 1930 the three Sneyds asked their father to apply to the trustees for more funds to keep them afloat. Evelyn Shove refused. She clearly believed she was protecting Ralph De Tunstall's interests, *he is an old man and in delicate health...* She obviously thought she was right to refuse to release any more capital, *I am sorry the sons have come to grief, but every business has bad debts & has to allow for these... I always felt it a mistake to start the business in Leek....*

It is hard to believe that a middle-aged lady with a private income, living very comfortably in London, really had a better understanding of the motor trade in North Staffordshire than did young Lionel and Ralph Sneyd. Without the extra capital the firm folded and Ralph De Tunstall Sneyd lost the whole of his investment. Deprived of his annuity from the proceeds of the business Ralph sued his sons. This was a legal device rather than a family quarrel (Lionel was writing affectionate letters to his father throughout 1930-31) and the three boys agreed to give him a rather smaller annuity, £150 a year [but still worth £6000], to be paid for with money from the shares they expected to inherit of the capital which formed his own trust fund! It was a most peculiar arrangement, entered into against legal advice, and it came further unstuck because Ralph De Tunstall lived so much longer than anyone expected. This meant that his income was much reduced in his later years.

Sneyd Brothers reflected its proprietors' eccentric background. For a time they housed the Fair View mummies - and various other parts of Ralph's collections - on garage premises. They also kept a monkey! Lionel had rescued it from an organ grinder who he thought was ill treating it - all the Sneyd children, and their parents, were animal lovers. It was a bad-tempered little creature and hated women; Lionel was the only one who could handle it and eventually it was sent to a zoo.

After the firm failed, Lionel continued in the motor trade, working for a firm in Southport and spending most of the week away from home. Ralph Clement did various jobs, ending up as the manager of the warping department of a textile mill and Billy eventually found work as bus driver.

All three of Ralph's sons had to make their own way in the world and mix with people their Great-Aunt Bertha - and their mother - had thought beneath them. But they were generally liked - and again, people who knew them described them as 'true gentleman.' Something of their father had rubbed off on them all.

When we first began working on the Sneyd diaries the person we heard most about from local people was Billy Sneyd - and no-one had a bad word to say about him. 'What a wonderful epitaph,' we said to each other. Billy was a drinker, well-known in all the local pubs, a comedian, a great raconteur who could put on the impenetrable Moorlands accent at will and entertain his fellow drinkers for hours on end. He had a fund of stories, not all of them true, and everyone claimed him as their friend. He could swear like a trooper but treated women with great respect.

When Frank and Chris took their mothers or sisters to visit him at Fair View, Billy became the perfect gentleman. 'He'd always put on a clean collar,' said Chris. 'The shirt might be dirty, but the collar had to be clean if he was meeting a lady!' They had liked him immensely. It was difficult to imagine Ralph De Tunstall with this hard-drinking, hail-fellow-well-met, bus driver son. Ralph was ascetic, he seldom drank and, as far as we could see, he did not have much of a sense of humour. He was a reader and a thinker; Billy was neither. They must have made an odd couple. Nonetheless, Billy had no choice but to participate in one of his father's more extraordinary ventures - his creation of an English version of Welsh bardic gorsedds....

Chapter 19
Ralph, Chief Bard of the Imperishable Sacred Land

'Cast your eyes over this, Most Learned One,' I said to Pam, thrusting a typed page at her as we climbed into the car. 'See what you think of it. It'll set the scene for today's jaunt, and with any luck you won't need to consult the map - we know the way to Bottomhouse don't we?'

As we drove out of Leek Pam read what I had written.

Thor's Cave, near Wetton, Staffordshire, September 1925

Clouds scud across the wide moorland sky, the wind rustles the withered summer grass and tugs at the voluminous cloak of the tall, thin, aristocratic figure who holds aloft the great two-handed sword. In front of him flutter the banners of St George - a red cross on a startling white ground - and the yellow dragon of Wales on a blood-red ground with the words 'Cylch Bardoll y Tir Sanctaidd Di-wyw', bright patches of colour on the barren hillside.

Behind the Chief Druid come the bards and bardesses, the men in green, the women virginal in white, their heads covered, and behind them the Welsh choir in national dress with their harp. The bardesses stumble on the uneven ground in their Sunday-best shoes as they carry the ceremonial Chalice of Inspiration and the Charger with the wild fruits and flowers. The bards hold the Knife of Efficiency, the Great Horn of Friendship, the Sword of Recollection, the Spirit Vase and the Spirit Lance. The land falls away sharply to the right and above them the cave's entrance stands open like a giant's mouth, boulders like jagged teeth at the entrance - ready to swallow them into its dark recesses. In the valley below, some two thousand people watch, spellbound, as the Druidic procession trudges up the rugged path.

Looking neither left nor right, the imposing figure of the Chief Druid leads the procession from fitful sun into the darkness of the cave and stops under the cathedral-like arches. Stepping forward in front of a natural stone altar, he half-draws the great sword from its sheath and in ringing tones asks first in lyrical Welsh and then in English - 'Is it Peace?' A moment's silence, then in unison the voices of all who are there fill the cave - echoes reverberating - asserting fervently, 'It is Peace.' He sheaths the sword and, placing it on the altar beside him, surveys the crowd...

Ralph De Tunstall Sneyd has opened what he believes to be the first Bardic Gorsedd to be held on English soil for over a thousand years...

'Well, it's all very atmospheric Marion - but we did say we weren't going to fictionalise Ralph...'

'I haven't! It's absolute fact - down to the very last detail. I've read two eye-witness accounts - both from people who took part in that first event. Amazing isn't it? Better get the map book out - we're almost in Bottomhouse!'

Pam studied the map short-sightedly, holding it just inches from her nose. 'I think if we turn left by the Green Man, towards Fair View and on through Onecote and then turn right towards Butterton we should end up at Wetton...'

It was a bright, very cold, early April day and we were exploring the area where Ralph had held his bardic ceremonies in the 1920s. It was the 'I think...we should end up at' bit that worried me! Pam's lack of map reading skills, enhanced by my inability to distinguish left from right, have got us lost many times in the past! Finding the small village of Wetton, some twelve miles from Leek, and Thor's Cave - which wasn't even marked on my road maps - did leave considerable room for error...

There was no river marked on the road we should have been on so I began to have serious doubts about the route when we saw a sign that said 'FORD. Cyclists dismount'. We turned a sharp bend and there was the river. But this was no ordinary ford. The road followed the river bed for a good forty feet. I edged along it, and stared in disbelief as a large snowflake drifted onto the windscreen. We emerged from the stream and immediately pulled up a sharp, twisting road and saw the sign 'Grindon.' We had gone wrong!

The scenery grew wilder and wilder. Sheer cliffs of grey limestone broke the skyline as I negotiated narrow valleys and steep single-track roads with hairpin bends. My driving skills were being tested to the utmost - but it was worth every strained mile. The trees, dusted with spring green, closed over us, the banks on either side strewn with pale primroses and white wood anemones.

The snowflakes ceased as an hour later we climbed up into Wetton and pulled thankfully into the Royal Oak car park. We gazed around at the cottages and houses of local limestone with slate roofs. They were all uniformly grey, a dead grey even in the bright, fitful sunshine which came between gusts of ice-cold wind. We went inside the Royal Oak. It was warm. Pretty landscape paintings and photos of old farming scenes filled the walls - but there were no photographs of the Druid ceremonies that had taken place here, even though we knew that Ralph had arranged for several hundred people to travel to Wetton to see them. Locals were chatting at the bar. The smell of chips pervaded everything.

'So this is where Ralph and Mr Wilson met to plan the ceremonies in 1925,' I said. 'Cosy - but I don't really see Ralph being comfortable in a pub, do you?'

The Reverend George Wilson had been Ralph's partner in organising the Druid Gorsedds. He was an interesting man, the minister of a rather 'way-out' Primitive Methodist chapel in Bakewell. He was a keen caver and pot-holer, and a prominent local archaeologist who, with a group of fellow enthusiasts, had been excavating Thor's Cave and other local sites since the early 1920s. We don't know how he and Ralph met, but somehow they came together and decided to create a version of the Welsh Gorsedds - bardic meetings - up on the Staffordshire moors.

'He used to go into pubs in Leek. Don't you remember that story Doug Pickford told us? His father used to meet Ralph in a pub. They got friendly - apparently they were both interested in the Robin Hood legend - they thought he came from Loxley near Uttoxeter. Anyway, Ralph asked Mr Pickford to teach him to play darts. Eventually he got quite good at it - though I think Doug's father said that he drank milk rather than beer! '

'That figures!'

We tried to imagine Ralph, dart player and Druid, sitting here in this pub talking animatedly to Mr Wilson, sipping milk and quoting the sixth century bard Taliesin as he did so! Ralph saw himself as the re-incarnation of Taliesin. He committed great chunks of Taliesin's poetry to heart and would quote it at length whenever he could get anybody to listen. He quoted from the poet in the ritual he prepared for the Gorsedds.

Primary Chief Bard am I to Elphin,
And my original country is the region of the Summer Stars,
Idno and Heinin called me Merddin,
At length every king calls me Taliesin.

I was with my Lord in the highest sphere
On the fall of Lucifer into the depth of Hell;
I have borne a banner before Alexander;
I know the names of the stars from north to south;
I have been on the galaxy at the throne of the Distributor...

Three of the Gorsedds had taken place in Wetton. We knew what the village was like in 1925 from newspaper pictures of Ralph, his handmaidens and bards, as they posed before starting the procession towards Thor's Cave. The actual colour of the houses was little different from the grey of the early newspaper photographs. Television aerials now broke the ridges of the roofs, the road was wider and better maintained - but essentially it had altered little.

The girl behind the bar had never heard of Druids in Thor's Cave - though she'd heard quite a bit about a lot of other things that went on up there, she said! She asked the other customers sitting at the bar. They had never heard of Ralph and the Druid ceremonies either. Strange that such extraordinary happenings should have so completely disappeared from local memory.

'Right, now what else have you brought with you,' said Pam, sipping her lager. I had done most of the work on the Druid ceremonies - Pam needed to see what I had found.

'These,' I pushed a pile of yellowing newspaper strips towards her - 'Here's Percy Brentnall's novel - and these are copies of newspaper reports of bardic meetings in Wales and Staffordshire.'

'Heavens! That's worth a LOT of Smarties!'

Pam studied the cuttings as I soaked up the atmosphere of the pub trying hard to see it as it had been over seventy years before - darker surely, but filled with locals, as now. Were the accents more broad? What did they discuss then? Farming? Rising unemployment?

'So, he'd been interested in Druidism since about 1906,' said Pam, looking at a Welsh newspaper report about an event at Holyhead in Anglesey and dated 1927. 'Ralph was there then as the representative for Staffordshire, and it says he had been a Welsh bard and member of the Gorsedd for over twenty years and *his tall figure has often been seen in Bardic Circles.*'

'Exactly,' I replied, 'he remained a member for the rest of his life. Do you remember we found his membership card for 1945 in one of Colin's trunks? He was fascinated by the Druids.'

Comparatively little is known about the origins of Druidism. Theirs was an oral tradition and much of it has been lost. Most of it what we do know comes from the Romans who wanted to make them appear as uncivilised as possible. Unlike the Romans, the Druids built no fine temples but gathered in open spaces near sacred oak trees. For the Romans, building was a hallmark of civilisation. Caesar, Cicero and Lucan all refer to human sacrifices at Druid ceremonies.

Caesar attempted to demonise the Druids further, saying that their chiefs were idle, avoiding manual labour, not paying taxes and spending up to twenty years learning verses and rituals and the pagan calendar by heart. But however biased and inaccurate the Roman accounts may be they are almost all we have.

Christianity absorbed many pagan festivals and traditions - including Druidism. Early churches were built on sites that were already believed to be sacred. Many pagan gods and goddesses became Christian saints - the early church carefully building on the existing pagan beliefs and absorbing them into its own canon to make it more easily acceptable to the new converts. So by the late 18th century when people became interested in the idea of Welsh nationhood and sought to recreate the old ceremonies, such rituals as survived had become essentially Christian. So they created new ones. It was Iolo Morgannwg, a Glamorgan stonemason, who invented the Welsh 'Gorsedd' in London in 1792. The word means 'circle' and referred to a group of bards who dressed in 'Druid' robes and met to celebrate music and poetry and the Welsh language. They became associated with the Eisteddfods which were revived in the 19th century and were then essentially competitions.

Ralph and Mr Wilson were heavily influenced by the Welsh Gorsedds but they did not copy them slavishly. For example, a photograph of the Archdruid of the Gorsedd Y Beirrdd in Ralph's handbook for Eisteddfods held between 1939 and 1945, shows a very different ceremonial robe from that which Ralph chose to wear. The Welsh robe was white - almost toga-like - and contained echoes of many other races and religions. The neck-plate is redolent of Celtic jewellery, the laurel wreath of the Romans, the bracelet is almost pure Saxon and the stole has many Egyptian images and hieroglyphs on it. The ceremony and the robes Ralph designed were almost entirely Christian. His was green, covered with the 'blood red cope' that he had worn two decades earlier as a knight. But he and Mr Wilson did try to introduce some pre-Christian elements into their ritual - the sword, the chalice, the horn, the spear and the alignment of the stones in a circle to satisfy astrological requirements.

Thor's Cave seemed made for their ceremony. Although it did not strictly adhere to the Welsh bard's tradition that the festival should be held in 'the face of the sun and eye of the light', Ralph pointed out pragmatically to sceptics that the procession through the village and the proceedings on the hillside opposite the cave earlier in the day did satisfy that tradition.

'Look at that letter he wrote to the *Leek Times*.' I pushed a photocopy of the very long letter towards Pam. 'He really did believe he was reviving an ancient local tradition...'

'I think modern scholars might take issue with some aspects of the history he put forward as fact,' she said, laughing as she read it out.

...many of the Romanised Britains were driven into Wales, Cumbria, and Cornwall, but the progress of the Pagans was arrested by a mysterious conquering hero, who united the British Chieftains in his defence of their sacred land, and who has been handed down in romance and legend as Arthur the Emperor and the upholder of Christianity.

The central part of Britain between the Trent and the Humber, with its almost impenetrable forests and mountains became the refuge of the Celto-Iberian race and of the Christian until it was eventually overwhelmed by the pagan hordes, and continued to be the home of poetry and song ...the time has come again to reinstate the Bardic system in its ancient glory, and as all such movements require a leader. I am willing in my capacity as bard and Troubadour to hold that position...

Still, I suppose it was convincing in its day!'

In another letter to the local newspaper shortly after the first Gorsedd in 1925, Ralph explained at length, and in most scholarly terms, what he saw as the connections between the myth of the Holy Grail, the legend of Osiris, pagan mythology and ultimately, Christian belief, and how he had tried to incorporate them into his ceremony. Both Ralph and the Reverend Wilson identified the area that is now the Peak National Park as the English stronghold in which these beliefs found refuge over the centuries, truly an 'imperishable sacred land'.

'Ralph must have simply loved all the dressing up,' said Pam. 'Think of all the letters he sent to Susanna when he was on his travels, raving over robes he had seen - Greek Orthodox, Jewish and many more. He must have had an absolute ball dreaming up the ritual, designing the robes and so on!'

'Absolutely. But what I find difficult to understand is just how he managed to get so many ordinary people to take part. Think of Nellie Birch and Millicent and Annie Blore. They were local farmers' daughters - but Ralph influenced them, got them there, and took them to Eisteddfods in Wales to hear poetry and music.'

We looked at the newspaper photos again. Nellie, who carried the 'Cauldron of Inspiration', wrote poems herself. She wrote one about that first ceremony. Her female eye noticed incongruous details - that Ralph wore sandals and Mr Wilson's son was in his scout uniform! Then there was Millicent who carried the charger with the first fruits and flowers at that first ceremony, her high-heeled strapped shoes peeping out below her white dress. She and her sister, Annie, were the elder daughters of Sarah Blore, the farmer's wife at Bottomhouse who used to read to Ralph when he was an old man. Their youngest sister, Nellie Hodgkinson, too young to take part in the ceremony, told us about his visits. We had even found one of Millicent's school books amongst Ralph's papers - she had written a long story for him about knights and their ladies. For Annie, Millicent and Nellie, Ralph De Tunstall Sneyd opened a door into a world far removed from the hard, repetitive grind of their everyday lives.

Dressed in the robes and wimples that they had made themselves - we had found letters from them to Ralph's housekeeper, Sarah Riley, asking for her help in choosing suitable material as they did not think it proper to worry 'Mr Sneyd' with such petty matters - the pretty girls stood smiling beside him. The photograph had probably been taken only a few feet away from where we were sitting.

Where Ralph was the dreamer, the artist, the poet, George Wilson was the man of action, the organiser. Between them they created a Midland Druid circle - the 'Bardic Circle of the Imperishable Sacred Land.' They must have been incredibly excited to feel that they were bringing to life again long-forgotten beliefs. To bring about their dream they needed each other's strengths - but in some ways Ralph was to be a sore trial to his friend.

Bourne House, Bakewell,
31st August

Dear Mr Sneyd,
I greatly appreciate all the trouble you are taking about the Gorsedd; without your help with reference to the dresses etc, we should find some difficulty in carrying this matter through properly.

But I must ask you to be good enough as to stick to the rules and decisions agreed upon. Confusion must not be introduced. You are sending out too many tickets. I have taken measurements and there will be room for no more than the 100 persons we agreed to invite apart from the choir and our own party...

You agreed that the press-men should be strictly excluded except for a representative of The Sentinel and the Daily Mail. This, under no circumstances, must be departed from. No cameras must be admitted except that the press representatives take a couple of good photographs for our own members only... Will you be good enough to secure the attendance of an additional police officer to assist the local constable in maintaining order? I am arranging for one way only into the cave, and it will be necessary for a policeman to stand for two hours to keep out all but ticket holders.

Please also send me a sketch of the stone circle to be placed in true orientation on the site of the old British Village at the top of Thor's Cliff... There need not have been any advertisement of the Gorsedd. I could have got the event into a dozen papers beforehand, but an unmanageable crowd would have been the result. Will you please try to be at Wetton on the 10th and 11th of September so that everything may be in perfect order, and every cause for confusion may be obviated,
Yours Fraternally,
George H Wilson

'Poor Mr Wilson!'

'Oh, I like this,' said Pam, 'What a wonderful description of Ralph and the way he planned the ceremony.'

'Yes, I thought you'd like that.'

She had moved on to Percy Brentnall's novel. Percy was heavily involved in the Gorsedds. He wrote the music for the Gorsedd Prayer which Ralph translated into English, he did much of the menial work of organisation and he carried the 'Great Horn' and the 'Sacred Spear' in the procession. Some time later he wrote a novel and many of the episodes in it are obviously closely based on Ralph's activities and the Thor's cave ceremony. The main character in his story, Dmitri Kortlander, is obviously Ralph - even down to the last detail of his clothing. But what was unexpected and new was the vivid description he gave of the way Dmitri/Ralph worked when planning his ceremony.

...his room was littered with papers, the toilet requisites had been removed from the dressing table, and in their place stood a typewriter, which machine, had by the look of it, written millions of words. It was clicking away; the elderly gentleman seemingly very engaged on what he was writing... the speed at which he manipulated the keys was certainly slow for he composed his lines without making any serious notes beforehand... his poetry had had good sales yet for a considerable time his writing had been dormant...

'I'd never thought of him typing you know,' I said. 'More quill pen!'

He had the bearing of an aristocrat, but he was a mystic. His clothes were cut to ancient style; he had worn that particular pattern for years. His crowning glory would appear to be his long white flowing hair, but his voice and manner of speech were certainly very arresting. The check design of his clothes seemed to fit in correctly with his entire personality, and, although commanding, the long black cloak he wore as an over-garment together with the wide brimmed hat stamped him out as a thinker, an author. He was not very conversant on modern matters; his mind, and his work bore on the past - bore on the mysterious, but at all times he was a gentleman in the full sense of the word. Quiet and inoffensive he was a lovely person to know. An aristocrat he was certainly, but he never allowed class distinctions to come into his path. He was just the same with a lord or duke as he would be with a newsboy... Perhaps some people thought him strange, but everyone always said he was a perfect gentleman - not just an ordinary gentleman - there was something about him that meant more than that ...there was something about him that was delightfully different; wonderfully strange.

Percy Brentnall was obviously hugely impressed by Ralph. His novel was invaluable and we were incredibly lucky to be able to read it. It was never published in book form but was serialised in a local paper. One of Percy's relatives cut out the extracts as they appeared and stitched them together. When she heard that we were writing about Ralph she gave them to her sister-in-law, Jean Bode, who passed them on to us.

Percy talks of 'The Chief Bard's secretary' - almost certainly himself - driving to Wetton to take articles in preparation for the ritual ...*the incense Thurifer, the Sacred Sword of Peace, the Grail Cup, the Charger on which the honey bread would be carried, the Cauldron of Inspiration which would contain cider, honey, meal, rowan, and milk...*

The description of the liquid in the cauldron is interesting - it closely resembles mead, a potent fermented drink made by Vikings which they sweetened with honey and flavoured with meadowsweet. Ralph seems instead to have used the bitter berries of the rowan - the witches' tree. Incense was burned in the cave. Heady stuff.

Chapter thirteen of the novel begins:

Crowds of people had come to the Manifold Valley on this Sunday. The little, picturesque, light railway had brought a load of sight-seers, some in sympathy with the movement, others perhaps with ridiculous intent, and fashionable motor-cars and motor-cycles, had brought their occupants to Wetton... some had invaded the village in motor-buses, while some had walked from Leek and from Buxton...

Amongst those in Bardic robes, the central figure was that of the Venerable Chief Bard, tall, and aristocratic in appearance, and with a wealth of snow white hair, he looked strikingly impressive in his crimson figured robe.

Cinematograph firms had sent their representatives to 'shoot picturesque trifles for their topicals' and the camera men, with characteristic enterprise, forced their way into the cave...

After having left the roadway, the procession had had to traverse several fields before it began the steep, treacherous ascent to the cave. After an arduous and hazardous climb the cave was at length reached. The Chief Bard took up a commanding position by a huge pillar of rock...

Only a limited number of the general public could be admitted to the cave to witness the mystical rites... a crowd of several hundreds watched the proceedings from the cave's mouth.

On the roadway, across the valley, were many other sight-seers, who did not venture on the strenuous journey to the cave...

Turning his face to the altar the Chief Bard proceeded with the next stage of the ritual which included several prayers, impressively and solemnly intoned in a firm, musical voice...

> *Here Incense rises*
> *Now it diffuses*
> *Its mystic Glory*
> *Spreading afar...*

Dmitri/Ralph had written the prayers himself.

Towards the end of the ceremony the bards and bardesses presented their symbolic gifts to the Chief Bard, to be blessed *...the Horn of Friendship, the Basket of Plenty, the Knife of Efficiency, the Cauldron of Inspiration, the Sword of Recollection, the Dish of Contemplation, the Spirit Lance and the Spirit vase. Having received the offerings, the Chief Bard placed them on the altar, and recited, in a thrilling, commanding, voice...*

> *Milk and honey, fruits and flowers*
> *Cake and ever-sparkling mead*

From Escavlon's fair bowers
Are a noble gift indeed.

Scarlet Rowan, berries bright,
Bardic apples, too are here,
Tinged with green, and crimson Light,
Drink from both in goblets clear.

Rose and lily fair,
Oak and mistletoe one sees,
Food and drink from barley rare,
Truly blessed gifts are these ...

From the newspaper accounts we know that after the main ceremony the 'Recorder', Mr Wilson, addressed the crowd about the historical significance of the valley and of Thor's Cave. Ralph admitted six new members into the Bardic circle - four bards and two bardesses. They came forward, bowing in front of him. He clasped their hands crosswise and said to each one, 'O, thou seeker of the Light, I initiate you into the Bardic Circle of the Imperishable Sacred Land.' More singing, more prayers, and the ceremony ended with the Chief Bard's own, heartfelt prayer,

For all who have gone before
For all who are with us now
For all who are yet to come
We beseech thee hear us...

The crowd dispersed and those who had taken part in the memorable event wended their way back across the windy moor to Wetton and retired to a local inn owned by a Mr Peter Bradbury where they were given tea. The first Gorsedd of Ralph's new Druid order was over.

'Right. I'm ready,' said Pam at last. 'Let's go and have a look at the cave.'

I packed up the papers we had spread over the table and with one last look at the room we left the warmth of the pub. It was cold, very cold outside and the wind sliced at our legs as we hurried to the car.

The barmaid had given us directions to the cave and I drove slowly out of the village so that we could observe the fields and the footpaths over them to the hills beyond. She had told us that there was one path that ran from the village towards the back of the cave and suggested that the procession would have gone that way. I stopped the car - we braved the icy wind and walked over to the hedge. We could see a path. Was that the direction they had taken? Back in the car we rounded a sharp bend in the road and gasped. Across the other side of the ravine the near-perfect arch of the mouth of the huge cave gaped at us - as if Thor was still howling at the world - black, ominous, stark against the sheer face of the grey cliff. Awesome.

'Stop at that lay-by,' cried Pam excitedly, reaching for her camera. 'This is magnificent - so much more dramatic than any of the photos we've seen.'

As I pulled into the lay-by Thor confirmed his presence. Without any warning, and coming from nowhere at all it seemed, a blizzard swirled angrily about us - filling and obliterating the valley, the cave, and for a few minutes the road itself, in a white-out. I clutched the steering wheel in disbelief. It would have been worthy of a sequence from a Hitchcock psychological thriller I felt. We were in very strange territory.

> *Once the baleful fire was gleaming,*
> *In that cavern far on high*
> *In yon mighty rock, and cauldrons*
> *For the awful gods stood nigh;*
> *Once the crimson blood was streaming...*

...was how Ralph had described the ancient ceremonies on the Moorlands in his poem *The Central Realm of England*. Local legend has it that human sacrifices were carried out in Thor's Cave and on the moors around. We could believe it. Now we could see what had so excited Ralph and why he had chosen this place for what he believed to be the first Druid ceremony to be held in England for over a thousand years.

We waited for the blizzard to clear and headed downhill.

'Now what?' asked Pam.

'Well ... another meeting was held the following year. The crowds were even greater and both Mr Wilson and Ralph must have felt that the spirit of the event was being spoiled and that it was in danger of becoming a circus, so in 1927 they moved it to Arbor Low in Derbyshire - a magnificent stone circle not very many miles from Thor's cave. Have you ever been there?'

'No, don't think so. Are you suggesting that we should...?'

'Read this,' I said, handing her a press cutting.

Saturday June 25th 1927

ENGLAND'S FIRST BARDIC CIRCLE
Desolate Scene at Peak Ceremony
Service at Ancient Ring of Stones

The extension of the bardic movement in this country entered upon a further stage on Saturday when the bards of the first bardic circle met on an isolated spot in the Peak at Arbor Low, near Bakewell in Derbyshire. Here there is a stone circle which is held to be second in importance only to those at Stonehenge and Avebury....

The Chief Bard of this circle is Mr Ralph de Tunstall Sneyd, himself a member of the Welsh Order of Bards and the recorder is the Rev George Wilson a well known Primitive Methodist Minister. There are 11 other bards in the circle including some women.

Saturday's ceremonies were carried through with due ceremony and in some secrecy ...situated in one of the bleakest and most exposed parts of the Peakland with an uninterrupted view of an immense stretch of undulating country the circle is almost ideally placed for astronomical observations...

Less than about half-a-dozen outsiders witnessed the meeting of the bards in this historic spot. A bitterly cold wind was blowing and rain fell at times... A farmhouse close by was the assembling ground, and from this the procession started, the good folk at the farm and one or two others being the only spectators of the gathering. Slowly and with great solemnity and dignity the bards walked in procession across three fields to Arbor Low, the men bards wearing green robes the women white edged with green. The red and gold banner of the bards bearing the inscription Cylch Barddol v Tir Sanctaidd Dwly headed the procession showing up weirdly against the more sombre background of the cloudy sky... Two new bards were initiated, one a man and one a woman - placing their hands in those of the Chief Bard. However, because of the unfavourable weather much of the ceremony and bardic ritual had to be omitted.

'They must have been mad!' said Pam. 'Do we know who was initiated?'

'Strangely enough we do. I did some digging about and guess who it was - Lionel and his wife, Irene.'

'Good heavens - I thought Lionel was far too down to earth... I suppose he had to humour his father...'

With the odd flake of snow still drifting over the car we pulled the dog-eared map book off the back seat and looked for Arbor Low.

'Well, if they didn't want too many people there you can see why they chose it,' I said. 'It's in the middle of nowhere!'

Arbor Low is, in fact, only a few miles from Wetton and we found it without too much difficulty. We pulled into the farm yard that Ralph had known and which now acts as a parking lot for the ancient stones, and in the fast fading light we braved the wind and looked over the rugged windswept landscape, trying to imagine Ralph, his son Lionel, Irene, Mr Wilson, the pretty handmaidens and Percy Brentnall trudging out in the pouring rain to celebrate the arcane ceremony that Ralph and Mr Wilson had invented. It beggared belief!

'I need tea,' I said. 'And somewhere halfway civilised, and WARM...'

The following year, and the last year that we can be certain that any ceremony took place, the Gorsedd was moved back to Thor's Cave. John Sneyd still has a copy of the ritual for the 1928 ceremony. Ralph had been ill for some time before it. Most of the work seems to have fallen on George Wilson's shoulders - perhaps it all got too much.

Haddon Road, Bakewell,
29th August 1928

Dear Chief,

I am distressed to hear you are unwell. Do please get fit for Sunday...

I am giving much time to arranging affairs for Gorsedd staying up late after my usual duties. It was midnight last night when I got the last letter written and I have done another large batch this morning. The press has been attended to and Gorsedd will be announced in all leading dailies and weeklies this midweek, and six to eight papers will have representation at Wetton... Do your best to get a choir ...Your sons' presence is indispensable and any compilations - poems etc ought to be in soon... You and Mr Rowson will be at Wetton by noon on Saturday I hope.

Will you ask Mr Brentnall to get last year's programmes from whoever has the remainder, and paste typewritten slips over the bottom of each title page giving the date. I enclose a slip giving wording and size. This is very important so that we may have programmes for sale.

I have secured a large reading room in case it is wet and may be able to put a circle of stones fixed in the true alignment on Friday or Saturday.

Sincere best wishes for your health,
Fraternally yours
G.H. Wilson.

And there the correspondence between Ralph and the Reverend Wilson seems to have ended. We have been unable to find any other records of Druid meetings amongst Ralph's letters and cuttings - though it does look as if he might have tried to organise another ceremony in 1929 as a taxi bill for that year survives and on September 1st and 3rd he hired a car and a driver (from his sons' garage) to drive him to Wetton. The round trip cost him £2 [£76] each time. Maybe organising the Gorsedds was just becoming too expensive.

Whatever we may think of the ceremonies that Ralph Sneyd and George Wilson created in the 1920s, one thing is certain - they did no one the slightest harm. They celebrated the good things - brotherhood, peace, beauty, music, appreciation of all life. They may even have made some of the gawping onlookers think. For Ralph, those ceremonies were the culmination of a lifetime of study and dreaming. After the ceremonies ceased he kept all the robes he had designed. They lay in a chest in his bedroom and were there until the day he died. He had, in effect, created his own 'church', ministry and set of ceremonies. No mean feat!

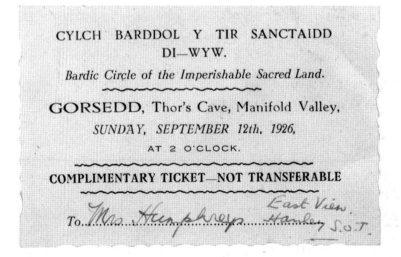

CYLCH BARDDOL Y TIR SANCTAIDD
DI—WYW.

Bardic Circle of the Imperishable Sacred Land.

GORSEDD, Thor's Cave, Manifold Valley,
SUNDAY, SEPTEMBER 12th, 1926,
AT 2 O'CLOCK.

COMPLIMENTARY TICKET—NOT TRANSFERABLE

To...*Mrs. Humphreys*... *East View,* *Hanley* S.O.T.

Chapter 20
Ralph's Spiritual World

Medical help might hasten your return to health - who is your doctor?
Reverend Wilson wrote in exasperation when Ralph was ill and it looked as if
he would have to run the 1928 Gorsedd single-handedly. Ralph suffered from
ill health quite a lot in his later years. In 1930 Evelyn Shove, his trustee,
commented that *he has several times appeared at the point of death &* [then]
taken a new lease of life ... and in numerous letters Ralph speaks of being ill
or recovering from illness. In August 1930 when it was clear that Sneyd
Brothers could not survive, Ralph again became ill. *All this business is
worrying him very much, the sooner it is finished the better* Sarah Riley wrote
protectively in a letter to Challinor and Shaw. The stress of coping with real
life was often too much for unworldly Ralph.

Some people took advantage of his naivety. Doug Pickford told us how
his father had tried to encourage Ralph to become a little more worldly-wise,
a little less trusting of the card-sharks and con-artists he met in local pubs. A
batch of correspondence survives that suggests that the Bradburys at
Bottomhouse also tried to put one over on old Mr Sneyd. For a time in the
1930s Thomas Bradbury rented some of the Fair View fields. Len, his son,
took it into his head that he wanted to live on the land and tried to bully Ralph
into renting him the bungalow occupied by Sam Riley - or, better still, building
him another one! Local people still believed Mr Sneyd to be extremely
wealthy. Matters had obviously become very tense by the summer of 1934.
Len Bradbury threatened to withhold his rent because there was building work
going on at Fair View that inconvenienced him, he went into the garden
without permission and took water from the pond, he locked gates, and, worst
of all, used Ralph's garage to skin a cow and left the skin there for several
days! Fortunately Sarah Riley had a vested interest in her brother remaining in
the bungalow and she kept copious notes detailing all Len's misdemeanours
and sent them to Challinors.

Ralph escaped from such unpleasantness - as he always had - by
retreating into the past. The ceremony we described at the end of chapter 14
was, it seems, one of many. The veneration of St George, the Knightly Patron

of Chivalry was, Ralph explained in one of his numerous letters to the editor of the *Leek Times... especially opportune in the present age as a protest against the debased ideals of ultra commercialism which sacrifice beauty and truth at the hateful shrine of avarice.* He must have found the 20th century an increasingly uncomfortable age in which to live!

Ralph's concept of chivalry was heavily entwined with Christianity and ideas about the Holy Grail. He believed - on no apparent evidence - that the Grail-worshippers (whoever they may have been) had had a series of centres - Glastonbury, Corbiere, etc, the principal centre in Western Europe being at Maladetta in Spain, which *is the Montsalvatch of the romances. I am convinced that the places I have mentioned were Colleges of esoteric Christianity where sacred rites were performed and where solemn initiations took place...* he told Mr Waite who had written about the Grail in the *Occult Review*.

As always, Ralph's pronouncements dissolved into generalisations and speculation and he interwove them with religious theories from Buddhism and Theosophy. *I have been in visible and recognised Communion with the Roman Catholic Church for over twenty years; but in the transcendental sense I claim to be a member of all religions....* he wrote grandly.

In 1922 he visited Winchester. The local paper reported that he came: *...as a representative of the Order of the Round Table of which he is a Knight and which claims to be a resuscitation of the original order founded by King Arthur. It is a mystic fraternity of poets and lovers of the beautiful that upholds religion, brotherhood, chivalry and culture. It teaches that there is an element of good in all things and the destiny of humanity is universal peace and happiness ...*

Ralph, with his tall, aristocratic bearing, his courteous, old-fashioned speech and his patriarchal shock of white hair, had obviously impressed the reporter. No-one remonstrated with him when he uplifted a sword, the symbol of knightly chivalry, in front of the round table in the Great Hall of Winchester Castle and presented a single red rose in honour of St George.

'Think about it,' I said to Marion, 'he must have brought that sword with him, on the train, all the way from Leek! He'd be arrested if he tried that today!'

'Wonderful! I warm to him!'

Ralph's own Order of the Round Table (as he sometimes called the True

Philosophic League) does not seem to have survived after 1890 as anything more than an idea, but as late as 1934 he was writing: *Having for the greater part of my life taken a deep interest in the Romance of King Arthur I refounded the Order of the Round Table about the time of the Indian and Colonial Exhibition in the Reign of Queen Victoria. Its ideals are Happiness, Harmony and Stability and it upholds Religion and Chivalry, Art and Science &c...*

'I just love the '&c'!'

'Who was he writing to?' Marion took Ralph's chivalric ideals more seriously than I could.

'Just 'Dear Sir' ...but I guess it was to do with one of these,' I replied, waving a couple of letters. One was from Edward Glenn who was co-organiser of something called the League of Chivalry which attempted ... *to bring back into modern life those small courtesies and gentle manners which are so characteristic of the old days of Chivalry...* The other letter contained a ticket from the Knights and Pilgrims of the Fellowship of the Knights of the Round Table of King Arthur requesting the pleasure of Ralph De Tunstall Sneyd's company at the opening of the Hall of Chivalry at Tintagel on June 5th 1933 and offering him a voucher for a cut price rail ticket! There was a surprising amount of chivalry about in the 1930s!

As the 20th century wore on, Ralph sought yet another way of escaping into a peaceful, spiritual past. He developed a serious interest in Buddhism. He'd first become aware of it when he read Colonel Olcott's *Buddhist Catechism* back in the 1880s, but not until after Harriett's death did he begin to study the subject in depth.

As well as being President of the Theosophical Society, Henry Steel Olcott was the first American ever to become a Theravadan Buddhist. With typical Victorian arrogance, he was shocked by what he saw as the ignorance of the Sri Lankans about their faith, and by debased modern Buddhist sectarianism. Like the Christian missionaries he so despised, he took it upon himself to teach the Sri Lankans what they should believe. He had some success. Each year, on February 17th, Sri Lankan Buddhists offer burning incense and light brass lamps to commemorate the anniversary of his death. Saffron-robed monks venerate his photograph and school children clad in neat, western-style school uniforms, offer gifts in his memory, praying 'May the merit we have gained by these good deeds pass on to Colonel Olcott and may he gain happiness and peace.'

Olcott was vehemently anti-Christian and proudly described his *Buddhist Catechism* as an antidote to Christianity. It is hard to see how Ralph could have made this uncompromising denial of God fit with his own devout Catholicism - but somehow he managed it. In the 1930s he became increasingly involved with Colonel Olcott's form of Buddhism. He converted part of his barn into a Buddhist chapel - the local press published an article about it in 1933 - and he collected Buddhist artefacts and statues of the Buddha. Eventually he had seven hundred of them! When once something caught his interest Ralph became obsessive.

Things ancient and spiritual absorbed Ralph's waking hours, and, if his notebooks are to be believed, his sleeping ones as well.

'Those two lecturers you went to see at the university...' Marion began. I knew what she was going to say. When I had visited the Educational Psychology Department at Leicester University to discuss why Ralph spelled so badly, I had taken some of his later writings with me, just to show how his spelling improved in later life and to see whether his adult handwriting gave any clues to his mental state. For convenience I had taken one of his notebooks - as it happened, the one in which he recorded his dreams had been on top of the pile. Both Professor Cooper and Dr Merry were interested in it - but not for the reasons I had expected. 'These aren't proper dreams,' they announced. 'Dreams are largely visual; these are all about ideas - they just aren't the sort of thing people dream!'

'So what were they if they weren't dreams?' asked Marion.

I shrugged.

One of the fullest descriptions is actually dated 1902 and was written out by Harriett. It covers eight pages of notepaper but is worth quoting at length because it contains so many elements that appear in Ralph's later notes about his dreams.

On the morning of [March 26th 1902] *I had a very curious dream... It seemed to me that I beheld a large number of the ancient order of the Culdees they were wandering in a valley situated in a beautiful and well-wooded country and around there were green and undulating hills, they were of stately appearance, some wore white robes, and others wore robes of a beautiful indigo colour I was impressed in my dream with the idea that the members of this ancient order, were the custodians of the wisdom of untold ages. They were poets and philosophers as well as being devout and ecstatic votaries of God and of Nature. It seemed to me during the 5th or 6th century an important episode which was called either the losing or the dropping of the keys took place...*

'We-ell - there's a fair bit of visual stuff in there - and he's talking about robes again,' Marion said. 'He must have had the dream then spent the rest of the day thinking about it!'

'Rest of the week more like!'

'Have you any idea what a Culdee is? They crop up rather a lot ...'

We looked them up. 'Culdee', according to the *Catholic Encyclopaedia*, was a much abused word. It derived from the Irish 'Ceile-De' and meant 'companion of God.' But the purple and white robes, the philosophy and the ceremonies were entirely Ralph's own invention.

'Personally I think the dropping or losing keys is the significant bit,' I said irreverently. 'My guess is that sometime on March 25th, say, Ralph lost his house keys. Harriett got cross with him - and this is the result!'

Marion looked disapproving. Once again, I was not taking Ralph seriously enough for her liking.

Ralph dreamed of seeing the eye of heaven as a circle of stones; he dreamed that the Adamic race lived for eight thousand years in the Holy Mountain; he dreamed of Atlantis and of the murder of four mind-born sons; he dreamed of Zoroastrian sun-worshippers, Zulus migrating and Arabs by the Caspian Sea. In his mind's eye he saw Romans in Iceland and knew the date when Arbor Low was built. Women dressed in indigo stood on buildings, dates of supposed significance came to him in his sleep. He dreamt of monks and nuns, Roman emperors, Scottish islands, religious ceremonies and Cadvan the American. He had visions that authorised him to compile rituals for the Culdees and attend services of whatever creed he chose and to gabble 'Glory be to the Father the Son and the Holy Ghost' each day after morning and evening prayers ...

'Gabble?' queried Marion.

'I think the exact phrase was 'say as quickly as possible'!'

He dreamt of Welsh bards fleeing to Picardy and slices of bread on white plates on round mahogany tables. He believed that the saint who founded Bardsey Abbey wanted him, Ralph De Tunstall Sneyd, to found a school there. And above all he dreamed of the Holy Grail; it was a pot of manna, it was a system that was *put before the Churches Egyptian and otherwise, but with the exception of the Celtic Church they failed to go on with it*; associated with it were twelve hermits and twelve knights and something called the 'Chismail

Feast', also two ladies in grey and nuns in indigo and the date 1594 was important for some reason.

Some of Ralph's interests were rather more mainstream. Archaeology fascinated him. As early as 1886 his great-aunt, Elizabeth Holley, widow of old Uncle John of Barton Bendish, was writing to Ralph about Mr Flinders Petrie's excavations. She also sent his private address in Bromley and suggested Ralph contact him because *One or two, properly qualified might go with him & they get their expenses.* But as far as we know, Ralph did not dig with Flinders Petrie. However, according to his son Billy, he did go abroad and work on several archaeological excavations - though when, where, how many and how often, we have as yet no means of knowing.

What we do know is that he and Billy excavated what they believed to be the site of a Saxon grave in the grounds of Fair View, but as with so many things, Ralph chose not to involve the professionals. The artefacts they uncovered have long since been dispersed and we have no way of knowing what evidence Ralph had for attributing them to the Saxons. His view of history tended to be romantic and he relied on his imagination and mythology rather than on anything as inconvenient as hard facts. A letter he wrote to the *Leek Times* illustrates this rather well.

...This realm, we may conclude [the Moorlands] *was the heart of the Hesperides and the heart of Logris, a land of dim forests and primeval mountains whose mysterious caves have sheltered countless hermits...*

....We may well conclude that to Ecton and Wetton came hardy Phoenicians in search of copper, with many a stranger from Southern lands who sought the Isle of the Sacred Apple; that in this region was to be found the secret wisdom of the blest abodes ...guarded well by the holy bards. Perchance the secluded Hamps and Manifold ... were seen and feared by lonely pilgrims, who told again in distant lands of Styx and Periphligetbon and Acheron and Cocytus... Perchance upon Soulshill 'twas thought that hero spirits gathered, who came from many a grim Tumulus to seek for blest Elysian fields, but stood awhile gazing westward e'er they passed beyond the river towards the mystic realm of sunset...

'Pure Madame Blavatsky!' sighed Marion, 'I've got pages and pages of that sort of stuff!'

'It's a real mixture, isn't it? Logris is the name for Arthur's Kingdom and the 'Isle of the Sacred Apple' is a translation of Avalon which was actually

Glastonbury ...'

'Which is some way away from Staffordshire!'

'Correct! The rivers are four of the five rivers of Hades that some, but not all, Greek myths suggest surround hell. Some just have the Styx. And the second one is actually Pyriphlegethon - I suppose he got close! Acheron is supposed to be based on an actual river, Epirus, which flows underground a lot of the time - like the Hamps and the Manifold. Similar geology, I suppose ...'

'Hesperides?'

'Nymphs who live in a beautiful garden in Arcadia - I suppose he meant 'land of the Hesperides' ...'

'And is there any evidence that the Phoenicians ever came to Ecton and Wetton?'

'Don't think so, but it's not impossible, they did come to Cornwall for tin...'

Ralph was a tireless writer of letters to newspapers and journals, and like the one just quoted, many of them come over as much less scholarly than he intended them to be. *How happy I should be*, he wrote to the editor of *Nature* in response to an article about a scheme to exterminate African animals that were believed to carry sleeping sickness, *if the news were conveyed to me that the man who is the ringleader of this diabolical scheme had himself fallen beneath the vengeance of a Lion or a Crocodile!*

In December 1922 he assured the editor of the *Times* that back in the mid 1890s *...returning from Olisund in Norway ... I saw what I believe to have been the head and neck of a Plesiosaurus* ...As ever, Ralph had a theory, unsubstantiated by any shred of scientific evidence, to account for his sighting of an extinct creature. *I believe that the descendants of the ancient Plesiosaurus may have become accustomed to greater depths of the ocean to escape the attacks of the Sperm Whale and the Grampus, and assumed a more perfect system of storing air and so remaining for long under water.*

Plesiosaurs were on the large side to have been eaten by whales, even killer whales (our name for the grampus) which have teeth and do kill squid and octopus. And they certainly weren't around in the Jurassic period to frighten timid little plesiosaurs into the depths of the sea! Ralph admits he only saw a grey head and a wide grey neck - it was probably a large seal!

'On the other hand,' interrupted Marion, who was fast becoming the champion of all Ralph's oddities, 'how about the sightings of the Loch Ness monster? Hundreds of people...' She rambled on and I stopped listening. '...you're just too prosaic!' she finished triumphantly.

Ralph in Wetton in 1925 before the procession to Thor's Cave

Thor's Cave

Millicent and Annie Blore
climb the hill to Thor's
Cave in their Druid robes.

OPPOSITE PAGE:
Photographs of Gorsedds
t Thor's Cave

BELOW:
The Blore family of
Bottomhouse. Mrs Blore used
o read to Ralph and her eldest
daughters were Druid
handmaidens at Thor's Cave.

The Manifold Light Railway on which Ralph organised many passengers to ride to the Gorsedd at Wetton

Ralph in his Buddhist temple, 1933

Ralph as a knight on
horseback at Fair View

Ralph at Winchester
Castle with his great
sword in 1922.

Part of the 'Chinese pirate ship'

17th century Bodhisattva

Colin and the Icelandic quern

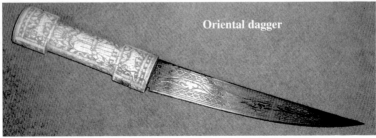

Oriental dagger

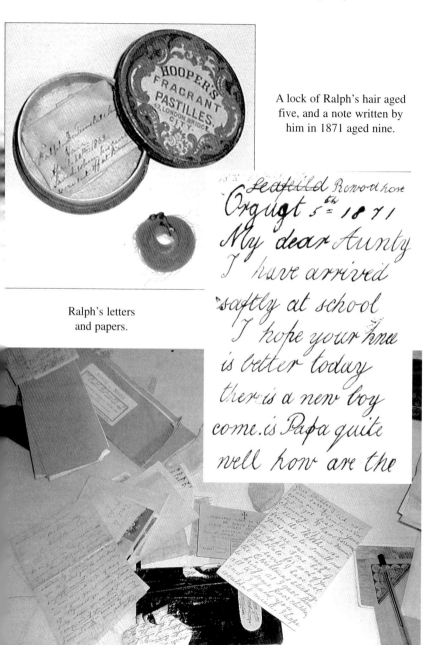

A lock of Ralph's hair aged five, and a note written by him in 1871 aged nine.

Ralph's letters and papers.

Ledfeild Rowodhose
Orgugt 5th 1871
My dear Aunty
I have arrived
saftly at school
I hope your hnu
is better today
there is a new boy
come. is Papa quite
well how are the

Detail of the Druid
gathering in Wales
with Ralph prominent
in the crowd.

This Welsh newspaper cutting
was captioned: *The Chief Bard of
Staffordshire compliments Miss
Kitty Sergeant aged 11 who won
a prize for pianoforte playing.*

Chapter 21
Memories of Ralph

Despite his wide range of interests it must have been lonely up at Fair View and the trip into Leek must have become more and more difficult. But well into old age, Ralph made the journey several times a week wearing his long black cloak and always carrying his little black bag full of books. There are still a few people around who remember him at this stage in his life. A number of people told us how he used to visit their families and talk for hours about abstruse subjects, oblivious of the fact that his hosts had jobs to do and homes to run. Some admitted that their parents dreaded these lengthy visits - but no-one was ever rude enough to turn him away.

For a time Ralph had a bicycle, and the late Harold Bode remembered how, when he was a schoolboy, Mr Sneyd would ride into town and leave his bicycle at Skinners in Derby Street. Their oil delivery van would take it back to him when it was next in the area - pedalling uphill all the way home would have been very hard work for an elderly gentleman. Presumably he got the bus back to Bottomhouse. Other people remembered how Ralph was shameless about cadging lifts. Sometimes he used to walk into Onecote and then decide to stretch his legs by walking home via Onecote Lane and Morridge Top - a triangular walk. By the time he reached Hopping Head he would be tired and would call in on his friends, the Smiths, and wait for Mr Smith to come home from his work as a joiner. Mr Smith's daughter remembered how, on those occasions, after his day's work her father was always expected to drive Ralph home before he sat down to his tea!

Other stories focussed on Ralph's oddity. Someone remembered how, at a function at Ipstones, he had spread mustard rather than butter on a teacake! Someone else told us that Ralph, a Buddhist who believed in re-incarnation, was convinced he would come back in his next life as a goat! Colin told us a story an elderly neighbour had recounted to him. One day, Ralph was walking home when he met an old woman, a tramp, a drunk, said to be 'rough as they come'. 'Hey mister!' she called, hoping to make some money to buy her next pint, 'yer can feel me c**t fer tuppence if yer want...!' 'Not today, madame,' Ralph replied, doffing his hat to her. His innate good manners would not allow him to be discourteous to a woman, however drunken and disreputable! Two generations on, his grandsons are equally courteous - Ralph's influence lives on.

Ralph's contacts spanned the social spectrum. On one of their drives out, on the Buxton-Ashbourne road, Frank and Chris and Billy passed a sign for a point-to-point meeting. On the opposite side of the road was a pub called the Jug and Glass. Billy commented that 'nowadays' (sometime in the early 1970s) this point-to-point was open to everyone, but in his father's day it had been a very special date in the calendar for the local gentry. On more than one occasion the Prince of Wales had attended with one of his mistresses and stayed in the pub. Well-known music hall artists would turn up to entertain them there. The Prince and his lady friends were treated like ordinary guests, and though everyone knew who they were they had to pretend not to recognise them. Billy claimed Ralph De Tunstall went to these point-to-points. 'How true all this is, I wouldn't like to say,' said Frank, 'but it makes a good story, doesn't it? When he told us about it Billy obviously believed every word of it.'

However odd people may have thought him, Ralph commanded a good deal of respect. As a little girl out with her father, Joyce Shenton remembers passing Ralph on the road near Thorncliff - a tall, upright figure pacing along with a long, slow, steady stride. 'That,' her father told her, 'is Mr Sneyd'. The Sneyds were no longer the local movers and shakers they had once been. People then had feared the family as much as they respected them. One of the things that John William Sneyd and his sister found it difficult to adjust to when they returned to Basford Hall in 1874 was that the obsequiousness they had taken for granted when they were younger - and which stemmed largely from fear of their father - was no longer forthcoming. Ralph De Tunstall had never known this deference and he didn't expect it, but nonetheless, even as an old man, to Joyce Shenton's father and all the farmers in the area he was 'Mr Sneyd' not 'Ralph' or even 'Ralph Sneyd.' It is difficult to define what makes a gentleman, especially one with little wealth or property - but, without exception, everyone who knew him remembered Ralph De Tunstall Sneyd as a gentleman of the old school.

By the 1920s and '30s, Ralph's birth family was little more than a memory jogged by the occasional letter from one of his elderly female relations. He continued to hear from his cousins, Dora and Harriet Bamford until their deaths. The last surviving letter from them is dated January 1936 and Cousin Harriet was still fussing about Ralph's health and advising him to wear a warm woollen belt and galoshes! She was eighty-three and would live another nine years. She and her elder sister, Dora, lived in Newport and were becoming more and more housebound and with less and less news to impart in their letters. Times were changing and they found it hard to cope. *I do hope your sons have work in these difficult times* wrote Harriet, troubled, as Ralph was, by the idea of a world in which gentlemen were dependent on their own labour for an income. Cousin Elizabeth Nelson wrote from Holme-next-the-Sea in a wobbly, old lady's hand, *I am not very well and so <u>old</u>.*

Aunts Fanny and Bertha also stayed in touch all their lives, trying hard to be supportive. They remembered Ralph's mother, Agnes, fondly, she was the prettiest of them all. She had such a sweet disposition and she was so musical, sighed her sisters. As the modern world became increasingly incomprehensible they dwelt more and more in the past and Ralph encouraged them. He had an insatiable appetite for information about the mother he had never known.

But mostly the letters are sad. They describe illness, bereavement and increasing frailty; Ralph's correspondents were old ladies struggling to come to terms with an apparently hostile world. *Is not this war terrible - there is no doubt that we are in the latter days and that this is the great war foretold in scripture* wrote Aunt Fanny miserably in 1917. Proud Aunt Bertha also ended her days in genteel poverty, almost blind, living in a grace-and-favour apartment at Hampton Court with her daughter. Young Bertha, like Ralph's sons, had to earn her keep and became a typist.

Slimy Uncle Gustavus eventually wormed his way back into Ralph's life. In 1914 he was corresponding with Stella at her boarding school - Gustavus always had a soft spot for pretty girls. By 1923 he was in correspondence with Ralph again, self-pitying letters about his own health, how he would have to give up the living of Chastleton because he could not find a curate and how he could no longer afford to live at Basford or keep it in good repair - though he might come back for a week or two in the summer. Ralph must have seethed.

The estate was slipping further and further away from him. Old Charlotte Sneyd died in 1940 and Woodlands was sold. The Townleys, her daughter and son-in-law, wrote to Ralph and offered him various 'heads' - presumably big game - and pictures of Etwall. He accepted gratefully. He had already bought some family pictures from Lady Wolseley in 1935 for what was then the exorbitant sum of £25 [£1,000]; ....*though I am not anxious to part with them,* she wrote, *I will not stand in your way to regaining them to your family.* Even in his late seventies Ralph was gathering together bits of the inheritance that he felt was rightfully his, to pass on to sons who had never really known or understood his world and for whom the Sneyds of Ashcombe Park were almost as remote as the ancient Romans.

There was endless correspondence with cousin Bertha Palliser over the patronage of the living of Dalbury. Ralph had scarcely known Bertha when they were young but by the late 1930s she was one of his closest surviving relatives and he determined that he and Billy would pay her a visit. She lived in East Molesey. The trip does not seem to have been a success - he was old, the journey made him ill and a doctor had to be called. *I was pleased to see you again after so many years,* Bertha wrote after the event, *but wish you had been well & able to get about & see things.* They would not meet again.

In his later years Ralph seems to have been desperate for company. He would visit Sarah Riley's nephew on the nearby farm and watch and talk while the milking was being done. More than once he got too close and his shoes were spattered with cow dung. 'Why can't those b*****s have tubes in their backsides?' he would ask indignantly. The bad language, delivered in Ralph's impeccable upper-class English, never failed to amuse.

He also visited his neighbours, the Blores at Bottomhouse. Sarah Blore would see him walking down the fields from Fair View towards their house with a book tucked under his arm; Ralph liked her to read to him.

'Why?' I asked Marion, 'he could read perfectly well himself!'

'They were always reading to each other when he was young,' answered Marion, 'remember all those books Aunt Susan used to read to him? And at school Mrs Cornish used to read aloud to the boys while they sketched in the evenings...'

One of the people who answered our appeal for information about Ralph De Tunstall Sneyd was Sarah Blore's youngest daughter, Nellie Hodgkinson, now a widow in her eighties. We called on old Mrs Hodgkinson one evening. It had been a hectic day, we had not left ourselves enough time and had other calls to make that evening. The Hodgkinsons, mother and sons, were very anxious to be helpful. They had got books from the library for us to see about the Sneyds of Keele - they'd even borrowed copies of our own books to show us, not having made the connection between the contact name they'd seen in the paper and the authors' names on *Finding Susanna* and *Thirty Pieces of Silver*! We appreciated their kindness but it was reminiscences that we were after. It was a small room, a gas fire was on full and everyone was talking at once. But in between the chaos we gleaned quite a lot of information.

The books Ralph brought for Sarah Blore to read were strange and difficult - when she stumbled over a word, Ralph would correct her. These reading sessions went on for an hour or two at a time - and yes, sometimes Mrs Blore would hide when she saw Ralph heading towards the farm, she had nine children to look after, she couldn't always spare two hours to read to 'Daddy Sneyd'...

'Did he have a cup of tea with you?' asked Marion.

'Oh yes! He'd always stay to tea afterwards - with bread and butter and home-made jam and cake - he always enjoyed that! He was on his own so much, you see - mother was sorry for him.'

'What did you think of him?'

'Well, the thing I remember the most was this - sometimes he'd bring an apple for us children, and he'd cut it into thin slices and give us a piece each - nine pieces and he'd still have half of it left they were that thin! When my mother was being a bit mean sharing things out we'd say - 'Oh - don't be like Daddy Sneyd!' Another thing. He always dressed the same - never anything different. He had these checked suits, black and white check, with plus fours and a waistcoat. Grey stockings and black shoes and a black and white trilby hat...'

That made sense. Old Mr Critchlow had told us how Ralph bought a bale of tweed sometime in the early 1900s. Everyone laughed at him at the time, but that bale lasted him for the rest of his life. The only problem was that every suit he had made looked exactly like the previous one! And now we knew the tweed must have been black and white checked.

'Anything else - anything at all?' Marion asked Mrs Hodgkinson.

'Well, maybe I shouldn't say this - but he had this odd laugh - Heh! Heh! Heh! Like that - a very odd laugh ...But he was a nice old man, we liked him well enough.'

It all added to our picture of Ralph.

Milly and Annie Blore, who had been Ralph's handmaidens at the Gorsedd at Thor's Cave, were Mrs Hodgkinson's elder sisters. She remembered them dressed up in their white robes - they were teenagers, she was a child of seven or eight. There were pictures in the family album she was sure, where was it? After some searching her son decided it was at his brother's house in the next street -Alan was a driving instructor, he'd be home soon and would bring it round. They called him on his mobile - several times. We sat sweltering in the little room, trying hard not to keep looking at our watches - we had to be somewhere else at eight and it was almost ten to.

Finally, Alan Hodgkinson arrived with the book. It was large and crammed full of little pictures and press cuttings - and Mrs Hodgkinson was easily distracted. We heard stories of uncles and cousins and nephews and nieces whose portraits we thumbed past - they were a prolific family. At last we found the pictures we were looking for, two young women in calf-length white robes with unbecoming hoods, in their best silk stockings and fashionable ankle-strap shoes with heels, their robes blowing in the wind as they stood in front of the family farm. Now we needed a picture of Sarah Blore... Eventually we found a nice one of her, with her husband, surrounded by their children. Alan agreed to take the pictures to Bruce for us. Now it really was time to go.

Our next call, a few streets away, produced two of Ralph's diaries, his Aunt Susan's autograph book, some drawings done by his Aunt Emily and a batch of books Ralph had had as a child - all purchased as a job lot some years previously when the contents of Fair View were sold. A fascinating find. We arranged to borrow the diaries and made copious notes and took photographs. Research was full of surprises, we told each other contentedly over a bottle of white wine in the Green Man that night. Our choice of wine was as eccentric as the rest of the project. We had broken our corkscrew, so we could only select our evening's celebratory tipple from the Leek Co-op's range of wines with screw top lids! It was surprisingly drinkable....

We were having great fun, but the luck that had pursued us when we were working on *Finding Susanna* was not with us. We had come to believe that Susanna Ingleby wanted her story told - she had seemed to help us at every turn and we had been able to reconstruct her life in great detail. Ralph De Tunstall must have wanted his story told as well - why else had he left so many notes? But there were so many things we didn't know.

'The thing that strikes me about Ralph,' said Marion, thoughtfully, sipping her wine, 'is how little he changed over the years. By the time he was eleven - earlier, even - his course was set. He was fascinated by the Middle Ages. He collected. And he was very religious. OK, as he got older he could pursue his interests in more ambitious ways - but they were the same interests.'

She was absolutely right.

But though Ralph may not have altered much, the world he lived in was changing rapidly. He saw the armistice of November 1918 and had much to be grateful for - both his sons had survived the war. No doubt he attended and enjoyed the 1918 peace parade in Leek. But of the young men who had joined up with Lionel and Ralph Clement almost half did not return. Ralph would have seen the erection of memorials in Onecote and Ipstones parish churches to those of his neighbours' sons who did not come home. He probably attended the carnival at Ball Haye that raised money to put up the great white Nicholson War Memorial in Leek in the centre of the old cattle market, and he may well have attended the ceremony when the memorial was unveiled in 1925.

He would have seen his neighbours' farms change hands several times in the course of his long stay at Fair View - and some would have had to sell up because their sons did not return from the front. But the little moorland farms themselves would have stayed much the same. Farming methods would have changed little, though Ralph would have seen a handful of forward-looking farmers buy tractors. He would have known of the formation of the Milk Marketing Board in 1933 which guaranteed milk prices and brought stability and some prosperity to the local farming community. He would also have noticed that the cattle in the fields and in Sam Riley's milking shed looked rather different. Up to the mid-1930s most farmers had shorthorns, which came in a variety of colours - white, roan, brindle and so on. Gradually these were replaced by black and white friesians which were better milkers.

There were greater changes in Leek itself. When Ralph was a young man there were over fifty silk manufacturers in the town but gradually the numbers declined. In the 1920s and 30s some firms went over to manufacturing rayon or 'artificial silk', some like the factory belonging to Ralph's friends, the Berminghams, went over to the production of sewing threads.

Leek grew. The area to the west had been expanding piecemeal in the early years of the century and by the 1920s reached as far as Burton Street. A new shopping street was developed on the site of what had once been the Globe Inn and the grounds of a big house called The Field. Council estates - Haregate, Abbotsville, Glebeville and the area around Station Street were developed in the 1920s and 30s, as were the private estates of Nab Hill, Big Birchall and an estate on the Newcastle Road on the site of a large 19th century house called Woodcroft which Ralph would have remembered. A new reservoir was built at Kniveden to serve the town's growing population.

Increasingly, from 1920, the roads around Leek would have carried motorised transport. By 1936 there was even a daily bus service from Leek to Bottomhouse and buses ran direct to Manchester from Leek. No doubt Ralph used them, and he got used to travelling by car   after all, his sons ran a garage. In the 1920s they charged him 7s-6d [£14] for the journey from Leek to Fair

View in one of their taxis. In 1929 he even bought a crash helmet from them for £1-10s-9d [£57] and a leather coat for £7-7s [£273]!

'Whatever must he have looked like?' laughed Marion, 'He was sixty-seven! Surely you didn't need special motoring clothes in the 1930s?'

'Maybe they were a present for one of his sons?'

Various people had told us that the three Sneyd boys had all had powerful motorcycles. They were remembered as strong, athletic, macho young men, racing their bikes around the fields and across the moors. We wondered whether their father had ever ridden pillion ...

He certainly flew. Just after the First World War he chartered a small plane, piloted by a Macclesfield man, Basil Lear, and took a trip over Fair View and his beloved moors, realising a lifelong ambition to have a birds' eye view of his world.

'Fancy even thinking of going up in a plane at that date!' exclaimed Marion. 'Even I didn't fly till the 1970s....'

'Lindbergh's first solo crossing of the Atlantic wasn't until 1927 and the first passenger planes didn't start to arrive until the 1930s, so he really was ahead of his time.'

Ralph continued to travel after his wife's death, and we know that once the war was over he went abroad again, but we cannot trace his itineraries. At first it seemed that his poetry would be a useful guide - at least to the journeys he took before 1929 when his book was published. From his poem *The Destruction of Rheims and Louvain,* we deduced that he visited France and Belgium while the war damage was still fresh. Ralph also wrote poems about Milan,Venice and Norway. Another poem described the 'Sandwich Isles'.

'Where are they?' I asked Marion.

'I don't know - but I think I've heard of them - vaguely...'

The following day, checking my emails, I found one from Marion, with an attachment, entitled *All you've ever wanted to know about the Sandwich Islands!* She had been busy on the internet. They are, it transpires, a string of eleven islands in the South Atlantic, somewhere near South Georgia. Miles away from any shipping route, they are volcanic, eighty-percent covered by glaciers, and - not surprisingly - uninhabited.

> *O sunlit islands, laved by summer seas!*
> *With spreading forests stirred by gentle breeze;*
> *Where starry maidens sit, with waving hair,*

Beside the shore, all crowned with blossoms fair.
(Isles Blest For Ever -The Sandwich Isles)

It did not sound much like first-hand observation to us, but then we discovered that the Sandwich Islands and the Sandwich *Isles* were not the same place at all. The Sandwich Isles was the name Captain Cook gave to one of the groups of islands in the North Pacific. Today we call it Hawaii! Did Ralph go there? Quite possibly, though we have no idea when.

Ralph's travels may well have been very extensive. Even his sons did not know the extent of his journeys. *I don't know whether you have ever been here,* Lionel wrote from North Africa before going on to describe Tunis, Carthage, Constantine, Tebessa and the other places he had visited. *Where was it you used to go for your holidays in Germany?* he wrote a couple of years later. Perhaps Ralph didn't talk to his children about his travels - or perhaps he talked so much they stopped listening!

Averil Scott-Moncrieff tantalised us with half-heard, half-remembered tales Ralph had told her when she was a little girl. 'He did go on rather. Once he got started he was unstoppable!' she told us. 'And Grannie never wanted me to listen to him...'

It was from Averil that we learnt that Ralph, while travelling in Africa (or was it the South Seas?) had somehow acquired a religious artefact that he should not have had. The location and details were hazy to say the least - but the burden of the story was that he was then pursued for miles by angry tribesman wanting their idol back! He also claimed to have been pursued by werewolves in Transylvania! They were colourful tales but added little to our knowledge - except to tell us that at some stage in his life Ralph had probably been to the Balkans, and back to Africa.

Many decades later some friends, William and Mary Overfield, wrote to Ralph with news of an amazingly cheap round-the-world cruise they were thinking of going on - would Ralph care to join them?

...an old friend and her husband ...are going for a 'World Cruise' in a Cargo-Passenger ship, the 'Durbania' ..sailing from Southampton on Nov 12th via Lisbon, Madeira, The Canaries, etc, Cape Town, Durban, Ascension, St Helena, Tahiti, Brisbane, Auckland, Melbourne, etc, these are just a few from memory and I may not have got them in the proper order, but we are seriously considering going with them and it is the chance of a lifetime and so remarkably cheap... The total cost for about six months is £112-10s [£4,500]

and no extras, it works out at about 10/6 per day or 1d per mile...

The *Durbania* was due to sail in November 1932 - Ralph would have been seventy that year. Did he go? We have no way of knowing, but he probably didn't - his final passport survives, with a rather rakish portrait of him with a cigarette hanging from his lower lip, and the only stamps it bears are for a visit to Germany in 1934. He wrote home to his housekeeper, *The Rhine and the Mosel are wonderfully romantic, around them are mountains crouned with castles, rising midst forests and vineyards...* It may well have been his last journey.

In the wider world, Ralph would have watched the unfolding of the Irish struggle for independence - Lionel was posted to Ireland in 1917 and sent angry letters home about *that traitor De Valera*. Ralph would have been shocked by the massacre of the Russian royal family and would have watched the rise of communism and the Soviet bloc. He would have been aware of Gandhi's campaign of civil disobedience in India. He must have noted the rise of Fascism. His cousin, Bertha Palliser wrote to him in 1939 stoutly defending Neville Chamberlain's appeasement of Hitler - *Mr Chamberlain knocked the ground from under Hitler's feet & deprived him of the excuse to overrun the whole of Czechoslovakia* - she argued with passionate underlinings for emphasis. He would probably have been pleased with her next, as we now know, startlingly inaccurate analysis - *I think the Pope has been splendid in standing up for the oppressed not only of his own Church but the poor Lutheran pastors & the cruelly treated Jews.*

We have no way of knowing what Ralph thought of 20th century life. Did he approve when women got the vote? How did he react to modern young women with cropped hair and skirts shorter than anything Harriett or his aunt would have considered decent? Did he read novels, or go to the cinema?

In some ways the modern world came late to the Staffordshire Moorlands. Up at Fair View they lacked electricity until the 1940s. Ralph believed that it was dangerous and unhealthy. The nearest telephone in 1936 was still in Leek and Ralph was never comfortable with the nasty, new-fangled contraption. *Perhaps you would let your housekeeper ring up & say when you would be here* wrote Mrs Townley tactfully in February 1940, arranging for Ralph to visit Woodlands to collect family items before the house was finally sold. We know he had a wireless, run, no doubt, on an accumulator, and he probably heard Churchill's portentous announcement on September 9th 1939 of the outbreak of yet another war in which his boys would risk their lives.

Lionel spent much of that war in North Africa and sent bright, overly-optimistic letters to his father assuring him (as early as 1941) that the Allies were winning and that the war would be over soon. He told his father as much as the censor would allow about the places he had seen and he grumbled endlessly about the heat and the flies and the dirt and made frequent references to young men back home who had managed to avoid the draft - *I think every man below thirty should have to serve.*

'Do you suppose he meant his brothers ...?' I asked.

'I thought Ralph joined up?' said Marion.

'I don't think so - he seems to have spent most of the war in Leek - maybe he was invalided out of the army? And Billy was never called up.

'Didn't Colin say he spent the war testing military vehicles?'

Lionel always sent his love to *the lads* as he called his brothers, but he probably did feel they had a comparatively easy war. Lionel was abroad when his only son was born and often asked his father for news of the little boy. *I shall arrive home to find John a toddler,* he wrote when little John was four months old *...he'll be going shooting with Uncle Ralph or on the beer with Uncle Bill before we know where he is!* Lionel and Irene had been married for many years before their baby arrived so it was doubly hard that he should miss so much of John's babyhood.

This war came close to home. Ralph De Tunstall saw the arrival of evacuee children and American servicemen in Leek; he would see bomb damage in the town and one German aircraft actually dropped a bomb between Ford and Grindon Moor - far too close to Fair View for comfort. Another plane crashed near Waterhouses - he may even have seen it, as many of his neighbours did, flying low over the moors for miles as the pilot struggled to regain control of his damaged aircraft.

He would experience food rationing - though, living in the country, Ralph was cushioned from the worst of it and he does not seem to have understood that food was scarce. His daughter-in-law remembered how, once during the war when he was staying with her, she took him his breakfast in bed - buttered toast and a little jar of honey. When she collected the tray the honey jar was completely empty - Ralph had eaten the lot! Ralph lived to see the end of the Second World War too, though at eighty-three he was probably too old to celebrate VE Day with his neighbours.

Chapter 22
Ralph the Poet

Getting to know Ralph has not been easy. As we have tried to show he was a complex man; gifted but unworldly, gentle but obstinate, loving but neglectful. But it is through his poetry that he reveals himself most clearly, and although we have quoted from his poems throughout this book, maybe it is now time to consider them as a whole and look at them as a collection.

A book of his poems was published in 1929 when he was sixty-seven. It contains 104 poems - some very long, the shortest a mere four lines. Analysis of the subject matter that Ralph chose in his collection illustrates, probably more clearly than anything else, what the important things in his life were. Of the 104 poems, almost half are about religion and the meaning of life as he saw it. Nineteen are devoted to Christianity, especially to the Virgin Mary; nineteen to Ralph's own philosophy of life which was firmly rooted in love and respect for nature and basic morality; four are about Buddhism.

Knowledge of his At-onement with Christ,
Is the heritage of the perfect Initiate,
Who has passed through many experiences,
And found celestial peace......

Christ shall be adored by all nations,
Under many names and by many rites,
And men shall come to Him
By many paths of wisdom!
    (Christ the Sovereign of Boundless Life)

Hail! Thou queen of realms of light!
Where the deathless lotus gleams;
Peerless virgin robed in white,
Golden hair around thee streams!
Crowned with stars for ever bright;
Mistress of celestial dreams!
    (Queen of Light)

In the highest heaven;
In the lowest hell;
In the heart of all things
There is Buddha!
    (*The Omni-presence of Buddha*)

The other major section is the one about chivalry and some of the longest poems in the collection are in this section. However, since these are so very closely associated with Christianity and the search for the Holy Grail they are really part and parcel of the religious poems. Of the rest, the biggest section by far contains the eighteen poems written to his dear wife, Harriett. There are seven to other members of his family - three to Susanna, two to the mother he never knew, and Etwall, her family home where he was born. There is one on the death of his great-aunt, Mary Sneyd-Kynnersley, but the only reference to his father is in a poem *Basford Hall in the Past* in which he describes its sad decay and the dismal life that his once-influential father had there as a lonely old man.

The master of this mansion
Is sprung of ancient race;
With beard white and stately
And strong and handsome face.

Oh, why should he be lonely
In this great hall forlorn?
Oh, when shall come the sunrise
And the resplendent morn? ....
            (*Basford Hall in the Past*)

Eleven poems describe places Ralph visited and in many of these travel poems descriptions of the places give way to mythology - especially Norwegian and Icelandic legends - so in part they are also religious and philosophical. Only five poems describe Leek and the surrounding countryside. Here are stanzas from two of them - *The Moorlands Wide* and *Rose Carnival at Leek.*

There scattered rustic homes are seen,
With walls of stone 'midst pastures green;
And lonely barns stand here and there,
Where herdsmen for their cattle care.

Rough fences, loosely built of stone,
Divide the fields around each home;

O'erspread with lichen grey and gold,
Uneven wind these fences old.

***

Leek, enthroned forever,
Near the winding river,
'Midst the Moorland Mountains,
And the woodlands fair.
Beauteous are thy daughters,
As the sunlit waters,
Who with thy fair children,
Ever can compare? .

The remaining two sets of poems could hardly be more disparate. Five are about the devastating First World War - the other six about fairies and fairyland - imagined lands of pure delight and fantasy.

Perhaps the most surprising omissions are that there are no poems about any of Ralph's four children or his massive collection of artefacts. The sole reference to his children is *In Memory Serene*, written after Harriett's death, which is really about idyllic family life in general. Perhaps in making his selection Ralph wanted to make sure that he was remembered, above all else, as a mystic, a profoundly religious and philosophical man.

Only one of the poems in the book - *The Land of the Dark Pine Tree* - is dated. Some of its 72 couplets are quoted below. It was written in May 1886, probably after one of Ralph's trips abroad, and it describes the local places that had meaning for him - Alton, Basford, Belmont, Cheadle, the Churnet Valley, Mosslee, Sharpcliffe and so on. Travel had featured largely in Ralph's life after he left school. He was a young man ill at ease with himself and his surroundings.

On a first reading he would seem in this poem to be yearning to escape back to the place he had just visited: *Why leave the palm-clad Orient fair, Where fragrant spices scent the air, For the land of the dark pine tree?* But in the end he hopes to find peace in his native land. The 'wanderings' in the last line reflects not just his physical wanderings but the wanderings of his mind.

....Beneath the eternal mountain high
The ancient town of Leek doth lie

Like lion's teeth the Roaches rise
As if to cleave the northern skies ......

By Westward Hall the river flows
And ever murmuring onwards goes

And Rudyard's beauteous waters gleam
Beneath the sun's expiring beam.

But when the Queen of Night rides high,
In her silver car through the starlit sky,

I fain would rest on thy fair shores,
And wearied with my wanderings pause.

Though all the rest of Ralph's poems are undated, it is obvious when some of them were written. There are poems in memory of his Aunt Susan who died in 1891; poems of ecstasy follow his marriage to Harriett in 1894; there are poems describing many of the places he visited - Iceland, Ceylon, Hawaii, Norway, Venice and Milan - which must post-date his journeys

'Have we ever found any reference, anywhere, in Susanna's letters and diaries to poetry?' I asked Pam in an email.

'No, not one,' came the answer after a day or so. 'I've checked everything. I don't somehow see her sitting reading poems do you?'

I had to admit I didn't. Novels - yes. Improving books of all kinds - certainly. But somehow not poetry. Yet another instance of just how far apart she and Ralph were in their tastes - and could it be that Ralph, realising this, did not let her know that he was a poet? When he was at school, his aunt had admonished him for daring to draw from his imagination - *copy, always copy*, she had urged. Perhaps he knew she would see writing poetry in the same light. And anyway the poems that he wrote contained his private thoughts and longings - dangerous ground, especially for his aunt's prying eyes!

Amongst Ralph's papers in the tin trunks we found hundreds of sheets of poems. Some were drafts. Some were corrected proof sheets of the poems that were finally printed in his published book. Some exist only on scraps of paper written in his own hand or copied by Harriett or Stella many years before the book was finally printed. Many are not included in the final selection at all. The photograph of him on the frontispiece shows a tall, suave, confident, good-looking young man but it is obvious from the content that not all of the poems in the volume were written when he was young. The ones about the First World War, for instance, cannot have been written before 1914 and by then he was already fifty-two years old.

His book of poems is labelled *Volume 1*. He presumably had planned for there to be a second volume. His poems reveal a man singularly out of touch with reality and obsessed by visions of unattainable love, peace and bliss, elements that were lacking in his life - as indeed they are in most people's lives. But unlike most people Ralph seems not to have given up his life-long quest for perfect love, a perfect place to live and perfect peace. In the last line of these two verses, taken from his poem *In Tranquil Peace*, he states his own view of what he was - a poet - and perhaps it is the lot of poets always to reach for the unattainable.

> *But, as I gaze,*
> *Those Isles dissolve and change!*
> *The Tranquil valley*
> *And the mountain range;*
> *The far volcano,*
> *With its lava flow,*
> *The knightly castles*
> *All dissolve and go.*
> *These forms are built*
> *Of clouds that change and glide,*
> *And sunlight that*
> *Makes splendid cloud and tide,*
> *But, though these wondrous*
> *Forms away may roll,*
> *They dwell forever in a poet's soul.*

In his poems Ralph recorded his dreams and desires and the places and people that were the bed-rock of his existence. But he remembered his childhood and some of the people in it through rose-tinted spectacles. When he was a little boy his aunt and Betsy, his nursemaid, had fed him with stories of fairies, knights and castles and taken him to see the crusader tombs at Mavesyn Ridware, igniting his lifelong passion for chivalry and romantic fantasy. It is small wonder that his memory of those early years in Armitage is that they were the most idyllic of his entire life. He longed for the fairy realm he had imagined in his childhood. It resurfaced in poem after poem.

> *Land of my childhood's dreams,*
> *Sweet fairy land!*
> *Land of silvery streams!*
> *Sweet fairy land!*

Fairy land where all is bright,
Dear land of mystic light;
True land of pure delight;
Sweet fairy land!
(Land of Dreams)

O fairy green, for ever blest!
The eyes of weary wanderers rest
On thee, and on thy varied sheen;
Beloved of nature, fairy green.
(Garden of Delight)

Oh, fain would I behold
Again, thy towers of gold,
Which, flower glades enfold,
In Fairy land!   *(Dream of Ardent Youth)*

He also immortalised his Aunt Susan in several poems, concentrating on her undoubted love for him.

O thou, who didst love me
In childhood's bright days!
Still now do I love thee,
And sing to thy praise.

Oh well didst thou sooth,
With thy beautiful smile;
And with tales of bright fairies,
The hours did beguile
(The Guardian of Childhood - Susanna)

The fact that his aunt had nagged and scolded him for years whilst he was at school, and afterwards, is conveniently forgotten.   It is the early years with her that he remembers with such affection.

But bright as his remembered childhood was, even then his own singularity, his obsession with collecting and his passion for Catholicism, set him apart from other boys his age. He wrote most poignantly as a young man, *Long had I wandered through the world alone; Few were my friends and lonely was my home...* And home, as we have seen, was lonely. Perhaps Ralph always saw himself as something of an outsider. Certainly as far as his father was concerned that was what he was. And although he socialised with all the people his father and aunt knew in Leek, took part in local activities and seems to have known a very wide range of people, he was right to say he had few close friends. Ralph was essentially a loner; he didn't fit in.

Nonetheless, he did not want to spend his life alone - he longed to find the perfect partner - someone who would engage fully with him in his unearthly kingdom. The repeated refrain in his poem, *Bright the Stars are Shining*, shows a young man longing for a soul-mate.

> *Swiftly, ye zephyrs,*
> *Bear me along!*
> *Soon shall my lady*
> *List to my song;*
> *Soon shall the breeze*
> *Bear my barque to the shore;*
> *Then shall the search*
> *For my loved one be o'er!*

And then he found Harriett Brookes. In her, unlikely as it seemed to his family and friends, he felt he had found the 'someone' he had been searching for, someone who was ready and willing to accompany him on his unrealistic journey. For Harriett, coming as she did from a practical working family, Ralph must have represented all that was exotic and beautiful. She threw herself into his religious pursuits, copied his poems, wrote some of her own - tried to live up to the idealised vision of her that he expressed in this poem *When We Wander in the Spring*.

> *When we wander in the spring,*
> *I will, of thy glory, sing;*
> *Love and light are in thy smile,*
> *Listen to my song awhile.*

And she did listen to his songs. And they wandered on the moors and read poetry to each other and conducted religious ceremonies of their own. He had found his fairy/lady/wife. Life was bliss. In poem after poem he portrayed Harriett, not as flesh and blood, but as a fairy princess or the lady of a knightly epic with himself as the knight. Then harsh reality cut in. Children were born and the children had needs too. In a household with a father literally 'away with the fairies' most of the time, and a mother who was doing her level best to live up to her husband's unrealistic perception of her as a perfect wife, companion, secretary, housekeeper, mother and muse, someone or something had to suffer. Harriett did her best, but in the end it was probably too much and her stroke at such a young age may have reflected the intense pressure she was under.

Though Ralph loved his children deeply - and from their letters they seem to have been genuinely fond of him too - one feels that it was love at a little distance. There are no poems to his children in Ralph's book, but amongst his papers we did find one written for his only daughter, his adored Stella. It is, perhaps, the most poignant of all - she was his *fairy child* whom he probably wanted never to grow up. We found several copies of Stella's poem - some in Ralph's hand with corrections and one in Stella's, folded and marked *Private*. It was a present for her tenth birthday.

> *Stella thou pride of the Moorlands wild,*
> *Thou art my love my fairy child.*
> *Gliding along so blythe and free*
> *List to the song I sing to thee.*
> *Love's sweet light is in thine eyes,*
> *Blue as the sea 'neath summer skies.*
> *Wavy and rich is thy soft hair*
> *Methinks I see the starlight there.*
> *Thy limbs are shaped with supple grace*
> *A rosy blush is on thy face*
> *Star of the Moorlands fair and free*
> *List to the song I sing to thee.*

It is a wonderful poem for any daughter to have had written for her by her father - but impossible to live up to. Stella, Ralph's fairy child, chose to marry James Shenton, a sound, hardworking slaughter-man with no pretensions to anything remotely 'airy-fairy.' She had had several children by him by the time Ralph's book of poems was printed, and perhaps the contrast between the memory of his fairy daughter and the wife and mother that she had become was just too much for him to bear seeing in print.

Ralph claimed that Shakespeare and Wordsworth were his favourite poets and maybe Wordsworth's poetry did influence him, as did that of other Victorian favourites like Tennyson and Longfellow with their simple rhymes and stirring subjects. But stylistically, Ralph's poems are closer to those of writers like William Morris and Dante Gabriel Rossetti, with whom he shared a passion for the mediaeval and the mythological - and both were talented artists. Ralph was certainly not influenced at all by the more challenging new writers - men like Robert Frost and T.S. Eliot. Nor does he seem to have read the great Catholic poet of the 19th century, Gerard Manley Hopkins.

Ralph's poems follow the traditions of 19th century poetry; they are not particularly innovative or original. He uses well-worn 'poetic' language - breezes are 'zephyrs,' valleys are 'verdant,' waters are 'lucid.' His lines rhyme, scan, come in regular verse patterns and follow well-established poetic forms - there is nothing avant garde about them. The refrain found at the end of each verse is a well trodden 19th century poetic device - and one Ralph used to good effect - sometimes movingly so. This is the last verse of one of his poems to Harriett.

> *Now, in long and sweet embrace,*
> *Lady-love, lady-love!*
> *Wrapped I gaze on thy dear face;*
> *Sweet lady-love!*
> *White-robed angel , hear my vow!*
> *I will love till death as now*
> *Lady-love, lady-love, sweet lady-love!*
> *(Lady-love)*

'Wrapped!' laughed Pam, 'Like a parcel! And even his publisher didn't realise he meant 'rapt' ...'

'Maybe he meant exactly what he said and was 'wrapped' around her, gazing at her as they lay in their marriage bed.' I replied. I like a nice bit of slushy romance!

But it is in his poem *The Weary War* that he uses repetition to its greatest and most moving effect.

> *A raven sat on an oak tree spread,*
> *Oh, the weary, the weary war!*
> *The clouds of thunder were overhead.*
> *Oh, the weary, the weary war!*
> *The earth beneath that tree was red,*
> *Oh the weary, the weary war!*
> *A wolf came through the forest wide,*
> *Oh the weary, the weary war!*

A noble feast he there espied,
Oh the weary, the weary war!
He lapped the stream with its gory tide,
Oh the weary, the weary war!

Here Ralph has used the refrain to encapsulate the length of the dreadful war and the change in public attitude from patriotic duty at the beginning, to the terrible sense of weariness and futility at the end. He also uses well-known poetic images - the raven as harbinger of death and the wolf as the bringer of tragedy. Perhaps the most chilling image of all is that of the stream - so pure and sparkling in his earlier poems, but now running with blood from which the wolf has his fill.

The draft of another (untitled) poem using repetition - in an almost prayer-like form - survived in the trunks. Someone had written it out carefully and neatly in a hand we didn't recognise.

All supreme Pontiffs and other Ecclesiastics
Of Christians and Buddhists,
Exalt the name of God forever.
All supreme Pontiffs and other Ecclesiastics
Of West and East,
Exalt the name of God forever....

Ralph ran through all the church dignitaries he could think of using the same formula - *Deacons and Archdeacons, greater Patriarchs and lesser Patriarchs, Metropolitans and Archbishops* - two whole pages of them. The section ended: *For all these chosen creatures, We praise thee Oh! Blessed One...*

Having found a form he liked Ralph went on to exploit it to the full, and urged all sorts of other people to exalt the name of God: scientists and artists, students and athletes, inventors and improvers, psychologists and physicists, astronomers and geologists, miners and farmers, warfingers and porters, wood-turners and sawyers, smiths and plumbers, photographers and phonographers, embalmers and taxidermists - five-and-a-half pages of them. No one was omitted it seemed - except possibly housewives!

Many of the longest poems in Ralph's volume were probably written for eisteddfods. They tell the age old stories of knights and their ladies: *Chivalry, Arthur's Court, Roland the Knight, Vivian and Merlin, Iseult and Tristram, Elaine and Lancelot,* they are full of brave deeds, of the search for the Holy

Grail, of Sir Gawain and King Arthur - of honour, purity and the tragic consequences of stepping outside the proscribed limits of courtly love. In the longest one, *Iseult and Tristram*, the hero and his love are doomed to die by his sword for doing just that.

> *But Tristram took his noble, knightly sword*
> *And kissed its blade, and said: 'Soon must I go*
> *And leave fair chivalry, by me adored;*
> *To pass the dark abyss, where waters flow*
> *In surging floods, from ladely caverns poured,*
> *'Midst gloomy realms of terror and of woe.'*
>
> *She came, and knelt beside her hero knight;*
> *He drew her down and clasped her wildly there;*
> *He crushed her slender body in his might;*
> *She yielded her sweet life with one short prayer.*
> *Short was her earthly life, and their delight!*
> *So passed Sir Tristram and Iseult the fair!*

In this next poem Ralph actually mentions bardic lore in the opening verse. Did he perhaps read this at one of the eisteddfods he attended?

> *Old Merlin, skilled in Bardic lore,*
> *Well versed in many a mystic rite;*
> *Who, into past and future saw;*
> *And, to whose inner sight,*
> *Was pictured many a secret thing!*
> *Sat in a forest near a spring,*
>   (*Vivian and Merlin*)

This poem, *Vivian and Merlin,* has recently been re-published as a small volume by a distant relative of Ralph's, the poet Steve Sneyd. Steve considered it to be the best of Ralph's poems.

In every poem in this group romantic love is celebrated, and in these, and in the ones written for his beloved Harriett, Ralph comes across as a very warm-blooded man, even though in 'courtly love' satisfying the desires of the flesh always seemed to end in tragedy!

> *Madly did Merlin kiss the fairy Queen!*
> *In the dim forest did he wildly love!*

                    ***

He kissed the damsel fair!
And she did blush and feel delight.

***

And now, Oh joy! At last, I see at last
Thy beauteous form near me reclining;
Thy love-lit eyes with glory shining;

***

Oh, give me love, and I will be your slave!
For love I live; for love I fain would die.

***

...As I clasp her dear form,
A soft rapture enthrals me,
Bright eyes and gold tresses
My sorrows dispel!

Perhaps his Aunt Susan would have been uncomfortable with the desires of the flesh so transparently displayed - but Harriett was enthralled - like the ladies in the knightly tales - by Ralph's ardour and the 'songs' he sang to her.

She was not the only person that Ralph managed to enthuse with his love of poetry. We mentioned Nellie Birch in chapter 19.   She was the daughter of a local farmer and one of twenty-two children - and Ralph persuaded her to write poems. We are grateful to Jean Bode for showing us a copy of Nellie's slim volume of poetry *Sunbeams and Shadows*. Published three years before Ralph's poems, in September 1926, by Fred Hill of Derby Street, Leek, it has Nellie's photograph inside. She is a smiling, attractive young woman with a smart 1920s bob. The foreword was written by a William Smith and Nellie dedicated the poems to her parents. Smith acknowledges that Nellie is no great poet but says that she wrote with simplicity and with genuine feeling. There is nothing profound or complex in her poems, she is, he says, *a smiling, vivacious, sympathetic soul, interpreting life as she found it.*   Many of her poems almost read like lyrics to popular songs of the period and one feels that they could easily be set to music.

And who in the world could wish better than this,
A big silvery moon and an hour of bliss,
A last fond embrace and one lingering kiss,
Then - 'Good-night.'

No, Nellie was not a great poet, but one cannot help but admire the determination of a country girl, from such a huge family, who had the courage to attempt poetry and who succeeded in getting a little book published. Contact with Mr Ralph De Tunstall Sneyd had certainly added a new dimension to her life.

We have quoted extracts from Ralph's poems throughout this book but perhaps we should end with a few lines from one of the poems which we think encapsulates him best.

> *But men, who have not*
> *Learned the truth sublime,*
> *By sages taught, that*
> *All should cease from greed,*
> *And reckless longing*
> *Leading oft to crime*
> *Are in poor plight indeed!*
>
> *Oh, may they quickly*
> *Find the mystic way!*
> *That leads from sorrow,*
> *And from sorrow's cause;*
> *Then shall they find*
> *All woe shall pass away.*
> *The high mysterious laws,*
> *Which govern all the worlds,*
> *Shall give them peace.*
>
> (*The Joyous Life*)

Chapter 23
The Death of Ralph
De Tunstall Sneyd

One summer Sunday in 1947, Ralph De Tunstall Sneyd went to bed as usual in the bedroom he had slept in for almost fifty years. Mementos of his travels were all around him, Harriett's clothes still filled one of the wardrobes, two large 17th century Dutch landscapes, of which he was particularly fond, hung on the walls. There was no electric light upstairs at Fair View though electricity had been installed on the ground floor a few years earlier. But it was June 22nd, the night after the summer solstice, and the sky was still light late into the evening. Ralph had no need of a candle as he sat up in bed looking through his stamp collection.

Perhaps as he looked he reminisced about where the various specimens had come from. There would have been stamps from letters he had sent home to his aunt from Australia and Iceland, even earlier ones that had come to her from her Cousin Emma in India and from his Uncle Dryden in New Zealand back in the 1860s. There would have been stamps he'd swapped with friends back in his schooldays at Leamington and in Debenham. Stamps from letters he'd written when he and Harriett were in Cape Town, and from when they, and later he, wrote home from Europe. Stamps from letters Lionel and Ralph had sent when they were overseas fighting in the two terrible world wars. Ralph's whole life could be read through his stamp collection.

The following morning Sarah Riley found him slumped forward in bed, the biscuit tin of stamps still in front of him. He was stone cold.

A few days later, after a funeral service at St Mary's in Leek, Ralph De Tunstall Sneyd was buried in Cheddleton churchyard, finally re-united with Harriett and his Aunt Susan whose grave he shared. He was dressed in his beloved Franciscan habit and on his coffin lay the great sword that he had carried to Thor's cave and raised before the Round Table in the hall of Winchester Castle. His tomb was draped with flowers and ivy.

The funeral was well attended; Ralph was a respected figure, the last of the Sneyds of Ashcombe Park, and the obituaries were glowing. We can do no better than to quote what his old friend Herbert Rowson wrote in one of them:

> *The death of Ralph De Tunstall Sneyd has robbed Staffordshire of one of her rich and rare characters, mourned alike by the wealthy and poor, the illiterate and the wiseling*

> *...He was a man of wide interests and tolerant attitudes and always willing to give a patient hearing even when he could not approve, never seeking to impose his beliefs on others. It was this many-sidedness that led a superficial observer to imagine him a man of many contradictions.*

> *In religion he was an eclectic. He was a devout broad Catholic worshipping at St Wilfrid's Cotton and at St Mary's church in Leek and in his own private chapel at Fair View. He was also a Theosophist and a sincere follower of that remarkable Russian woman, Madame Helena Petrovsky* [sic] *Blavatsky. A true Buddhist of the reformed Hindu church, he was well-versed in all the pagan sacred scriptures before their decline. A reverent Druid, he resurrected the ancient cult in Thor's Cave, restored at his own expense, the pageantry of an eisteddfod; and initiated many followers into the ancient rites and instructed them in the tenets of an Absolute Divine Force of Love residing in an Imperishable Land. In his own quiet inimitable indulgent way, he modestly taught us the unity in all cults before they declined and optimistically pointed out that the scientist of today was rediscovering the ancient theory of Relativity. I'm afraid at the time most of us felt his thoughts were a bit too high browed for us but a few are realising that his teachings were predictions of coming events and his forecasts those of a great soul. When he took us apart he spoke seriously about the Lost Word, or as he preferred to express it, his quest for the Holy Grail. He took a modest interest in the Old Catholic church and perhaps a more silent one in Archbishop Leadbeater's Liberal Catholic church and in Dr Annie Besant's works.*

> *He followed very cautiously the activities of H.P.B. and Dr Annie Besant as first Grand Masters of the Co-Masonic Lodges. He thought the women's movement a step in advance in the social civilisation of the world but was not greatly interested in politics.*

> *With the sponsoring of the Druidical worship went a keen interest in*

folklore and antiquarian research all over the world, and in his chapel and house many such scientific curios were to be found.

In the realm of thought this same many-sidedness was evident. He was an idealist in philosophy; a scientist of no mean knowledge; and possessing an imaginative sensibility that sent him exploring in the faery lands of poesy, his favourite poets being Shakespeare and Wordsworth.

He was a Conservative in politics, partly by hereditary and early training and partly because he lived chiefly in the country and was never intimate with the mechanised squalor of our towns and cities in this industrial age.

He was a man who preserved what Kipling called 'the common touch'. One cannot do justice in a few words to so versatile a character

Despite a few inaccuracies it is a pretty full summary of Ralph's life. But in some ways Ralph De Tunstall was not a *versatile character* at all. He had set his course as a boy; the things that absorbed him then continued to interest him throughout his long life. His father and aunt had dismissed him as foolish and useless, an embarrassment and a disappointment. Most of his relatives and neighbours saw only an otherworldly eccentric, and the young men he had grown up with soon despaired of him ...*Leave the 'ancient type' & 'universal' stuff alone. Put the 'English Catholic Vade Mecum' in the fire. Leave Darwin alone...* his erstwhile school friend, William McCombie Hutchins, wrote irreverently in October 1888.

Up on the Staffordshire Moorlands and in the town of Leek people are still very accepting of difference. There is a certain pride, a desire not to judge or be judged. Ralph was strange, yes, but the Moorlands bred eccentrics. He was a local man, a gentleman, he harmed no-one and he was treated with amused tolerance - and respect.

But because he was so gentle, so unassuming, so unconcerned with things of the world, little now remains to remind us of Mr Sneyd of Fair View. Fewer and fewer people now remember him. Billy revered his father and kept the house as an increasingly dilapidated shrine to his memory. But Billy died in 1976 and the house was cleared and sold. Ralph's collections are dispersed and forgotten, his book of poems is long out of print, no-one worships in his Chapel of the Holy Grail. The True Philosophic League and its members are long dead. No memory remains amongst the villagers of Wetton of the first English Gorsedds which drew thousands of tourists and reporters to their village, not once but three times, in the 1920s. Even the letters and notes and memorabilia that Ralph saved so carefully now lie jumbled in trunks in an attic.

> *Golden moments flying,*
> *Flying far;*
> *Soon shall I be lying*
> *Beneath a star.*
>
> *My lute shall fall in pieces,*
> *There to lie;*
> *Its subtle music ceases*
> *When I die.*
>
> *They that cared not for me,*
> *My songs shall sing;*
> *And they that ridiculed,*
> *Shall blossoms bring.*
>
> *And those that found on earth*
> *No place for me,*
> *At length, an answered riddle*
> *In my heart shall see.*
>
> *(Golden Moments)*

The End